THE COMMERCIALISATION OF ACCOUNTANCY

The Commercialisation of Accountancy

Flexible Accumulation and the Transformation of the Service Class

Gerard Hanlon

St. Martin's Press

657
H241c

First published in Great Britain 1994 by
THE MACMILLAN PRESS LTD
Houndmills, Basingstoke, Hampshire RG21 2XS
and London
Companies and representatives
throughout the world

A catalogue record for this book is available
from the British Library.

ISBN 0–333–61856–4

Printed in Great Britain by
Ipswich Book Co Ltd
Ipswich, Suffolk

First published in the United States of America 1994 by
Scholarly and Reference Division,
ST. MARTIN'S PRESS, INC.,
175 Fifth Avenue,
New York, N.Y. 10010

ISBN 0–312–12291–8

Library of Congress Cataloging-in-Publication Data
Hanlon, Gerard.
The commercialisation of accountancy : flexible accumulation and
the transformation of the service class / Gerard Hanlon.
p.   cm.
Includes bibliographical references and index.
ISBN 0–312–12291–8
1. Accounting.   I. Title.
HF5635.H24   1994
657—dc20   94–16014
                                                        CIP

To Bernard and Nora Hanlon

Contents

List of Figures

List of Tables

Preface

This book examines the nature of professional work in the private service sector. It particularly focuses upon accountancy. It tries to explain the nature of this work and the nature of the control processes experienced by the people who carry out such work in terms of the altered regime of accumulation that has emerged within the global economy in the past decade or more. The book postulates that this new regime has changed the way in which professional people experience their work. Basically it states that this professional work has become more commercialised and that the old notions of public service, objectivity, etc., if they ever were appropriate, are now redundant and have been replaced by a more blatantly commercial relationship. In the light of this, new mechanisms for controlling and socialising young professionals have been developed. These new mechanisms entail three components: technical ablility, social skill and commercial capacity. This latter component is a product of the new regime and is increasingly important in assessing who will and who will not make it to the very top of the accountancy profession. This 'commercialism' is, the study suggests, of growing importance within the private sector professions more generally and has been developed as one part of the overall attack on labour by capital in its search to restore profitability. This strategy and the emphasis placed on commercial skill helps to distinguish the private sector service class from its public sector counterpart. As such it is central to the fracturing of the service class within what has been called flexible accumulation.

GERARD HANLON

Acknowledgements

This book, like any other body of work, is the product of time and effort on the part of a large number of people – from those who participated in the actual research to those who put up with behaviour such as not getting a 'proper job' over the past number of years. I would like to take this opportunity to pay my regards to at least some of these people.

Firstly I must thank Dr James Wickham from the Sociology Department at Trinity College Dublin for his generous time giving, hard work, perseverance and ability to criticise me on the numerous occasions when it was required. I sincerely hope this work does him credit. Secondly, I would like to thank Professor John Jackson, also from Trinity's Sociology Department, and Dr Peter Armstrong from the Management School at Sheffield University for their helpful comments on an earlier draft of this work – my PhD thesis.

Thirdly, I must thank the EC Commission for providing me with a Research Fellowship from the Human Capital and Mobility Programme. Without this I would not have been able to work in the very stimulating environment that exists at the European Institute in the LSE. Lastly, I must thank all those who were kind enough to give me their time for interviews and for filling in questionnaires – I hope my sometimes apparently inane questions did not bore them too much.

GERARD HANLON

The author and publishers thank the following for permission to reproduce copyright material:

FAS/ERSI, Dublin, for Table 1.1 and Figures 1.2–1.4, from T. Corcoran *et al., A Review of Trends in the Occupational Pattern of Employment in Ireland 1971–90* (1992).

University of Bristol, for Table 2.1, from P.W. Daniels *et al., UK Producer Services: The International Dimension*, and for Figures 2.5, 2.8, 2.9 and 2.10, from A. Leyshon *et al., Large Accountancy Firms in the UK: Operational Adaptation and Spatial Development* and *Internationalisation of Professional Producer Services: The Case of Large Accountancy Firms*, respectively *Working Papers on Producer Services*, 1, 2 and 3.

The Accountant, for Table 2.2, from G. Jones, 'Wide Variance in Growth Reshuffles League Table' (June 1989).

Routledge, for Figure 2.12 from E. Davis *et al.*, 'What Internationalisation in Services Means: The Case of Accountancy in the UK and Ireland', in H. Cox *et al.* (eds), *The Growth of Global Business: New Strategies* (1993).

Basil Blackwell, for Figure 1.1, from D. Harvey, *The Condition of Post-modernity* (1989).

Thomson McLintock, for Figure 2.1, from R. Winsbury, *Thomson McLintock – The First Hundred Years* (1977).

GEC, for Figure 2.2, from N.A.H. Stacey, *English Accountancy 1800–1954* (1954).

Financial Times Business Information, for Figure 2.7, from J. Bohdanowicz, *Who Audits the UK?* (1984).

NESC, Dublin, for Figure 5.1, from *The Economic and Social Implications of Emigration* (1991).

NBST, Dublin for Figure 5.2, from J. Wickham, *Technicians and Engineers in Irish Electronics Plants* (1987).

Every effort has been made to trace all the copyright-holders, but if any have been inadvertently overlooked the publishers will be pleased to make the necessary arrangement at the first opportunity.

1 The Post-industrial Mirage: Polarisation and the Rise of the Producer Service Economy

It is indisputable that over the past two decades the global economy has restructured itself. However, what is not beyond dispute is the nature of this metamorphosis. A number of different positions have been mapped out; Bell (1974, 1976) and others have argued that we are entering a post-industrial society, on the other hand Lash and Urry (1987), in a somewhat similar tradition, have suggested that what is actually taking place is the disorganising of capitalism. Alongside these theses a set of counter-theories has emerged. These counter-theories are primarily coming out of the Marxist tradition; Sassen (1988, 1991) believes that what we are experiencing is the increased flexibility of capital. This flexibility has arisen from capital's need to weaken a powerful labour movement in the core areas of the global economy. Primarily what is taking place is the desire by capital to increase profitability hence in many respects, although by no means all, the transformation is part of capitalism's dynamic development. Harrison and Bluestone (1988) would also strongly argue this case.

The purpose of this chapter is to disentangle these theories and try to explain why economic restructuring emerged and the role of the service sector in this process. The remainder of this study then seeks to locate the role of accountants within this restructuring. It does this largely by describing the altered nature of socialisation experienced by this key group of controllers within late twentieth century capitalism.

DEINDUSTRIALISATION AT THE CORE

This section deals with the processes that have taken place in the UK and the US occupational structures although it will also briefly examine recent changes within the Irish occupational hierarchy. There are a number of reasons for concentrating on the UK and US as opposed to other states such as Germany or Japan. Historically Ireland has formed part of the UK economy and as such has been very heavily influenced by Britain. It could

be legitimately argued that even today Ireland forms part of the UK labour
market and is thus greatly influenced by UK labour trends (see Chapter 5).
The USA has also had a major impact upon the Irish economy via direct
foreign investment (DFI) by US multinationals. American multinationals
are possibly the biggest non-Irish feature of the Irish economy outside of
the EC superstate. Another motive for concentrating on these states is the
fact that Ireland is part of the Anglo-American accountancy tradition which
is significantly different to the accounting tradition of Continental Europe
(see Chapter 2). The final reason for concentrating on the Anglo-American
axis is the similarity, highlighted by Corcoran *et al.* (1992), of the changes
in labour trends experienced in all three states in the 1971–90 period.

What have these trends been? They have largely entailed an expansion
of both professional work and low skilled service employment, and a
decline of work in traditional manufacturing. All of these trends I would
suggest have polarised the occupational structure of all three states. That
manufacturing employment has declined in the UK and the USA is beyond
question. Between 1970 and 1986 the percentage of the US labour force
engaged in manufacturing declined from 27 per cent to 19 per cent
(Harrison and Bluestone, 1988: 28). Likewise in the UK, manufacturing
employment fell from 35 per cent of total employment in 1950 to 26 per
cent in 1981 (Harris, 1988). During the 1980s the British decline was even
more pronounced, 25 per cent of manufacturing jobs were lost between
1978 and 1985 (Sassen, 1991: 24, n. 2). This decline has largely been concentrated in the old industrial centres of both the UK and US economies.
Martin (1988) has estimated that between 1979 and 1986 75 per cent of the
manufacturing job losses in the UK were concentrated in the industrial
regions of the North. It has been the old, relatively skilled, trade unionised,
working class areas of the economy that have borne the brunt of this devas-
tation. These trends have weakened the labour movement to such an extent
that in the USA only 15 per cent of the workforce was expected to be
unionised in 1990 (Harrison and Bluestone, 1988). Within such an environment US manufacturers were paying relatively less per hour in 1986 than
in 1973 (Harrison and Bluestone, 1988).

If manufacturing employment is in decline then what has replaced it?
The answer lies in the service sector. Whilst manufacturing shed jobs the
service sector created them. Services now employ 65 per cent of the UK
workforce, this figure having risen from 61 per cent in 1981 (Allen, 1988).
Martin (1988) estimates that the service sector has created 3 300 000 jobs
in the UK between 1971 and the mid-1980s. Yet again the USA has undergone a similar change (Sassen, 1988; Harrison and Bluestone, 1988). However, what these aggregate figures hide is the shift within the service sector.

In the 1970s service employment growth came largely from public services but throughout the 1980s the source of job creation was the private service sector (Sassen, 1991; Barras, 1984). This private service work is regionally concentrated. In the UK during the years 1979–86 66 per cent of the service jobs created were based in three southern regions (Allen, 1988). A situation thus is emerging wherein the bulk of the manufacturing job losses are based in one area and the majority of new service sector jobs are located in a different region. This has led to increased regional inequality in Britain (Gillespie and Green, 1987). Such a feature is exacerbated by the fact that the public sector has diminished its role as a job creator; the public sector exhibits more spatially egalitarian job creation policies.

Like the US and UK, Ireland's occupational structure has undergone a major transformation in the past twenty years. The broad changes in the Irish structure are highlighted in Table 1.1.

Within these aggregate shifts there are three processes which are noteworthy, from our point of view, about the Irish changes. The first is the relative decline in the importance of manufacturing employment. In 1971 30.5 per cent of the working population was employed in manufacturing, in 1990 the figure was 28.4 per cent. Second is the vastly increased importance of the service sector, all the jobs created can be accounted for by services. Its share of total employment jumped from 43.5 per cent to 56.7 per cent between 1971 and 1990. The third noticeable feature about these changes is the movement within the service sector away from non-marketed services (roughly the public sector although this is a rather crude breakdown) to marketed, that is private, services. The trend in new jobs to come from the private as opposed to the public sector was particularly pronounced in the 1986–90 period when all of the service sector growth was concentrated in marketed services. In contrast to this period the 1970s witnessed a rapid growth in the non-marketed sector with the expansion of the

Table 1.1 Sectoral changes in Irish employment, 1971–90, (000s)

Year	1971	1981	1986	1990
Manufacturing	320	363	306	320
Services	457	587	607	639
Non-Market	123	193	206	202
Market	334	394	401	437
Agriculture	272	196	168	167
Total	1049	1146	1081	1126

Source: Modified from Corcoran *et al.* 1992, Table 2.3.

Irish welfare state (it could be suggested that the Irish welfare state was created in the 1970s). In 1971 the non-marketed sector employed 26.9 per cent of Irish service workers yet in 1981 this figure rose to 32.8 per cent, by 1990 it had declined to 31.6 per cent.

This broad situation is reflected in the EC more generally. Between 1970 and 1985 services increased as a percentage of total employment, rising from 47 per cent to 59 per cent. In the same period manufacturing's share fell from 41 per cent to 33 per cent and agriculture's share fell from 12 per cent to 8 per cent (Commission of the European Communities, 1989: Table 17). These industrial job losses were largely based in the old industrial heartlands, whereas the bulk of the service work that emerged was more evenly spread.

At a descriptive level all of the theorists would accept that these changes in the occupational structure have taken place. However, there is tremendous dispute as to what these alterations mean for the future social order and where these innovations originated from? Finally, what is the relationship between the service sector and manufacturing? It is to these issues that I will now turn, starting by examining the latter debate first.

THE SERVICE SECTOR–MANUFACTURING RELATIONSHIP

The interaction between the service and manufacturing sectors has long been a cause for discussion. Gillespie and Green (1987) have suggested that there are basically three views concerning the growth of services:

(1) Services divert resources away from manufacturing. This is because they are unproductive; this is supposed to be particularly true for the public service sector.
(2) Because of the greater demand elasticity of services, as income rises there is a disproportionate rise in the demand for services. This will eventually lead to a form of post-industrial society.
(3) Production and services are intimately linked in a self-service economy. This has led to the growth of two different forms of services – the producer services which are sold to intermediate consumers and the consumer services which are sold directly to the final customer.

The first two reactions view services and manufacturing as quite separate. Both implicitly give primacy to one or other sector. Theory (1) looks on services as parasitic and as taking resources away from manufacturing. Manufacturing is seen as a basic industry because it can export and hence generate multiplier effects. It was largely this view that led writers such as Brown and Sheriff (1986), Sargent (1986), and Cairncross (1986) to bemoan the loss of the UK's manufacturing base. Similarly Harrison and Bluestone (1988) have suggested that the deindustrialisation of the USA has severely weakened the US economy and will eventually damage the American service sector. They argue that 25 per cent of the services bought in the USA are paid for directly by manufacturing and hence services are, to a large degree, dependent upon manufactures (Harrison and Bluestone, 1988: 35). There is much to be said for this viewpoint at a national level. Massey (1988a: 242) has highlighted that a 1 per cent drop in UK manufacturing exports would require a 33 per cent increase in service sales overseas to offset the decline. This growth would be difficult for a large number of states to attain simultaneously. Sassen (1991: 56) has demonstrated that although the international trading in services has increased, up from 7 per cent of all services in 1970 to 11 per cent in 1980, the figures are still very low when compared with manufactured and agri-cultural products. The percentage of these latter two commodities traded internationally in the same period increased from 30 per cent to 55 per cent and from 32 per cent to 45 per cent, respectively. Hence international trading in services is still too restricted to lead to a service led multiplier effect on a global scale.

There are a number of reasons for this limited international trading in services (see Chapter 2 for an analysis of these in auditing). But this is not to say that services will not increase their tradeability. Some of the fastest growing areas of the service sector are highly traded (Sassen, 1991). One example of this high tradeability is the experience of New York. New York has been losing corporate headquarters since the 1960s yet it has increased its dominance of the financial and producer services sector. This suggests that these services are bought from New York based producers by non-New York based corporations. Thus producer services act as a basic industry for the New York region in a way that previously they had not. As a result of this one in three of the New York working population is employed in the producer service area. Thus for key cities producer services are increas-ingly important as a basic industry.

The same cannot be said for provincial cities and towns. Leyshon et al (1989) have argued that the vast majority of producer service employment growth can be explained by the growth in local demand and in the local economy. I would suggest that this is true for non-global cities[1] (see Sassen-Koob, 1984; Sassen, 1988, 1991; Freidmann and Wolff, 1982). The reason for this is simply that producer service multinationals do not locate their key rapidly growing internationally orientated functions in these provincial cities. These services are to be found in the major urban centres of the world economy. The traditional producer services such as the audit[2] are locationally tied in a way that the newer services, for example management consultancy, are not (see Chapter 2). This has led Sassen (1991: Table 3.15) to suggest that the US accountancy firms directly exported $350m worth of services in the latter 1980s. Sassen also argues that if one considers the sales of American accounting affiliates overseas this figure reaches $4.2bn (Sassen, 1991: 56). I would suggest that this second figure is incorrect as most of this latter money stays within the country of origin and very little is repatriated to the USA due to the nature of the international organisational structures within accountancy (see chapter two). However, the overall point is correct: the producer services are increasingly a basic industry in certain locations.

Having stated the above, the fears expressed by some of the authors mentioned are justified from a national viewpoint. As will be highlighted later on in the chapter the move to services has had some very negative consequences for the social structure of the core states. But this viewpoint is quite simplistic in certain respects. As Harrison and Bluestone (1988) argue, the switch to services has led to an increase in the profitability of capital and it is this, not the nation-state, that is the cornerstone of capitalism. The growth of the service sector, especially throughout the 1980s, has given capital expanded flexibility and hence allowed it to develop strategies for extracting greater profits.

The second method of viewing services is derived from the concept of income elasticity. We are told that as income rises the demand for services expands disproportionately and we move into a service or post-industrial economy. This theoretical position is most closely identified with Bell (1974, 1976). I will not explain the post-industrial thesis in great detail due to the familiarity many readers will have with the theory. There are primarily five components to Bell's argument. First, there is a move away from the production of goods to services. Second, the pre-eminent group or class in society is the professional–technical status group. Third, the axial principle of post-industrialism is theoretical knowledge; the scientific discovery and application of this knowledge becomes the dynamic force within society. Fourth, society becomes much more future orientated through its control of technology. Fifth, decision making is passed over to an 'intellectual' elite. Within all this change the nature of work and the experience of employment improves, profitability gives way to what Bell (1974) calls a 'socialising mode', wherein distribution is made largely through rational–technical decision making rather than property ownership, and society becomes much more meritocratic. These transformations arise due to the emergence of a professional cadre who control the forces of production. This is a bloodless form of managerial revolution.

As one would expect there have been a number of criticisms of the Bell theory. These concern one central issue – profitability. The importance of profitability has not diminished in the past twenty years. Because of this the other features of the post-industrial thesis, i.e. improved work quality, emergence of an independent managerial–professional elite which dominates society, the centrality of theoretical knowledge, allocation of surplus value through rational decision making as opposed to property ownership and so on have not come to pass. Because of the significance which profitability still holds today the service sector is increasingly operated along the same lines as manufacturing – work is often degraded, services are becoming increasingly concentrated, labour is subject to tight control etc. (Sassen, 1991; Kumar, 1978; Allen 1988). Post-industrialism has as a result largely been discredited; however, its legacy is still important. Some of this legacy is to be found in the writings of people from the Disorganised Capitalism school, which will be addressed shortly.

The final approach to the service–manufacturing relationship is to see them as interrelated. This method concentrates on the producer services and the development of a self-service economy. It has been most clearly expounded by Gershuny and Miles (1983). This thesis suggests that the service sector will not be a panacea for manufacturing job losses and that the increased demand for services must be linked to the socio–technical structure and the nature of the production process. Gershuny and Miles argue that much of the demand for services has been for producer services and that this has been stimulated by the changing nature of the production process. In contrast to the post-industrialists they believe that the increased demand has not been generated by income elasticity.

> The familiar pattern of declining employment in manufacturing and the growing employment in marketed services is not reflected in the final consumption figures. Indeed trends are generally quite contrary. The manufacturing employment proportions declined while the manufacturing consumption proportions increased. The marketed services – employment proportions all increase whereas, for the majority of countries, the equivalent consumption proportions decrease. This quite clearly excludes one of the common explanations of the growth of marketed services employment. We must conclude that this growth may reflect low productivity growth in the sector, or a fast growth in demand for intermediate services, *but not, in general, in final demand for marketed services*. (Gershuny and Miles, 1983: 101 emphasis in original)

Hence Gershuny and Miles argue that it is the changed nature of the production process and/or low productivity that has created the demand for
marketed services. (The issue of low productivity has been disputed by
Barras, 1984. He has highlighted how the private service sector is closing the
gap on manufacturing and how private services have been investing more
heavily in capital than manufacturing firms.) The other side of this growth is
the emergence of a self-service economy. The move away from the final consumption of services leads to increased manufacturing growth. Because of
the low productivity and high prices of services people begin to buy manufactured goods and to serve themselves. Hence they buy a video rather than
go to the cinema and this in turn stimulates the production of videos. On a
large scale such a transition leads to renewed manufacturing growth. The
former point, i.e. low productivity has partially been criticised already (see
the arguments made by Barras) and because of this and its rather tenuous
connection to the rest of this book the idea of a self-service economy will not
be developed any further (for a more in-depth discussion see Allen, 1988).

However, there are also a number of other areas of Gershuny and Miles'
work that have also been criticised. To some extent it is technologically deter-
ministic. It places great emphasis upon Kondratieff cycles and technological
innovation and thus implicitly stresses the role of technology as the dynamic
force within society rather than profitability. A second criticism of Gershuny
and Miles' work is that the manufacturing sector is still in some sense deter-
minant because it provides 50 per cent of service demand (Gershuny and
Miles, 1983: 108). This assumption cannot be left unchallenged.

The service sector is increasingly independent of manufacturing. This
process has developed during the 1980s, largely after Gershuny and Miles
wrote their seminal book. Sassen (1991, especially Chapter 3) has demonstrated how the nature of DFI has altered over the thirty–forty year period
since 1950. In the 1950s this DFI was largely located in the primary sector
–raw materials or agricultural products for example. During the 1960s and
1970s this investment was primarily concentrated in manufacturing traditional products such as the car. This form of investment was driven by the
search for cheap labour and new markets hence it was largely aimed at the
periphery. In the 1980s there has been yet another change, DFI became
concentrated in the new high technology manufacturing areas and in private services. The latter accounted for 40 per cent of foreign investment
and was the fastest growing sector in DFI. This must be put in a context
wherein total DFI had expanded dramatically in the 1980s, up from
$545 bn in 1984 to $962.8 bn in 1987 (Sassen, 1991: 36). Increasingly this
investment is concentrated within the core. The fact that from the mid-
1980s onwards the globalisation of services has outstripped that of

manufacturing is evidence, according to Sassen, that the service sector is increasingly independent of manufacturing. In previous eras service sector internationalisation always followed, and was highly influenced by the overseas expansion of manufacturing (see Chapter 2 for an analysis of this in accountancy).

The second way within which the dependence of services on manufacturing has lessened and indeed been radically changed is in the area of corporate development and strategy. In the increasingly complex world of late capitalism manufacturing firms, and firms generally, need the expertise and assistance of producer service firms such as advertisers, law firms, accountancy practices and so on more than ever before. This has altered the relationship between the two sectors.

> What were once support resources for major corporations have become crucial inputs in corporate decision-making. A firm with a multiplicity of geographically dispersed manufacturing plants contributes to the development of new types of planning in production and distribution surrounding the firm. (Sassen, 1991: 11)

The relationship is not parasitic nor are the two divorced, rather it is one of complementary association. Both sectors are increasingly interwoven into the production process (Wood, 1988).

Despite these criticisms, the work of Gershuny and Miles is significant. It highlights the importance of the connections between manufacturing and services. This has encouraged others to examine the affiliation closer and to link it more closely to the search for profitability (Sassen, 1988, 1991; Harrison and Bluestone, 1988, Allen 1988, Wood, 1988).

The three opinions on the service sector have all contributed to the theories that emerged in the late 1980s about the future of the 'service economy'. There are really two schools of thought about the changes that the advanced economies have undergone in the past two decades. Both take from one or more of the viewpoints just examined. These two schools are the Disorganised Capitalism–Flexible Specialisation school, and the Flexible Accumulation school. It is to an analysis of these two theories that we now turn. Firstly we shall examine the Disorganised Capitalism thesis.

A DISORGANISED TRANSITION?

A number of features that have emerged since the 1960s and beyond have led several authors to suggest that capitalism has moved away from an 'organised' to a 'disorganised' structure. The clearest expression of this thesis is to be found in Lash and Urry's book *The End of Organised Capitalism* (1987). This disorganisation encapsulates all areas of society – the economic, the cultural, and the political. If one had to pick the central feature of the Disorganised Capitalism argument it would be the demise or demotion of everything 'Big' – Big unions, Big capital, Big cities, Big political parties, Big classes, etc. – no one object, issue, or conflict dominates society any more. What is now taking place is the fragmentation of the class structure, increased emphasis on the local, a move towards deurbanisation and so forth. All of this leads to a fundamental shift in the way politics and economics are conducted, in the way in which issues come to the fore and, at a cultural level, a move towards post-modernity and a decentring of subjectivity.

Within this theory a dichotomy is presented between capitalism's development throughout this century until the 1960s and its development since then. In the period before the 1960s capitalism was characterised by increased concentration of capital, the growth of large labour movements representing the interests of what Lash and Urry call the 'core working class', the decline of small firms and the self-employed, the centrality of manufacturing to the economy, the increased bureaucratisation of control, the growth of the state and some form of corporatism, the growth in the size of industrial plants amongst other things (for a fuller account of these points see Lash and Urry, 1987: 3–10). In the period after the 1960s there was a move away from these features to a new set of characteristics which have come to define Disorganised Capitalism. Lash and Urry list fourteen such points, as they do for the Organised Capitalism era, of these fourteen points only the seven most salient ones for this work will be highlighted (once again I refer the reader to Lash and Urry, 1987: 3–10 for a more detailed listing):

(1)   Decline of the nation-state and the growth of global capital which led to a deconcentration of capital at a national level.

(2)   The growth of white collar work and an educationally based stratification system which leads to individual achievement and mobility plus the growth of new social movements, for example the green movement which detract from class politics.

(3)   Decline in the absolute and relative size and power of the core working class as the advanced economies deindustrialise.

(4)   Growth of manufacturing in the periphery which facilitates a change in the occupational structure of the core. This allows the advanced states to emerge as service economies.

(5)   The move to the periphery of manufacturing leads to a decline of regional economies within which the manufacturing sector has shaped the social and political relations.

(6)   With deindustrialisation industrial cities begin to decline and there is a move towards deurbanisation by the service class which further hastens the demise of the city.

(7)   There is a decline away from collectivism and national bargaining and towards new forms of flexibility both in capital–labour negotiation and in terms of work organisation.

This Disorganised Capitalism bears a resemblance to the Post-Industrial theory put forward by Bell and others. Lash and Urry (1987: 162) acknowledge this fact; however, they stress that the similarity is superficial and based largely around the issues of the greater importance knowledge, education, and science have plus the rise of a service class – something like, although not the same as, the post-industrial professional–technical strata. The reason that the Disorganised Capitalism and Post-Industrial theories are different lies in the fact that for Lash and Urry capitalist social relations continue to exist and there is a level of capital accumulation within society that allows for the continuation of the capitalist class' domination (Lash and Urry, 1987: 7). As a consequence of this the managerial–professional class, although central to the overall disorganising process, are not a direct obstacle to capital accumulation nor capitalist social relations.

The second way in which Lash and Urry stress that their work is different to that of Bell is the fact that they do not suggest that the working class necessarily lose their power and/or importance. The core working class remains a powerful force within Disorganised Capitalism; however, its struggles are increasingly sectional and are not capable of being reduced to simple class politics.

Many of the changes that characterise Disorganised Capitalism have occurred. This is not the objection to the theory. The objection stems from the fact that the Disorganised Capitalism theorists provide an inadequate explanation as to why these changes have taken place. Lash and Urry argue that the traits of Disorganised Capitalism are interrelated, hence the decline of class politics can be linked to the decline of the core working class which in turn can be linked to the spatial mobility of manufacturing capital and so on. This would lead one to assume that the cause (or causes) of these interrelated happenings come from one single or from a number of related sources and that the issue or issues would relate to profitability – the central tenet of capitalism. Despite the fact that in their introduction Lash and Urry emphasise the importance of capitalist social relations and capital accumulation they pay scant regard to the notion of profitability. A nice example of this is the move towards flexible specialisation and the 're-emergence of craft industries'.[3] Lash and Urry (1987: 199) highlight three causes for the move away from mass production techniques to smaller craft based, high technology plants. These are changes in technology, changes in taste, especially a rejection of mass consumerism and a move towards post-modernist demand forms, and competition from the periphery in the mass production arena. What each of these three causes fail to adequately explain is the role of capital within all of this change. For example, peripheral mass production is largely a result of core capital's spatial movement; added to this is the fact that much of the work performed in these small, flexible, craft based production units is often carried out for large scale capital. Indeed very often large scale capital has reduced its core workforce and outsourced this labour in order to reduce its operating costs hence these firms often entail a deterioration of working conditions (Murray, 1988; Harrison and Bluestone, 1988). The key feature in all of this is capital's desire to increase profitability through the manipulation of space, labour, technology, and taste (Harvey, 1989). Reading Lash and Urry's account of flexible specialisation one could be forgiven for thinking that it simply emerged from a vacuum. This move to flexible specialisation is important because it touches on the issues of deindustrialisation, new forms of production and labour control, new spatial configurations of production and so forth; in essence many of the core features of Disorganised Capitalism. Yet what is presented is largely descriptive rather than explanatory; it is incoherent in the sense that it does not pull out the central cause of this change.

Lash and Urry argue that possibly the largest single factor in the demise of Organised Capitalism has been the emergence of a service class, that is managerial–professional workers. This class is the key group within Disorganised Capitalism. It is this class and the issues that concern it – for instance the differences between the public and private sector service class – that dominate the political agenda of the disorganised era. Entry into this class is largely regulated via education and credentialism. There are a variety of issues within this that I reject (see Chapter 6). Suffice to say at this point that Lash and Urry accept that the rise of this class was not inevitable, it came about due to the emergence of bureaucratic control within US capitalism originally and later on in European capitalism (for a fuller discussion of bureaucratic control see chapters 3 and 4). Hence they acknowledge the role of labour control and of profitability in the development of this class yet they inexplicably fail to carry forward such an acknowledgement in their examination of the period of Disorganised Capitalism.

The second Disorganised Capitalism thesis that has been put forward has been presented by Offe (1985). I will only examine this study very briefly because although aspects of it are interesting it has not been as influential as the work of Lash and Urry (at least in the English speaking world). Offe suggests that the labour market is an inadequate mechanism for solving the production–allocation dilemma. There are a number of reasons for this; the uniqueness of labour as a commodity; the restrictions that operate on the labour market – trade unions, employers' organisations and so on; the contemporary functional disturbances that are currently impacting upon the labour market (see Chapter 6 for a more in-depth look at these issues, or Offe, 1985, especially Chapter 2); and the differentiation of the labour market along ascriptive lines (Chapter 4 deals with this in relation to accountants). Offe thus suggests that the labour market should be completely or partially replaced as a means of solving the difficult relationship between production and distribution. Offe feels that people should be given new support systems, essentially new means of self-identification, that are not based around the current ideas of work and employment. The labour market should be made more fluid so that people can enter and leave it with greater ease. The chief need for these requirements comes from the fact that large numbers of people are either outside or rather tenuously attached to the labour market because of the four points just outlined. Effectively one could suggest that large numbers of people have been marginalised. Offe's book *Disorganised Capitalism* is a collection of essays and hence, I would suggest, is not as fully developed as the work of Lash and Urry. However, it presents some interesting points on both the nature of the labour market and the service sector which I will use later on in this book. Having stated this, as a self-contained theory I would argue it is inadequate and it is one with which Lash and Urry have little sympathy.

In light of the arguments and criticisms described in the past few pages one may legitimately ask, as Cooke (1988) does, to what extent are the changes in capitalism today the product of disorder or the product of some emerging new order or merely an intensification of an old order with some new innovations? I propose that what we are witnessing is the emergence of a new order. It is with the presentation of this that we will now proceed.

FLEXIBLE ACCUMULATION – TOWARDS THE HOMOGENISATION OF ECONOMIC SPACE?

The fundamental feature of this argument is that the changes which have taken place in the past twenty years are largely attributable to the search for increased profitability by capital. This search led to a move away from what has been termed Fordism to a more flexible form of accumulation. Gordon *et al.* (1982) have highlighted how capital and labour compromised in the post-war era in order to achieve stable growth and consistently high profit margins. This compromise led to the creation of a welfare state, it shifted conflict from the industrial to the political arena, it gave consistent wage increases based on productivity deals to workers, it became management's prerogative to organise the production process, and, finally unions became more conciliatory in nature.

However, perhaps the two most important features of this compromise were the segmentation of the labour market and the development of bureaucratic control. The labour market was divided into three sections. One was the independent primary sector – this consisted of middle class, professional, career orientated employment. Second was the subordinate primary sector which consisted of blue collar, skilled and semi-skilled, trade unionised work. Third was the secondary labour market, made up of poorly paid, non-unionised, insecure employment which exploited largely female and/or migrant labour. The latter market is often forgotten in an analysis of Fordism. It allowed Fordism a degree of flexibility which was often manipulated by employers, for examples see Castles and Kosack's (1985) description of the 'flexible treatment' meted out to immigrants in various European states.

The logic of the Fordist or segmentation system was based around the notion of a fine division of tasks and the development of an internal labour market. Work and the internal labour market were controlled through a complex web of rules and procedures. This facilitated control because workers, at least those outside the secondary labour market, were guaranteed two things, job security with some form of promotion based upon seniority, and rising living standards provided they obeyed the rules laid down. This whole order centred on mass production techniques and mass consumption and was in many ways, as Lash and Urry have described, Organised Capitalism. Fordism lasted all the way through the post-war boom because it was highly profitable (for a more detailed look at this period see Gordon *et al.*, 1982; Edwards, 1979).

The reason for the demise of Fordism is to be found in the crisis of profitability that emerged in the late 1960s, early 1970s. Harrison and Bluestone (1988) highlight how in the USA wages and income grew whilst corporate profits fell between 1965 and 1973. Likewise within the EC the profitability of capital fell by 40 per cent between 1967 and 1975 (Commission of the European Communities, 1989: Table 42). Why did the rate of profitability suddenly fall in the late 1960s? Harrison and Bluestone put forward a number of reasons. The market for many of the products upon which the Fordist era was based had become saturated. With the renewed economic strength of Europe and Japan corporations from all the advanced economies were selling similar products in an increasingly saturated market, thus there was overcapacity and low productivity. Labour was still powerful and capable of maintaining the concessions it had gained from capital and, indeed, with the upturn in militancy labour was threatening to gain even more concessions. Lipietz (1987) on the other hand suggests that the falling rate of profitability came from the increasing organic composition of capital, which in turn led to the low addition of surplus value to products. This was exacerbated by the fact that capital merely increased the price of goods which led to inflation; firms then tried to get around this by borrowing which in turn led to problems servicing debts and then to job losses and so on. I favour Harrison and Bluestone's explanation. They have demonstrated how American capital could no longer simply pass on the cost to the customer because of the increased international competition, hence Lipietz's argument about passing on the price to consumers looks weak. Whatever explanation one prefers, there is no disputing that a crisis did emerge and it was one to which capital had to respond. This need for a response led to a major reappraisal by capital. This basically entailed a shift from a Fordist regime of accumulation to a flexible regime (see Lipietz, 1987 for a further discussion of regimes of accumulation). The main aim of this shift was to restore profitability by weakening labour (Harrison and Bluestone, 1988).

One of the noticeable features of this restructuring was the emergence of a New International Division of Labour (NIDL) (Lipietz, 1986, 1987; Cohen, 1987; Harris, 1988). This entailed the exporting of manufacturing to the periphery where labour was between five and ten times cheaper at the very least (Harrison and Bluestone, 1988). This spatial movement was prompted by a number of factors. One was, the existence of a huge cheap labour reserve in the periphery. Second was, the separation of the conception and execution of tasks within the labour process, and within this, the division and subdivision of individual tasks to such an extent that they required minimal skill (this process was begun long before capital's recent restructuring). Third was, the development of communication techniques that allowed multinationals to plan production on a global scale. One could add a fourth reason for this globalisation of capital – the search for markets. Lipietz (1987) argues that many of the locational tendencies developed by capital at this point were driven by the need to overcome tariff barriers. It must be stressed that this process of spatial mobility was not solely core driven. Metropolitan capital required willing political regimes in the periphery and semi-periphery (see Chapter 5 for an analysis of Ireland's 'willing regime'). All of this meant that foreign direct investment changed its nature during the 1960s, it became concentrated in the periphery as opposed to the core (Lipietz, 1987) and peripheral investment was aimed at the manufacturing sector rather than the primary sector (Sassen, 1991). Harrison and Bluestone (1988: Table 2.1) demonstrate how in the 1965–80 period US foreign investment by private capital jumped from \$49.5 bn to \$213.5 bn and repatriated profits, which grew even faster, rose from \$5.2 bn to \$42.5 bn. Added to this is the fact that while domestic US manufacturing was losing its share of world trade US foreign subsidiaries were expanding theirs. This latter expansion has compensated for the loss of profits by US domestic firms and now accounts for 33 per cent of pre tax profit for US capital.

All of this suggests that US capital has attempted to sidestep the falling profitability in the USA by moving overseas. It is in this light that the deindustrialisation of the core should be examined. However, it is not being suggested that the exportation of manufacturing capital is the sole reason for the core's deindustrialisation. Martin (1988) has highlighted a number of other factors such as the rise of the Newly Industrialised Countries (NICs), international competition which has led to the closure of inefficient firms, development of new technologies and the increased capital intensity of manufacturing generally etc. Lipietz (1986, 1987) has also argued that although core capital originally created low skilled, low paid work overseas, under a system which he calls 'bloody Taylorisation', there emerged a form of 'peripheral Fordism' under which peripheral capital developed some independence with which it began to compete, albeit in a relatively limited number of areas, with the core (witness the rise of Korea). However, what I am suggesting, and what many others have already argued, is that the creation of this NIDL and the deindustrialisation of the core which parallelled it were key elements in capital's attack on labour.

The reason behind this deindustrialisation and its impact upon the core working class is ignored by the Disorganised Capital thesis. They would have us believe that this spatial reorientation on the part of capital was part of some largely incoherent or unstructured change in capital; it was not. The spatial mobility of manufacturing allowed for a whole series of other assaults on labour. Martin (1988) highlights how the decline of manufacturing employment was concentrated in those areas of the economy that were blue collar and heavily trade unionised with a strong commitment to the broader labour movement. These processes further facilitated the weakening of labour. Spatial mobility allowed capital to play one geographical area off another by threatening to move if labour made 'unreasonable' demands. The response of many regions to this was to make themselves more attractive, that is increase capital's share of the total product by diminishing their own.

We thus approach the central paradox: the less important spatial barriers, the greater the sensitivity of capital to the variations of place within space, and the greater the incentive for places to be differentiated in ways attractive to capital. The result has been the production of fragmentation, insecurity, and ephemeral uneven development within a largely unified global space economy of capital flows. (Harvey, 1989: 295–6)

This internationalisation of capital has facilitated firms in extracting a whole series of concessions from labour. In the early 1980s US labour accepted pay freezes for the first time since 1964 (Harrison and Bluestone, 1988). Capital also implemented moves towards bargaining at plant level as opposed to the, typically Fordist, national level bargaining which had characterised the previous forty years or so. This allowed capital to compare plants and use the 'efficient' factories as benchmarks from which to lower the demands or increase the productivity of other plants. In essence it pitted one factory against another.

Capital began to move away from the Fordist compromise in other ways. There were increases in the outsourcing of goods, thus the role of subcontractors grew. Many of these subcontractors employed people that had previously been employed by the large corporations and had benefited from a whole range of improvements won during the last forty years. As capital restructured these people were made redundant and found themselves doing the same work only now they worked for subcontractors and received less pay and poorer conditions (Murray 1988, Harrison and Bluestone 1988). Even within the large corporations new systems of pay were devised. Two tiered pay structures were introduced for identical work. New employees spent longer and longer on probation periods thus receiving less pay than older employees. There was a growth in the use of part-time workers. These changes have been highlighted by a whole series of writers (Sassen, 1991; Harrison and Bluestone 1988; Harvey 1989; Corcoran *et al.*, 1992; Commission of the European Communities, 1989). In the USA part-time workers increased from 8m to 18m between 1980 and 1985, thus in 1985 they represented 17 per cent of the total workforce (Harrison and Bluestone, 1988: 45). In the UK in 1989 part-time employees made up 24 per cent of the total labour force (Sassen 1991; Commission of the European Communities, 1989: 53). Between 1978 and 1984 the percentage of British women workers working for less than sixteen hours a week rose from 25 per cent to 33 per cent (Sassen, 1991: 240). Likewise in Ireland the use of part-time workers increased although not as rapidly as in the UK or the USA. Between 1979 and 1990 the percentage of the labour force working part-time grew from 5 per cent to 8 per cent (Corcoran *et al.*, 1992: Table 2.8). In the EC more generally part-time work has also expanded (Commission of the European Communities, 1989). In effect the increased use of flexible or temporary workers led to the further segmentation of the labour market (see Figure 1.1).

The primary feature of these policies is that they are designed to give capital increased control and flexibility over labour. The peripheral groups allow for flexibility in two ways. The first peripheral group entails the use of people with common skills, for example secretaries, in jobs that are routine and have no career opportunities. These people allow for numerical flexibility through high labour turnover and natural wastage. The second peripheral group allow for even greater numerical flexibility through the use of part-time workers, short term contracts and other such measures, these people have even less job security and less career prospects than the first group.

The core workforce is smaller in number than it would have been under Fordism. This group is also functionally flexible, something that it would not have been under the previous regime. These employees are central to the firm and as such capital tries to shield them from the exigencies of the marketplace, this is not the same as saying that the issue of profitability has been downgraded, as we shall see.

The other groups, which are not connected in a direct way to the firm, also facilitate flexibility. These groups have grown throughout the 1980s,

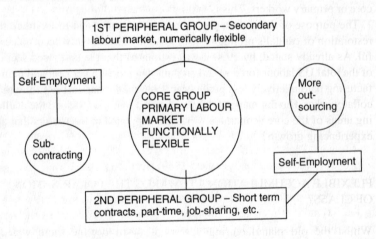

Source: Harvey, 1989: 151.

Figure 1.1   Labour market structures under flexible accumulation

there has been an increase in the use of subcontractors, office temps, self-employment and so on. The growth in self-employment was quite dramatic in the past decade, in the UK their ranks have swelled by 136 000 per annum on average (Hakim, 1989: 287). A similar trend has been noticed in the USA where between the mid-1970s and the mid-1980s self-employment grew by 15–20 per cent (Steinmetz and Wright, 1989). Likewise in Ireland self-employment has expanded from 9.5 per cent of the total non-agricultural workforce in 1971 to 13.2 per cent in 1990 (Corcoran *et al.*, 1992: Table 2.7). Similar trends have been experienced in the EC as a whole. There are a number of reasons given for this expansion. It cannot be accounted for simply by the increase in unemployment (Hakim, 1989; Steinmetz and Wright, 1989). The growth can be explained only partly by an increase in the numbers of unemployed but it must also be attributed to the development of producer services which have a higher level of self-employment than other areas of the economy, and the increase in self-employment in traditional sectors of the economy as part of a move towards increased flexibility (Steinmetz and Wright, 1989).

The idea of the flexible firm is largely derived from Atkinson's (1984) work. What has been described are trends rather than what is actually being adapted by capital in a holistic sense. Hakim (1989) has advocated that the complete flexible firm is a myth. However, capital is implementing many of these processes even if in an eclectic way. Most organisations have sought further to fragment the labour market through expanding their use of peripheral or secondary labour market workers and reducing their dependence on core or primary workers. This is in direct contrast to Fordism.

The purpose of these strategies is to weaken labour and to facilitate the restoration of capital's profitability. In this they have largely been successful. As already stated, by 1990 it was estimated that the unionised section of the total US labour force would amount to a mere 15 per cent and manufacturing paid relatively less per hour in 1986 than it had in 1973 for a blue collar worker. Having mapped out the changes that have shaped the declining areas of the core economies, what has happened in the sectors that are experiencing growth?

FLEXIBLE ACCUMULATION – TOWARDS THE POLARISATION OF CLASS?

Whilst the old manufacturing sectors were in decline there was an upsurge in employment within the service sector and, indeed, in new areas of the manufacturing base. Within services the area of job creation was the private sector as public sector growth was limited by a political shift to the right on behalf of the state (Sassen, 1991). Indeed in some instances the state was strongly advocating the growth of the private service sector at the expense of public services via subcontracting, the curtailment of civil service employment conditions for state employees, and other policies. This was especially true for the USA and the UK (Harrison and Bluestone, 1988). The shift on the part of the state is further evidence of the decline of the Fordist regime of accumulation.

Why in the late 1970s and particularly the 1980s did the private service sector grow rapidly? The answer is closely tied to the changes that were occurring in the manufacturing sector although the relationship is not one of dependency. With the internationalisation of the production process, of markets, and of the financial system there emerged a need for tighter controls on behalf of capital. Specialised producer services provided these control mechanisms and they have allowed capital to manipulate an increasingly complex global system. The central issue at the heart of this growth is thus the issue of control. Capital required new methods of controlling a spatially dispersed production system and it required new methods of managing a global financial system. This latter system is a control mechanism in itself. The financial system allocates surplus value to those areas that give the greatest return hence it penalises those sectors that give a low return both by moving capital spatially and/or by moving it from one sector of the economy to another. Both of these strategies have grave consequences for labour (see Chapter 6 for a further discussion of this).

> Increased capital mobility does not only bring about changes in the geographic organisation of production and the network of financial markets. It also generates a demand for the types of production needed to ensure the management, control, and servicing of this new organisation of production and finance. (Sassen, 1991: 23)

Thus the process of internationalisation, of which the NIDL was just one feature, led to a major growth in the producer services sector. Essentially these services were a means of controlling the new system.

Because of its growth and its strategically important control functions in the world economy I believe that this is a key economic sector, if not the key sector, within capitalism today. As has been suggested this sector is increasingly independent and it has evolved into a basic industry in areas deemed to be 'global cities'. Friedmann and Wolff (1982) and Sassen (1991) have argued that it is from these cities that the world economy is run. Head offices of multinationals buy in these services to enable 'rational' decision making in the operation of far flung corporations, in many instances these head offices are not located in the same city as the producer service firms. Moving towards the end of the twentieth century it is, to overstate the point, a case of all roads leading to the global city and the producer service sector. Within these cities producer services employ roughly one in three (Sassen, 1991). The importance of these cities and the status of their producer services, especially their internationally orientated products, has led to the creation of an international labour market for professional workers which has had debilitating effects on the periphery (see Chapter 5).

What is the composition of this sector in terms of job quality? The most noticeable feature of producer services is its polarisation. Only 2.8 per cent of these workers are in the middle income section of the total labour force. This compares with construction and manufacturing where 50 per cent of the workforce are employed in the middle income sector (Sassen-Koob, 1987). There are a variety of reasons for this polarised structure. Producer services are largely made up of two types of occupation – high skilled professional work and low skilled, clerical or manual employment. For example, work in a management consultancy firm or a legal practice entails the use of highly specialised professionals or clerical/secretarial staff. Added to this is the fact that this sector is very poorly organised by trade unions and is subject to some of the most detrimental features of the flexible firm strategy discussed earlier, for example the service sector is where the bulk of part time employees work (Commission of the European Communities, 1989). On top of this the vast majority of part-timers are female and hence at the bottom end of the service sector occupational hierarchy (Sassen, 1991; Harvey, 1989).

Not only has the producer service sector got an almost non-existent middle income category but it also has a wider range of income than manufacturing. Thus the poorly paid are more poorly paid than their counterparts in manufacturing and the highly paid are more highly paid than their equivalents in manufacturing; as a sector it has a greater scale of inequality than manufacturing (Harrison and Bluestone, 1988). Thus its growth within the advanced economies has serious implications for the equality of the social structure. Harrison and Bluestone (1988: Figure 5.4) have highlighted how during the last decade or so of Fordism the inequality gap was being bridged by the nature of employment growth. They suggest that between 1963 and 1973 of the new jobs created, as compared with those in existence, low wage employment declined by 10 per cent, middle income employment grew by 90 per cent, and high salaried employment rose by 20 per cent. In marked contrast to this, during 1979–86, when producer services provided the bulk of the new jobs, the figures were + 35 per cent, + 50 per cent, and + 15 per cent, respectively. The middle income share had shrunk dramatically. All of this leads one to believe that the private service sector has a very different, and indeed very negative, occupational structure when compared with manufacturing.

> The financial sector, as well as the other service activities which sur-round it, is structured very differently than manufacturing. It tends to be staffed by well-paid, white-collar professional and technical workers at one end, and poorly paid, semiskilled and unskilled workers (whose collars may be blue, pink or white) at the other. The general rule, with a few exceptions is: men at the top, women at the bottom; whites at the centre, workers of colour and immigrants at the margin. (Harrison and Bluestone, 1988: 55)

Alongside the harsh employment structure of the producer services is the development of a similar manufacturing structure in the most advanced areas of production at the core. More than anyone else Sassen (Sassen-Koob, 1987; Sassen, 1988, 1991) has examined these twin processes. A major component of capital's restructuring has been the downgrading of manufacturing. Because of the fine subdivision of tasks that has taken place in the most advanced, and indeed in other, areas of the manufacturing sector much of this work has been degraded. This is particularly true of industries like electronics although it is also widespread in more traditional manufacturing industries such as textiles. These industries have expanded recently in terms of employment. However, the growth areas are unionless, often made up of immigrants, and in the worst instances the labour is sweated in conditions reminiscent of pre-Fordist capitalism. The features that allowed for the break up of the old industrial centres and for the spatial mobility of manufacturing have also facilitated the re-importation of manu-facturing, or its renewed growth, in certain core regions. The difference is that this time manufacturing development is increasingly on capital's terms. Truly this is the homogenisation of economic space par excellence.

> Though inadequate, the evidence points to a massive growth of sweat-shops and industrial homework in garments, toys, footwear, and increas-ingly electronics in both cities [New York and Los Angeles]. (Sassen, 1988: 160)

Sassen (1991) has suggested that London, and to a much lesser extent Tokyo, are developing similar features to New York. Within this area of the manufacturing sector there is once again a relatively well paid, if much smaller, labour pool and a larger, poorly paid workforce. Like producer services these new manufacturing growth areas have increasingly high wage differentials. These differentials are determined by issues of class and, possibly more importantly, gender and race.

The growth of a highly unequal reward system, the expansion of a whole range of low skilled employment opportunities, and the possibility of gentrification has led to the emergence of an informal economy in many of these global cities. These cities have also experienced large scale immigration from the periphery. These migrants supply labour for the expansion of a downgraded manufacturing sector, low skilled service employment such as waiting or office cleaning, and indeed for the relatively rapidly expanding professional labour market (Hanlon, 1991). Cohen (1987) has argued that the core has become dependent upon such migrant labour and/or second generation migrants. This has led to the growth of some third world features in many of these cities. All of which has brought great benefits to capital.

Much of what has been described in the last few pages is based upon the experience of major cities such as London and New York. It must be stated that these cities are noted for their particularly high concentration of producer service employment and their lower level of manufacturing employment than the countries within which they are based. As such these cities are the most pronounced expression of a producer service economy and thus other areas of Britain or the USA will not have developed these tendencies to the degree described, nor are they likely to. Having stated this, these trends are emerging across large areas of the core: producer services have grown in many areas, manufacturing employment has declined in many areas, and new areas of manufacturing employment growth experience different conditions to what had existed previously, therefore, to some extent manufacturing has been downgraded, that is non-unionised, feminised, and experiences the use of flexible strategies and so forth throughout certain core economies.

In light of what has just been presented it becomes evident that there is a coherent pattern to the alterations that have emerged. What has being highlighted is the interrelatedness between these processes and the search for increased profitability. When examined the decline of traditional manufacturing, the decline of the core working class, the weakening of the labour movement and class politics, the demise of the nation-state, the move away from collectivism, etc. do not appear as something haphazard. All of these things appear as a result of the pursuit of surplus value. However, I am not suggesting that these occurrences were inevitable or predetermined. It is conceivable that the exporting of manufacturing to the periphery could have facilitated more autonomous development for these recipient regions but this did not take place due to a fine division of labour, the repatriation of profits and so on. Although Lash and Urry's Disorganised Capitalism thesis describes many of the characteristics of capitalism today it does not explain from where they originated. These features emanate from the attack on labour by capital in the latter's bid to increase the rate of profitability.

Has this pursuit of profitability been successful? The answer is 'yes'. Harrison and Bluestone (1988) have demonstrated how during the 1980s capital's rate of profitability in the USA returned to the levels it had achieved in the 1960s, although it did not reach the peak rate it had achieved in that decade. Likewise in the EC profitability has grown continuously since 1981. In 1981 it was a mere 62 per cent of its 1960 figure, by 1989 it had risen to 85 per cent (Commission of the European Communities, 1989: Table 42). However, this profitability has been bought at a price. Unemployment rose in most of the major economies and despite some fall in the mid- to late 1980s it is still a lot higher than it was when Fordism was in place (Harrison and Bluestone 1988; Commission of the European Communities, 1989). On top of this is to be added the poor quality of much of the work and the working conditions that have replaced the traditional manufacturing employment structure. The new areas of growth appear to be highly polarised. These features led to an increase in inequality of 18 per cent between 1975 and 1986 in the USA plus the apparent abandonment of any aspiration towards full employment (Harrison and Bluestone, 1988: 118). This was in marked contrast to the growth in equality during Fordism. There appears to be a somewhat similar gap emerging in the UK wherein a sizable minority of workers are being left behind in terms of skill and rewards (Lovering, 1990; Gallie, 1991).

THE FLEXIBLE ACCUMULATION REGIME AND IRELAND

How have these processes affected Ireland? Ireland is neither a part of the core nor of the real periphery, it lies somewhere in between in what has become known as the semi-periphery (Breen *et al.*, 1990). In terms of industrial skill Ireland also lies somewhere in between the advanced economies and the NICs. Ireland was also a recipient of DFI over the course of this restructuring rather than a donor. Therefore, one may wonder how these processes have impacted upon Ireland.

The Irish employment structure changed rapidly throughout the 1980s. During the 1971–81 period there was a net increase of 173 000 jobs within the Irish economy; 70 000 of these were in the public sector, 45 000 were in the manufacturing sector and 58 000 were in the private service sector. In the 1980s this altered drastically. Between 1981 and 1986 manufacturing employment fell by 60 000, public sector employment increased by only 13 000 and the private service sector increased very slightly. During the 1986–90 period this situation altered yet again; public sector jobs declined by roughly 4000, manufacturing and construction increased by 14 000 (the bulk of this increase was concentrated in the new manufacturing growth areas such as electronics), and the private service sector grew by a much larger 36 000 jobs (Corcoran *et al.*, 1992: 16). All of these changes are in line with those that took place in the advanced economies albeit that some of these processes occurred five years or more after they had emerged in the USA or the UK. This is acknowledged by Corcoran *et al.* (1992: 9) who suggest that if Ireland's agricultural sector is ignored the occupational structures of Ireland, Britain, and the USA in the late 1980s, early 1990s are very similar. Considering the fact that we are concerned with trends towards, what could loosely be called, flexible labour policies such an analysis is adequate; however, it leads one to assume an altogether too favourable image of the Irish social structure. If one accepts that 15 per cent of the Irish workforce are engaged in agriculture and that many of these have been marginalised (Breen *et al.*, 1990), that there is an unemployment rate of roughly 20 per cent, and that over the course of the 1980s between 150 000 and 200 000 people emigrated, then the Irish social structure appears to be quite peripheral and very different to that of the UK or the USA. Put simply Corcoran et al's proviso is a rather large one.

The growth of the service sector would lead one to assume, if the experience of other economies is anything to go by, that self-employment, part-time working, and the proportion of females in the labour force also grew. As already touched upon self-employment and part-time work both expanded. Self-employment in the service sector grew rapidly in the years between 1971 and 1990 (see Figure 1.2). During the nineteen year period from 1971 self-employment expanded by 72 per cent. However, this expansion was not even across economic sectors nor time. The bulk of the growth, some 70 per cent of the total expansion, came about in the 1980s. By economic sector there was also uneven development. Building's expansion in the 1980s was insignificant. Manufacturing roughly doubled in terms of self-employment which was in marked contrast to what had occurred in the 1970s. The greatest period of self-employment growth in manufacturing was in the latter half of the 1980s and it would seem reasonable to assume that much of this could be accounted for by the flexible strategies of capital. This would have led to a number of different types of

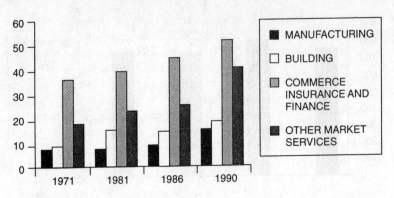

Source: Corcoran *et al*. 1992: Table 2.7.

Figure 1.2   Self-employment by economic sector (excl. agriculture), 000s

self-employed personnel, from low skilled outsourcers for large firms to highly skilled and specialised subcontractors. Much of this is in line with the arguments put forward about the new, high technology, growth areas of the manufacturing sector in the advanced economies. It should be remembered that in the latter 1980s it was these industries that were growing rapidly in Ireland.

The commerce, insurance and finance sector experienced the greatest increase in self-employment between 1971 and 1990, it grew by some 42 per cent overall, the bulk of which was concentrated in the 1980s. Within other market services, which include personal services and professional services, self-employment more than doubled. Yet again this increase, 70 per cent of it, was concentrated in the 1980s (see Figure 1.2). This growth reflects the increased use of outside expertise by large firms and the high levels of self-employment that are to be found in the 'post-industrial' sectors more generally (Steinmetz and Wright, 1989).

The increased participation rate of females in the workforce also reflects changes taking place within the Irish occupational structure (see Figure 1.3). During the 1970s both labour forces expanded but by far the greatest relative expansion was in the female labour force, it grew twice as quickly as the male workforce, 25 per cent as opposed to 11 per cent. This reflects the nature of employment change in the 1970s. Both the service sector, public and private, and the manufacturing sector were growing. Expansion within services was over twice that of the manufacturing part of the economy (see Table 1.1, p. 3), which would help account for the greater relative increase in female workers at this time, given the higher concentration of women in the services. But in both labour forces the trend was positive.

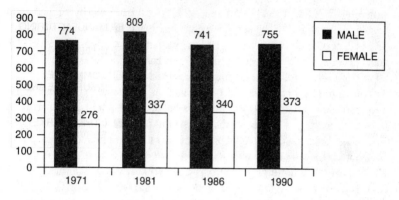

Source: Corcoran *et al.*, 1992: Table 2.2.

Figure 1.3   The male and female labour force changes, 1971–90, (000s)

In the 1980s there was a noticeable reversal of this tendency. Male unemployment grew by 33 per cent, the male labour force shrank by 6 per cent, and the participation rate amongst males fell by roughly 10 per cent. On the other hand the female labour force grew by 10.5 per cent and the female participation rate increased by 4 per cent. The one downside to all of this was the increase in female unemployment which nearly doubled during 1981–90.

I would suggest that these changes reflect the changes taking place within the economy, notably the shift from manufacturing to services, especially private services. As manufacturing became relatively less important to the economy and growth disappeared during the early 1980s before picking up again slightly (Table 1.1, p. 3) the traditional areas of male employment were adversely effected. If Sassen (1988, 1990) is correct then even the small upswing in manufacturing employment growth in the late 1980s, which was concentrated in new areas such as electronics, may have brought no respite to the male labour force as much of this work is low skilled, poorly paid, and because of this, occupied by females. The area of real employment expansion, the private service sector, is also noted for its widespread use of female employees. Yet again these trends are broadly in line with those in economies such as the UK and USA – male manufacturing employment declines while female service employment increases (Martin, 1988; Sassen, 1988).

Ireland has also undergone similar trends to both the USA and Britain in terms of part-time work. Ireland's level of such work is low by international standards, it stands at 8 per cent of the total workforce or 92 000 people. As with the USA and the UK (Sassen, 1991) the vast majority of part-time work is to be found in the service sector; in Ireland this sector accounts for 75 per cent of such employment, and the vast majority of part-time workers are female, again 75 per cent. A mere 3 per cent of the total male working population are employed part-time in comparison with 17 per cent of the female working population.[4] The growth of part-time work was rapid throughout the latter 1980s. In the years between 1986 and 1990 part-time work expanded by 40 per cent whereas the full time workforce grew by only 3 per cent. Amongst the male labour force part time employment grew by 31 per cent and amongst females it grew by 42.5 per cent (Corcoran *et al.*, 1992: 23–4). The rapid growth in part-time work, from an admittedly small base, is closely tied to the expansion of the private service sector.

Thus in five broad areas: manufacturing decline, private service sector growth, increased instances of part-time work, an increase in self-employment, and an increased feminisation of the labour force Ireland is in line with international trends in the advanced economies. If one accepts that the above description is accurate then one has to ask whether the Irish occupational structure has undergone the same polarisation tendencies as that of the USA and the UK. I would suggest the answer is 'yes'.

Between 1971 and 1990 the total numbers employed grew by 7 per cent but within this there were some quite significant changes. Agricultural workers fell from over 25 per cent of the total workforce to roughly 15 per cent (Corcoran *et al*, 1992: Table 2.3). Within the non-agricultural changes there was an upward shift in the skill level within the economy. There was a rapid growth in the professional, associate professional, and managerial groups, these occupational groups increased by 80 per cent, 80 per cent and 60 per cent respectively. Other areas of growth were sales workers, personal service workers, security employees and clerical staff for example. At the lower end of the occupational hierarchy labourers, transport workers, foremen, etc. declined (see Figure 1.4).

That significant changes have altered the occupational structure is beyond doubt. However, how are these changes to be interpreted? The most noticeable feature is the increased size of the elite end of the occupational structure. Between 1981 and 1990 occupations such as; 'managers/ proprietors', 'professionals', and 'associate professionals', grew from 21.7 per cent to 26.3 per cent of the workforce whilst the middle sector, 'skilled manual' and 'clerical', stabilised at around 30 per cent. The lower skilled working groups, 'sales workers', 'security workers', 'personal service workers', and 'semi and unskilled'[5] remained stable at 25 per cent (see Figure 1.4). This is in marked contrast to other economies. In the USA of the top ten fastest growing occupations for the 1984–90 period six are low

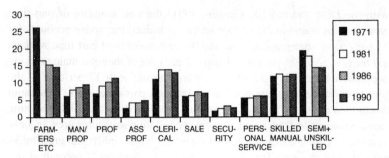

Source: Corcoran *et al.*, 1992: Table 4.6.

Figure 1.4   Employment by occupation, 1971–90, per cent

skilled and low paid while three are elite occupations, only one is in the middle income category (Harrison and Bluestone, 1988: 71).

However, there is a problem with Figure 1.4, and that is that it ignores the unemployed. The very rapid growth at the top pales almost into insignificance when compared with the 224 per cent increase in unemployment between 1971 and 1990, up from 61 000 to 210 000 and standing at 297 000 in 1992 (Coghlan, 1992). If one includes unemployment figures plus figures for agriculture and emigration then the structure begins to look a lot more polarised with both the top and the bottom growing rapidly, particularly the latter, and the middle remaining stable at best. Although this is not the place to pursue the matter, it may be that with the homogenisation of economic space the core is peripheralised to some degree, as Sassen suggests, and alongside this the periphery takes on certain aspects of the core, such as the emergence of elite professional and producer service workers on a relatively large scale.

On the evidence just presented it appears to be the case that Ireland has undergone many of the processes experienced by other economies during the past decade. It is in the light of these features that accountants were chosen as the subject of study. In many ways accountancy is central to the Flexible Accumulation regime.

FLEXIBLE ACCUMULATION AND ACCOUNTANCY

Accountancy could be said to typify Flexible Accumulation or at least the elite occupational aspects of this new structure of accumulation. It is one of the fastest growing occupations in the fastest growing sector of the advanced economies. That the financial and business service sector grew rapidly throughout the 1980s has been well established. In Ireland the annual rate of increase in employment amongst professionals in the Business, Finance, and Legal sector was 10.2 per cent between 1971 and 1981, 3.3 per cent between 1981 and 1986, and 5.4 per cent between 1986 and 1990. It increased from 0.6 per cent of the total working population to 2.2 per cent in 1990 (Corcoran *et al.*, 1992: Table 5.3.1). This outstripped the growth of all other professionals. The increase in the number of chartered accountants was even more impressive. In 1980 there were 4033 chartered accountants in Ireland, North and South, in 1989 the figure was 6817; this is a growth rate of 69 per cent, the equivalent figure for England and Wales was 36 per cent (Hanlon, 1991).

Accountancy is also growing in other ways. In the UK between 1978 and 1986 the fee income of the top twenty accountancy practices jumped by almost 400 per cent, up from £258m to £1.4bn (Leyshon *et al.*, 1989: Table 17). In Ireland too fee income has risen; in 1987 it was worth Ir£85m to the largest eight firms (Fitzgerald, 1987) and in 1992 the largest ten firms shared Ir£225m between them, an increase of roughly 265 per cent (McManus, 1992). (There is also another area of growth. The number of practices rose throughout the 1980s, up from 400 to 700. The area is characterised by high levels of self-employment, of the 828 practices in Ireland only 32 had five partners or more (Rowe, 1988: 141).

These trends alone make accountancy worth examining as does the fact that very little sociological analysis of accountancy has been carried out to date. However, it is also interesting for a variety of other reasons. Although the evidence is sketchy, due to the fact that it was not an integral part of this project, accountancy appears to be highly polarised in terms of occupational, and indeed class, structure. Accountants, twenty years after they have qualified earn, on average, Ir£40 000 per annum, after five years qualified they earn Ir£22 000 per annum (LSCA, 1990: Table 2) hence it is a highly lucrative profession. However, the bulk of the non-professional staff within these practices, who make up about 15–20 per cent of the total workforce, are paid a lot less. These people are engaged in clerical and secretarial functions and earn between Ir£7500 and Ir£11 000 with the majority gravitating towards the former figure. Thus there appears to be two extremes in terms of salary; roughly Ir£9000 per annum or, if one is a 45 year old professional who has stayed in practice for twenty years, Ir£40 000 per annum. All of this would lead one to suggest that accountancy is in many ways the classic 'post-industrial' occupation in Steinmetz and Wright's (1989) sense of the term rather than Bell's (1974) use of it[6].

Lastly, and I would argue most importantly, in the highly dispersed and yet tightly controlled economic system that has emerged accountants are a key part of the control orientated producer services. I would suggest that the engineer possibly represents the 'ideal image' of Fordism whereas the accountant is the key image of Flexible Accumulation. Accountants and accounting controls are present in all areas of organisational life today. In many ways accounting is the meta-language of Flexible Accumulation and it is found in all areas of social activity from the stock exchange to the hospital. One nice example of this link between Flexible Accumulation and accounting meta-language is the emergence of the debate concerning agency theory within accountancy. Agency theory in accounting seeks to limit the divergence between the actions of an agent in reality and the actions desired by the agent's principal. The basic theoretical argument is that a principal, that is a person who employs, has authority over, or delegates work to somebody else, desires certain actions from an agent, that is the subordinate within the relationship. However, because of human nature which, so the theory tells us, is based around self-interest, risk aversion and so forth this principal–agent relationship is fraught with danger; the agent may well act in his or her self-interest to the detriment of the principal. For instance take profit related bonuses and a board of directors. If directors are only paid a bonus when profits are over £1m then in a year when profits are £900 000 directors may seek to write off an unusually large series of depreciation costs and/or other costs in order to limit such costs next year and hence increase next year's profits and their bonus. Such an action limits this year's profitability which may not be in the interests of the owners, particularly those seeking high dividends. If new accounting techniques can tightly control such a relationship at costs lower than those of not monitoring the relationship then these techniques are worthwhile. Theoretically any situation within an organisation involving subordination or delegation is a principal–agent relationship and hence susceptible to accounting control. These controls allow for increased information about and monitoring of every principal–agent relationship within an organisation. They could thus be used to increase capital's flexibility. Although agency theory has existed for some time in economics it only emerged in accounting in the late 1970s (Eisenhardt, 1989; Watts and Zimmerman, 1990). The emergence of this theory at a broadly similar time as the push towards Flexible Accumulation could have been a coincidence, however, I would favour Armstrong's view (Armstrong, 1991) that the two are related and that this agency theory should be seen in the light of the profession's 'collective mobility strategy' (see Chapter 6). The whole point communicated by this theory is that the cost of every individual relationship, every individual person, and every individual action can be calculated. Surely this is Flexible Accumulation, or if one prefers – Thatcherism, Reaganomics, or Enterprise Culture in a nutshell. Accountancy, like other producer services, is intimately bound up with controlling the process of Flexible Accumulation. Because of this it is both interesting and important to analyse how these people are socialised into their controlling functions (see Chapters 4 and 5) and to examine the role that this occupation, along with other elite occupations, will play in the changing class structure of flexible capitalism (see Chapters 3, 4, and 6).

At this point I should explain what I, rather than others, mean by the term 'Flexible Accumulation'. It refers to all the labour force and economic changes outlined but I also use it in a broader sense in order to highlight other, and what I believe to be very central, features to this regime of accumulation. The shift from Fordism to Flexible Accumulation has basically entailed an intensifying of the process of labour market segmentation so that the subordinate primary market has shrunk, the secondary labour market, which gave Fordism a degree of flexibility, has grown, and finally, there has been a significant shift within the composition of the independent primary sector – the service class. This latter alteration has been made up of three processes. First, an ideological upgrading of the issue of commercialism so that profitability has emerged to be of paramount cultural importance (Keat and Abercrombie, 1991). Second, the labour market changes outlined, which in turn were grounded in the increased vigour with which the search for profitability was conducted, have meant that numerically those service class occupations most directly involved in the search for profit, for example accountants, have grown the most rapidly hence altering the shape of the service class. Lastly, the intensified search for profit and the new, or renewed, emphasis on commercialism has changed the organisation, the control processes, and the ideological outlook of many service class employees. It is this last point that forms the core of this book. However, the book should be read with the overall picture outlined in the last few pages in mind, the difference between my work and the work of other authors such as Harrison and Bluestone is simply that I am interested in how this exacerbated search for profitability has affected dominant rather than dominated groups.

RESEARCH METHODOLOGY

What follows is based upon quantitative and qualitative research. This research entailed the conducting of 55, taped, semi-structured interviews with accountants in both practice and industry, the latter accounted for four interviews. The bulk of the interviewees, 29 in total, were recently qualified although still under contract. The reason for this was simple, these people were about to make a number of very important career choices and as such would have thought seriously about issues such as emigration, leaving practice, sources of work satisfaction, what superiors looked for in potential promotees and so forth. Ten of the interviewees were partners, four were directors or senior managers, and twelve were assistant managers or managers. These people were chosen to provide a possibly different outlook on issues such as those just listed. 31 of the interviewees were from the largest six multinational practices, known as the 'Big Six', the others were from small and medium practices or industry. Needless to say for the purposes of confidentiality all names, of people and firms, have been altered or left out. This book builds upon my Ph.D thesis which was completed at Trinity College, Dublin. Thus the majority of the research data was collected in Ireland during my time at TCD. However, some supplementary interviews were carried out in the USA during October 1993 while I was based at the LSE.

The interviews themselves were semi-structured. A number of broad areas were covered in each interview (see Appendix 1) although flexibility was allowed so that the interview could pursue areas of interest as they cropped up. All the interviews were taped and they lasted roughly one hour each. These interviews were carried out singly except in two instances when for reasons of time two people were interviewed together.

The quantitative research (also conducted from TCD) involved the conducting of two surveys, one with 400 accountants based in Ireland and the other with 250 Irish accountants based overseas.[7] The response rate of those based in Ireland was roughly 30 per cent and for those abroad it was roughly 40 per cent, the overall number of respondents being 220. The survey population were picked out by using a systematic random sample gathered from the complete list of members held by the ICAI. The two questionnaires covered a similar range of issues which arose largely out of the semi-structured interviews. The area in which the two questionnaires differed most largely concerns the issue of emigration (see Appendices 2 and 3 for a presentation of the two questionaires).

It should be noted here that this book does not deal with the issue of gender at all, although this is an important area given the increase in the female participation rate within accountancy and the professions in general. There are two reasons for this. First, given the recent influx of females into Irish accountancy it would have proved difficult to make insightful comments on their future within the profession as so few women have been in it long enough to have been reasonably expected to have made significant strides up the career ladder. In the light of this age related problem it would have been difficult to prove or disprove the importance of gender as an issue within accountancy, although intuitively the author expects it will prove to be an issue in the promotion debate. Second, given the problems outlined just now, to look at gender in any serious way would have meant that many of the other issues addressed in this book would have had to be sacrificed. This was something I was not prepared to do despite the attractions in examining the nature of female participation in an elite occupation such as accountancy.

A second and possibly more contentious weakness within this work lies in the fact that what is presented is a theory of change and yet the research methodology provided only a static investigation of socialisation and migration. While this is recognised, the argument for the rise of the commercialised class does not depend on it. Hopefully, these issues can be taken up in future work. Having highlighted this weakness I would still strongly defend the work as I believe that a combination of my empirical research and evidence from elsewhere makes the theory highly plausible at the very least.

Having mapped out the broad terrain within which I hope to place the chartered accountancy profession we will now turn in Chapter 2 to the historical development of accountancy.

2 The Formation of a Polarised Profession: Economic Concentration and Geographic Dispersal within Accountancy

Accountancy has become the preeminent qualification for business in the Anglo–American world. This is not because it has some inherent quality rendering it absolutely essential to the planners and strategists of modern business, rather it has to do with the historical development of Anglo–American capitalism. Many writers have shown that other major economies have managed sufficiently well without giving accountants a pivotal role. In Germany and Sweden engineers appear to fulfil the managerial role occupied by British accountants (see Lawrence, 1980; Glover and Kelly, 1987 for Germany and Jönsson, 1991 for Sweden). This chapter will only briefly examine the emergence of accountancy as *the* business qualification in the UK and the USA as this topic has been adequately researched elsewhere (Hannah, 1976; Stacey, 1954; Jones, 1981; Tricker, 1967). The chapter accepts the important role of the accountant within modern business and concentrates on the development and growth of the large international accountancy practices. These practices are commonly known as the 'Big Six'.

Why should I focus the chapter's attention mainly on the Big Six? Largely because these practices dominate the profession globally. In 1981 they audited 493 of the Fortune 500 corporations in the USA and all of the companies quoted on the New York Stock Exchange (Tinker, 1985: xvii). In Britain the top eleven practices in 1984 (mergers have since reduced this number) controlled 1254 of the largest 1872 firm audits (Bohdanow-icz,1984: Chart 2). It is the same practices that dominate on both sides of the Atlantic (and elsewhere). As will hopefully be highlighted throughout this book, everything about these organisations is international – their outlook for the future, their clients, their labour markets, their resource structures and so forth. It is through their international expansion that they came to dominate Irish accountancy (Robinson, 1983). The dominance of these firms has led one writer to rather romantically state

The Big Eight are the glamour capitals of accounting. They inhabit a land of prestigious fat-fee accounts and work with an all-star cast of clients the likes of Exxon, TWA, General Electric, Ford, the Hughes Empire, Chase Manhattan Bank, ABC, and the Oscars. This association with the high and mighty gives the Big Eight an aura of excitement. (Stevens, 1984: 13)

It is the task of this chapter to map the route by which small practices in the nineteenth century became depositories of excitement in the late twentieth. What follows is largely a general history and although quite detailed it does not examine all the historical issues that have emerged. For a more in-depth account of this history see Jones (1981) or Stacey (1954).

THE HISTORICAL BEGINNINGS, 1850–1900

There appears to be a general consensus that the first place where accountancy practices were significantly developed was Scotland. Accountants emerged in Glasgow and Edinburgh in the 1840s and 1850s. In Edinburgh they were working mainly around administrative areas and law, whilst in Glasgow they moved more firmly into commerce. Accountants were involved in work such as: insurance and actuarial services, insolvency, debt collecting, etc. The profession was viewed as an extension of the legal profession (Jones, 1981). These Scottish bodies applied for and were duly awarded royal charters – Edinburgh (1853), Glasgow (1855), and Aberdeen (1867) – although they did not merge into the one Institute until 1951.

As the profession began to emerge south of the border it did so, not surprisingly, in the industrial centres. Thus the first English accountancy bodies were established in Liverpool (1870), London (1871), Manchester (1873), and Sheffield (1877). In 1880 these bodies were incorporated into the Institute of Chartered Accountants in England and Wales (ICAEW) under a royal charter. These accountants came from the growing bourgeoisie and, for a whole series of social reasons, the profession was made up of non-conformists rather than Church of England believers (for a further discussion of these events see Stacey, 1954).

The history of these practices is intertwined and intimately connected with the rise of Anglo–American capitalism. A number of processes in the period 1850–1900 facilitated the emergence of an accountancy profession. The most obvious and important feature of this period was the continued growth of industry and the consolidation of the Industrial Revolution which had taken place in the preceding century. However, a number of other factors took place that greatly benefited accountants, the most important of which related to changing state policy. State activity aided accountancy primarily in three ways:

(1) The increasing role of state legislation, particularly the Companies Acts of 1844, 1847 and 1862. The 1844 Act permitted the creation of joint-stock companies via the granting of limited liability. This later led to the separation of ownership and management, which in turn gave an increased importance to the role of auditor as watchdog. Other legislative changes such as the various Factory Acts (Marx, 1976a) lessened many of the abuses perpetrated on labour and, as a result, put increased emphasis on costing and efficiency, a feature that is probably of more importance today (Jönsson, 1988). This indirectly benefited the accountant. It was not inevitable that the accountant should benefit from such a process Jönsson (1991) has highlighted how in Sweden costing and cost accounting came to be dominated by engineers.

(2) The growth of taxation from 1800 onwards. This created work for accountants in two ways – first, to collect and calculate tax on behalf of the state and second, to help individuals avoid paying it.

(3) Increased educational facilities from 1850 on enabled accountants to widen the pool from which they recruited. These changes, plus events more generally such as the increased size of organisations, the increased division of labour, the greater complexity of production and so on meant there was an increased need for specialised knowledge. Accountants provided aspects of this knowledge and thus the growth of the profession accelerated.

At the beginning of their business life these accountancy practices had a different market in comparison with the one they later developed. The main sources of income were from book-keeping, insolvency and bankruptcy, investment trusts, life assurance etc. whilst auditing was a lot less important. Although the Municipal Corporations Act 1835 allowed anyone to establish a business provided they made use of an auditor, it did not greatly increase the importance of auditing within the profession. This was partly because it was a restricted piece of legislation geographically but, more importantly, because *anyone* could perform the audit. Accountants did of course gain from the Act but this was largely because of the increased bankruptcies that followed it (Stacey, 1954).

The audit became compulsory for all firms with the Companies Act 1900 (it was, however, only in 1948 that audits were limited to qualified accountants). In contrast to this the German experience was different. In 1914

German law *allowed* shareholders, but did not oblige them, to appoint auditors (Gallhofer and Haslam, 1991). The fact that previous to this German law did not allow shareholders to demand the appointment of auditors reflects the interest the German state had in facilitating capital accumulation by the management rather than guaranteeing the absolute rights of the shareholders as was the practice in the UK. Jönsson (1991) has also argued that in Sweden shareholders were largely regarded by the state as mere speculators and, indeed, accountants were viewed as a vested interest and as such could not be trusted to act impartially. One consequence of these features was that the notion of the audit giving a 'true and fair' account of the company's finances for the investing public was given little, if any, importance. In such an environment it was the state that assumed the role of public watchdog and the 'public' did not merely consist of investors but the whole of society, including labour. All of this hampered the rise of the accountant to the top of the management ladder. Yet again in comparison with the UK the investing public and stock exchange in Germany were relatively small whereas the banks played a large role in providing industrial capital to industry; this meant that auditors did not have the role of providing accurate information to an otherwise poorly informed public. An altogether different situation emerged wherein the German banks created their own auditing wings to ensure the safety of their investments (Gallhofer and Haslam, 1991).

However, to return to Britain the Companies Act 1900 consolidated the audit as the centre of a large practice's business (it had been growing as an increasing percentage of the business in the two decades preceding 1900). Because the audit was an annual requirement it gave some measure of assured growth and stability to the profession. It was on the basis of these changes that accountancy moved into the twentieth century.

1900–40: THE EMERGENCE OF LARGE SCALE PRACTICES

A number of features which have since shaped accountancy emerged in the first half of this period. These were;

- The increased domination by London
- The establishment of practices abroad
- The growth in the status of the accountant.

Each of these factors has had a lasting impact upon the profession worldwide.

The Increased Domination by London

The increased role of London came about because of the fact that it dominated the economy generally. Most of the large UK corporations had their HQs in London. As a result, an accountancy firm needed a London office if it was to take advantage of this very lucrative market. It is at this time that Scotland, possibly the major force within the profession heretofore, begins to lose out. Many Scottish practices started to follow their clients to London. As the clients of the Scottish practices grew they went South and the practices followed suit. This was noticeable for both Brown, Fleming and Murray (now part of the Big Six firm Ernst and Young; see Jones, 1981) and Thomson McLintock (now part of the Big Six firm KPMG; see Winsbury, 1977). Thomson McLintock opened a London office in 1914, in part as a response to the growth of work generally in London, but also because many of their clients had London bases and in order to keep these clients McLintock had to have people in London permanently. The move south was directly precipitated by the bankruptcy of the Northern Equitable Insurance Company which had moved its HQ from Glasgow to London. In order to carry out the bankruptcy work Thomson McLintock created a London branch. In many respects this flow to London became self-perpetuating.

This shift meant that there was a great deal of work to be found in London simply because this migratory trend was noticeable in all areas of business. One consequence of this was that the London accountancy offices became powerful and they soon outstripped their head offices at generating fee income(see Figure 2.1). In 1933 the London office was only nineteen years in existence yet it had a fee income roughly four times that of its 56 year old Glaswegian counterpart.

Another feature which accelerated the growth of London was the nature of the economic changes taking place in Britain. After World War I the traditional industrial areas like Scotland and the North of England went into decline, whereas London, the south generally, and the Midlands, benefited from the new economic growth centred around car production, chemicals, electrical engineering and so on. This meant that although the Northern practices gained work by way of insolvency and bankruptcy, this work only led to short term profits, whereas the south gained from the formation of new clients and the creation of new long term annual audits. These processes further tilted the balance of power towards London (Jones, 1981).

Because of the nature of accountancy partnerships the London offices were soon able to exert their new-found strength. The terms of a partnership are renegotiated periodically and if a successful resolution cannot be

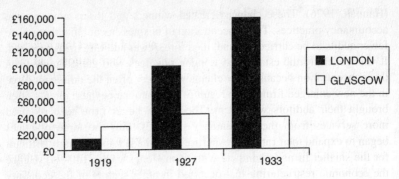

Source: Winsbury, 1977: 23.

Figure 2.1   Fee growth of Thomson McLintock's London and Glasgow Offices, 1919–33

found the partnership is dissolved. As these London offices grew they demanded increased authority and a greater share of the profits when renegotiation took place. It was very difficult for the non-London partners to refuse. If they did refuse it meant they would lose many of their London based clients, as these clients were often more loyal to the particular partner or manager they dealt with than the firm. Thus the non-London partners would have to establish a new London office and start from the very beginning again. This would prove more difficult the second time around as they would not have the same degree of business moving to London that they had originally and, added to this, was the fact that the London market had now got long established practices thereby making competition more intense. In the light of these pressures many renegotiated on London's terms.

This friction was noticeable amongst the Thomson McLintock offices. The London office came to resent Glasgow's interference and in the 1930s stated that it wanted to appoint its own staff as partners. This and other features, such as the fact that London felt Glasgow was charging too much for inter-office work, led to a split. When the split came it benefited the London office most; London was allowed operate all over Britain whereas Glasgow was confined to Scotland. These firms reunited in 1954 at the behest of London which was then engaged in establishing national coverage. In this latter partnership London was very much the senior firm (Winsbury, 1977; Stacey, 1954).[1]

The last factor which greatly helped London, and in many ways began to polarise the profession in terms of size, was the series of amalgamations, mergers, and takeovers that occurred in the UK during the 1920s and 1930s

(Hannah, 1976). These changes created winners and losers amongst the accountancy practices. The concentration of business meant that there were fewer audits to be carried out and, therefore, fewer auditing firms required. It was generally the established London practices who gained most from this concentration because their clients were very often the dominant force in the new enlarged firms. As a result of this dominance these clients often brought their auditors with them. These new, larger firms also required more services from the accountancy practices, thus the large practices began to expand their range of expertise. This made it increasingly difficult for the smaller firms to compete with them (Jones, 1981: 140–74). Hence the economic restructuring that occurred in other sectors of the economy had a very significant impact upon the nature of accountancy's growth. Many of these large audits were secured through close personal ties and by the penetration of the commercial and industrial elite by the senior partners in major accountancy practices (Jones, 1981).

All of the above changes ensured that by 1940 the accountancy profession in the UK was dominated by a relatively small number of large London based firms.

The Establishment of Practices Abroad

The international expansion of the large practices was prompted by many of the same processes that encouraged the move to London. In the 1920s and 1930s many of the major London firms began to establish contacts overseas. Many English firms had developed US connections as early as the turn of the century, for example Whinney, Smith and Whinney had links with Ernst and Ernst of the USA in the early 1900s (Jones, 1981), George A. Touche and Co. linked up with John B. Niven and Co. to form Touche Niven and Co. to cater for transatlantic clients, and Price Waterhouse opened an office in New York in 1890 which later became Jones Caesar in 1895 (Richards, 1981). After this these firms began to establish contact with accountants in other Commonwealth countries such as South Africa, New Zealand, Australia, or Canada. These were not full mergers; rather they were agreements to cooperate on international projects. These agreements concerned issues such as costs, standards and so forth but not areas of firm strategy or structure.

During the inter-war period these London firms expanded into Continental Europe. However, the nature of this geographical enlargement was fundamentally different from previous cross-border endeavours. These offices were established by the major English firms from scratch rather than via links or mergers with existing practitioners. This was largely because the Continental Europeans had a relatively weak accountancy tradition. Thus by World War II there was a German Price Waterhouse and Whinney Smith and Whinney and Brown, Fleming and Murray between them had established the Continental *Treuhand* practice. These firms and others like them were to service international clients (referred from the HQ in London) *and* they were also to actively court local business; this latter point was a new departure. Many of these firms severed their UK connections during World War II although they did not go out of business – Continental *Treuhand* became one of the relatively few strong Continental practices. The fundamental reason for this international expansion was the need to follow clients if they were to be satisfied and maintained as clients (Jones, 1981: 180). This international expansion reinforced the gap that had emerged between the elite London practices and the other firms.

These international moves, as briefly pointed out, had led many practices to look towards establishing contacts with the USA. Many US practices were formed by British accountants who had at one point worked for the big London firms, e.g. Touche Niven and Co's 'American' founder had worked for Touche's of London (Richards, 1981). American practices came to dominate the global accountancy profession as US industry, and the US economic system more generally, became supreme within the global economy. From about 1920 onwards most of the innovations within international accountancy were made in the USA. Many of these innovations were related to the changing corporate structure of companies, the development of multi-locational plants, and the emergence of the holding company and later on the multi-divisional organisation (Hannah, 1976). These changes took place in the US before they did in Britain, reflecting the earlier concentration of business in the USA. One example of this process is the fact that the publishing of consolidated accounts – simply the detailing of profits and losses for each individual subsidiary company by its controlling organisation – was legally enforceable in the USA in 1918 whereas in Britain this law was only passed in 1948 (Jones, 1981: 152). The publishing of consolidated accounts was a means whereby investors had access to more information about the company's finances.[2] The larger companies in the USA and the greater dynamism of the American economy ensured that the leading US practices developed specialisms, such as management consultancy, earlier than their British counterparts and that they grew to a larger and more powerful size. The beginnings of these processes occurred around World War I and the inter-war period and meant that during the post-World War II boom it was the US firms and not the British ones that dominated the profession worldwide.

The Growth in the Status of the Accountant

As already mentioned, when the accountancy profession first started it was viewed largely as an extension, and a low status extension at that, of the legal profession. The relatively humble social origins of accountants in comparison with other professions such as medicine, the clergy, or law further disadvantaged the profession in terms of prestige (Stacey, 1954). However, by 1940 this had altered. Accountancy had become an established profession, guaranteeing its members a good living and, for those who were successful within the occupation, it assured a path into the commercial and industrial decision making groups of the day. There were a number of events which facilitated this elevation in status.

One, the concentration of industry plus the internationalisation of capital benefited a small number of accountancy practices. These practices became important business entities in themselves. Because of their own organisational importance the partners within these practices came to yield considerable corporate muscle in their own right.[3] However, other more important features aided the profession's rise.

Two, the outbreak of World War I and its unexpected length put the British economy under great strain. The state abandoned its *laissez-faire* policies and directly set about creating a war economy. Within this unusual situation accountancy received a huge boost. Accountants were moved into areas of general financial supervision on a large scale for the first time. As rationing became more widespread new accounting techniques, such as cost accounting, were introduced. The aim of these policies was to make divisions and departments more accountable.[4] These policies were initially implemented in the Department of Munitions but they very quickly spread to other sections of government and to private companies. This created a situation wherein

> the principal domain of accountancy had been public practice during the first decade of the new century, as a result of the war, their talents and skills found employment in such diverse capacities as managers, commercial superintendents, cost and stores accountants, factory accountants, and cost investigators. (Stacey, 1954: 97)

The war meant that for the first time industry began to use accountants as managers and overseers rather than simply as auditors or insolvency experts and so on. Once again this was not predetermined. In Germany accountants did not benefit from the war for two reasons. First, the German state was slower to move to a war economy with greater state control than Britain and second, throughout the war the German state placed little emphasis on cost control; instead it favoured a policy of allowing industry high, some would say exorbitant, levels of profitability in order to stimulate production (Gallhofer and Haslam, 1991)[5] Much of this was in contrast to the British economy where the war also brought other changes such as increased taxes and more complex tax legislation. These also provided a boost to the profession. After the war costing was increasingly used by companies to control their different sections and to plan the organisation and structure of firms. In this new environment accountants were central. The prestige gained by accountants during the war was recognised in 1924, when the Companies Law Amendment Committee was established. This committee was comprised of both accountants and lawyers, indicating that in the eyes of the state the profession had come of age.

The third feature in the accountant's elevation of status was closely related to the adoption of new techniques during the war. It concerns the introduction of accountants into the strategic decision making groups within companies during the inter-war era. As more and more UK companies reorganised and became multi-locational they began to use cost accounting methods (Hannah, 1976). Many of these methods were beyond the grasp of existing managers, who would have come from a non-accounting background; they thus invited accountancy practices in to help reorganise the firm. Having done this it is likely that many of the accountants involved in this process were asked to stay on with the company. As a consequence of these events accountants increasingly joined as part of a management team (Jones, 1981: 156–63). Thus the process whereby accountants from the auditing team joined the management of a client company was created. As a result of these changes accountants increasingly began to work outside practice (see Figure 2.2). The increased importance of the accountant at this time is evident from the growth in the membership of the ICAEW. During the 1910–20 period membership grew by 27 per cent, in comparison during the following decade it rose by 72 per cent (Jones, 1981: Appendix 2), suggesting a rapidly increasing demand for accountants.

Within practice there were also changes. *The Royal Mail Steam Packet Company* case (1931) enshrined the role of the accountant as public policeman in the eyes of the public. This was a fraud case concerning the fact that the directors of the company paid shareholders a dividend from a large, secret, reserve fund which they had set up. The effect of this was that shareholders received a dividend even though the company was losing money. Because of this the shareholders were uninformed about the company's difficulties and the share price was therefore kept artificially high. The auditors were aware of this situation but had kept silent as they felt that their allegiance was to the board of directors rather than the public owners. When the truth became known a trial was held at which many

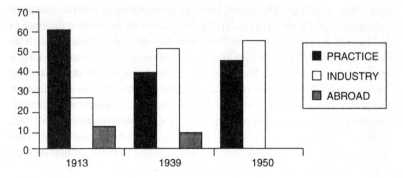

Source: Stacey, 1954: 215.

Figure 2.2   Percentage composition of ICAEW membership, 1913–50

accountants from the leading firms, such as Thomson McLintock, were called to give evidence. The ruling of the court was that the practice had been fraudulent and that the auditors should have informed the investors and thus acted as a public watchdog. This ruling cleared up any ambiguity that may have existed about the Companies Act 1900 and explicitly made the auditor a public representative who was trustworthy, independent, and knowledgeable (although there is still a debate about whether or not the auditor's primary function is to highlight fraud, see Chapter 4). In many ways this judgment was a culmination of the growing separation of ownership and management (Stacey, 1954: 70) and I would argue the acceptance of the UK state of the profession's independence and pivotal role of the shareholder. In direct contrast to the UK state in Sweden after the collapse of the Krueger empire in 1932 the state began to perform this watchdog role and treated investors and accountants with scant regard (Jönsson, 1991). Likewise, as stated, the German state actively encouraged the creation of secret reserves or was at best ambivalent about them until 1920 at least (Gallhofer and Haslam, 1991).

What must be borne in mind about the issue of status is that the large practices and their employees gained immensely. It was the senior members of these practices that gave evidence in court and sat on governmental committees, it was these groups that helped reorganise large corporations and held the important state departmental posts during the war, not the small practitioner who did the books for the local corner shop. Although smaller accountants did possibly gain as a result of this prestige their working environment did not greatly alter. They were divorced from this glamorous corporate world. It is accurate to say that by 1940 the UK profession was well on its way towards polarisation, both in terms of practice size and the nature of the work carried out by accountants. Small practitioners worked for individuals and small firms preparing accounts and giving limited tax advice, whereas their larger counterparts were engaged mainly in auditing whilst training, and, as they got increasing experience, management services and corporate tax. After World War II the trends examined throughout this section intensified. These features, along with an increased propensity towards merger, created a situation very like the one we have today.

POST-WAR ACCOUNTANCY

World War II presented many of the same problems for the government as World War I had. Basically these difficulties concerned how to plan, control and coordinate a war economy. In the UK this involved the establishing of committees to oversee production and distribution. Accountants were placed on these committees which assessed the demands of the state, manufacturers, and consumers (Stacey, 1954). Added to this was the increased need for productivity, thus enabling cost accounting to grow in importance still further.

In the post-war period, partly as a response to their role during the war, the Companies 1948 Act gave certain accountants the sole legal right to perform an audit.[6] The 1948 Act also made it illegal for a holding company not to present consolidated accounts (see earlier). State action also brought other benefits to accountants.

The large practices also received a great boost from the government's nationalisation scheme. Roughly 20 per cent of the UK's industrial capacity was nationalised after the war. This ensured the further creation of very large industrial organisations. Each of these new, enlarged firms required a single auditor. It was the large, London based practices that received these audits. The smaller practices had neither the expertise nor the capacity to carry this work out (Stacey, 1954: 224–30; Jones, 1981: 208; Richards, 1981: 92). Nationalisation also helped certain accountants in another sense. These new, state firms placed greater emphasis upon the internal audit and the monitoring of the company from within. This meant that growing numbers of accountants could leave practice and find work in industry. This again favoured accountants from the big practices because from their training they had experience of large organisations and the accounting systems that were implemented in these organisations, unlike their smaller counterparts (this advantage still exists today, see Chapter 3).

With this increased size of business, partly as a result of nationalisation but also due to the increased numbers of mergers and takeovers in the private sector (Hannah, 1976), the accountancy practices began to amalgamate. This process really began to emerge in the 1960s and it is best highlighted by taking one of the Big Six firms, Ernst and Young, as an example (see Figure 2.3).

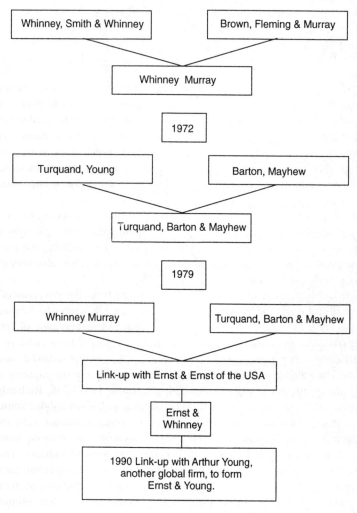

Figure 2.3   The merger process of one major UK practice since 1965

As is shown in Figure 2.3, these large London, and indeed US firms, went through a period of rapid expansion via mergers with firms of equivalent size. This change was not merely confined to Ernst and Young change was also occurring amongst other firms for example Thomson McLintock, Peat Marwick and others (for a chronological account of many of these mergers see Jones, 1981; Richards, 1981; Winsbury, 1977). The mergers with other large firms took place to give the firms greater size thereby giving greater expertise, capacity and international scope. These firms were also merging with provincial practices in order to gain a national geographical coverage. It was decided by most of the London practices to expand nationally through mergers with local firms because it would prove too difficult to grow via organic development. These difficulties arise from the reluctance of clients to leave their existing accountants and because of the importance attached to having local people who are both known in and are aware of the regional business environment. The provincial firms were willing to merge due to the gains that could be achieved i.e. the referred work deriving from London's multi-locational clients and membership of a large national, or indeed international, practice brought status. Although it made economic sense for many of the large practices to merge, there is a possibility that many of these amalgamations were prompted by fear and as a reaction to similar moves by rivals (Jones, 1981: 221). One consequence of the tendency towards larger practices was the dropping of the legal requirement in 1967 by the state which restricted partnerships to a maximum of twenty partners.

Related to the national merger boom was the continued growth of practices overseas. As highlighted, many of the large practices had connections abroad prior to World War II. In the post-war period this expansion grew dramatically. Again it was related to what was occurring in other sectors of the economy. During the decades 1950–70 the percentage of Top 100 UK manufacturing firms with interests abroad increased from 29 to 58 per cent. The UK was not alone in this process other major economies were also involved in this global growth, especially the USA (Armstrong *et al.*, 1984). This led to increased cooperation between the British and American accountancy practices. They began to combine and establish, or re-establish, Continental European firms. Thus in 1969 Whinney Murray and the American practice Ernst and Ernst formed Whinney Murray, Ernst and Ernst. This Continental European firm was formed to serve multinationals. Its partnership reflected Anglo–American dominance with 13 of the 29 partners coming from Britain or the US. One other example of Whinney Murray's worldwide growth was the fact that Turquand Young, who were strong in Asia, looked after Whinney Murray's Far Eastern clients. These geographical features were important factors in the mergers which took place in 1979 between the firms concerned (see Figure 2.3).

It became increasingly important to have a connection or an office overseas during the 1960s and beyond. International practices increased their client base through referred work, kept large clients because they had international connections, maintained their size in some instances simply through referred work, lost portfolios if they could not provide an international link up and so on; these features led many of the large firms abroad (Winsbury 1977; Jones 1981; Richards 1981).

What is noticeable about all these mergers is the desire to achieve an adequate spatial coverage. There is also a strong wish to achieve a favourable geographical fit. Thus a firm that is strong in Asia and is weak in America will merge with one that has the opposite characteristics (this particular example is closely identified with the mergers in Figure 2.3). This trait is still prevalent today. The reason for the importance of geography is due to the spatial expansion of firms in other economic sectors and the fact that the audit has to be carried out on site. This latter point meant that a local office was a prerequisite for carrying out an audit (with the advent of the computer audit this may alter, see Chapter 3).

Another aspect to the growth of multinationals was the fact that they required a new level of expertise and new services. Many of the specialisms which exist today originate from this time. It is at this point that services such as international tax, corporate planning, computer services and so on really begin to emerge.

The growth of the world economy, the creation of new services, the offices abroad, etc. all ensured increased profitability for the large practices. Between 1960 and 1975 Touche Ross and Co.'s fee income increased by 2200 per cent and between 1975 and 1979 it grew by 130 per cent (Richards, 1981: 44). Although Touche Ross' growth was exceptionally high other firms also achieved large increases. However, the downside of all of this expansion was that again in the UK it was the London offices which gained disproportionately. By the end of the 1970s there was clearly an elite of about twenty UK practices that dominated the profession. The smaller firms could not compete with these practices for corporate clients nor for the highest quality staff. The profession was very firmly polarised. The medium practices were under pressure either to merge or run the risk of losing their larger and/or growing clients to these London based rivals. Medium and small firms also found it more difficult to attract the top recruits, these people wanted to join the largest practices (Stevens, 1984). There had thus emerged two, largely separate, labour and business markets but before examining this situation today a brief look at Irish accountancy is required.

IRISH ACCOUNTANCY

The evolution of Irish accountancy has been quite different from that of the British profession. There have been a number of reasons for this but the primary one concerns the relative underdevelopment of the Irish economy and the predominance of agriculture. The first Irish accountants operated from the 1860s, in 1866 there were 27 practitioners operating. It was also in 1866 that the oldest firm in business today, Craig Gardner (now part of the Big Six firm, Price Waterhouse), was established. In 1888 these accountants received a royal charter and thus the Institute of Chartered Accountants in Ireland (ICAI) was formed.

As has been noted previously, the old industrial areas of England and Scotland were where British accountants based themselves (excepting Edinburgh). This process reflects the fact that the chief impetus for the growth of the profession was the development of large scale capitalism, especially the joint-stock company. Ireland lacked this form of development and as such practices had to make do with an exceptionally high number of very small accounts. The fee income was derived from areas such as insolvency and bankruptcy (like their British counterparts), but also from areas such as debt collecting and land agency. This latter feature stems from the high number of absentee landlords in Ireland (Farmar, 1988: 16). Thus in 1870 only 14 per cent of fee income for Craig Gardner came from limited companies whereas 50 per cent of fee income came from accounts worth less than £7 per annum. Three fees made up 20 per cent of Craig Gardner's income yet these three averaged less than £16 per annum each (Farmar, 1988: 23). In comparison with this a large London firm could have ten–fifteen clients paying fees of more than £500 each and an exceptionally large fee would be over £4000 (Jones, 1981: 63). Thus the client base amongst Irish firms was made up of a large number of small accounts simply because of the nature of the local economy. This presented the firms with a problem in that they could not develop the expertise needed to attract large companies, and as such they were viewed as inexperienced in comparison with their London rivals. Because of this the bulk of what large Irish organisations there were, for example Guinness, Power's Whiskey, Jameson's Whiskey, Bank of Ireland, Great Northern Railway, Great Southern and Western Railway, used London accountancy practices (Farmar, 1988: 45). In light of this fact it is not surprising that as late as 1884 the audit only comprised 17 per cent of Craig Gardner's business.

However, in the 1890s this began to change. The change coincided with the launch of a large number of public companies throughout the decade. In the 1890s 40 major Irish firms were launched on the Dublin stock exchange and the number of new limited companies that were registered increased from 50 per annum in the 1880s to 150 in 1897. All of this activity led to increased business for accountants and to an increase in the importance of the audit. This meant that by 1904 the audit was the mainstay of the largest Irish practice. This growth must, however, be put into perspective. Despite the increased volume of business throughout the 1890s, in relative terms, Irish practices fell behind their London counterparts. In 1874 Deloittes' (now a Big Six firm) fee income was £7600 and the fee income of Turquand Young (now also a Big Six firm) was £13 586 as opposed to Craig Gardner's (the premier Irish practice) fee income of £6762. In the intervening twenty years the gap had increased dramatically, Deloittes earned £25 814 in 1887 and in 1895 Turquand Young earned £41 184, whereas in 1895 Craig Gardner earned only £11 800, less than half that of Deloittes and a quarter that of Turquand Young (Farmar 1988: 38; Jones 1981: 263–4). Thus the slow growing Irish economy restricted the development of practices and facilitated the dominance of London. One example of the strength of the London economy was the fact that in the 1900–14 period company launches were averaging 4000 per annum. This growth acted as a magnet by pulling resources towards London.

Craig Gardner decided in 1897 to establish a London office. The reasons for this decision centred around the fact that London was a very rapidly growing business market but there was also the prospect that E. and J. Burke Wine Importers, Gardner's biggest client throughout the 1890s, were contemplating a move to London. As with their Scottish counterparts, the London office began to grow quickly. In 1899 this office contributed £1000 to the Dublin headquarters. It was not long before the London office had grown too large to be simply controlled from Dublin. Until 1903 the business was run as a branch office but when the partnership came up for renegotiation a new arrangement was reached. A new partnership Craig Gardner and Harris was created in London. This new partnership remitted three-eights of its profits to Dublin. In 1910 the London firm was earning more than Dublin and Craig Gardner's Belfast office put together. At this point the London firm broke away completely and formed Harris, Allen and Co. Harris, Allen and Co. eventually went on to take Craig Gardner's largest client account away from the Irish practice. It is quite likely that if the firms had not split altogether in 1910 then the centre of power within Craig Gardner would have shifted to London during the following decades. By the outbreak of World War I Irish accountancy had become a backwater, much the same as Scottish accountancy had. The Irish firms had a high percentage of small accounts and even their large clients were quite small by international standards. Craig Gardner, Ireland's largest practice, had a client base very similar to that of a small or medium English practice. The events which took place after World War I firmly reinforced this pattern.

With the advent of the audit as the major component of fee income, the profession's growth became increasingly dependent upon the growth of the economy in the long term, that is upon the creation of new profitable companies that would guarantee substantial amounts of audit work. However, World War I interrupted a period of economic growth in Ireland. Craig Gardner's fee had grown by 30 per cent between 1910 and 1913, with the outbreak of war this growth ceased. As stated, the economy of Ireland, especially Southern Ireland, was primarily agricultural (Meenan, 1970). This meant that the role of the accountant in Ireland was not as significant as that of his or, in the very rare instances, her British counterpart during the hostilities. There was little need for Irish accountants on governmental committees nor was there much scope for the implementation of cost accounting techniques within Irish industry, which was of a limited nature. Where firms were large enough and strategic enough to be important within the war economy they used London accountants. Thus although Irish accountancy did gain from the upgrading in prestige that the profession received after the war, it did not move as directly centre stage within the economy as its British counterpart. This was due to the fact that the economy was not industrial.

In the post-independence Ireland this weak industrial base continued to stifle the growth of the profession. Ireland's economy largely stagnated during the inter-war period (Crotty, 1986). This negatively affected Irish accountants and in 1926 there were just over 700 (Farmar, 1988: 128). Added to this poor showing was the fact that in real terms Craig Gardner's fee income was less in 1922 than it had been in 1914. During the 1920s there was little new industrial growth. Between 1922 and 1930 only 50 public companies were registered and about 100 small private firms were registered annually (Farmar, 1988; 129). This ensured that new work was very difficult to come by. Thus the Irish profession did not achieve anything equivalent to the development the London practices encountered. For example in 1930 fee income for Craig Gardner amounted to roughly £30 000 (Farmar, 1988; 127) whereas for Whinney, Smith and Whinney's London office on its own the figure was £61 598 (Jones, 1981: 265).

With the emergence of a Fianna Fail government in the 1930s and the implementation of protectionist policies there was some move towards industrialisation (Crotty, 1986: Meenan, 1970). Many of these new industrial firms were semi-state bodies such as Aer Lingus, Coras Iompair Eireann and so on. However, these new, and by Irish standards large, audits appear to have been granted on a political basis. Many of the Irish, Catholic, Nationalist practices such as Kennedy Crowley benefited from this development, whereas the Anglo–Irish practices like Craig Gardner received very few state audits despite their larger size. The other side of this coin was the tendency of the large Protestant firms, for example the banks, to use Protestant accountants. This meant that the growth of large practices was further restricted.

The substantial lack of industrial development in Ireland from 1920 through to 1960 forced accountants to operate in a very restricted market. As stated, much of the industrial development that did take place was state sponsored and as a result, the winning of audits depended upon having the correct social and political connections. To some degree this ensured that practices remained small because the original large practices were Anglo–Irish and thus lost out to smaller Nationalist firms. One dramatic example of this political patronage concerns the Irish Hospital Sweep Stakes. This account went to Craig Gardner (in itself this was an anomaly). The reason Craig Gardner received the portfolio was due to the fact that Joe McGrath, one of the principal organisers of the Stakes had worked, with his brother, for Craig Gardner before joining the IRA. The Sweep Stakes also demonstrate how small the Irish market was: in 1935 the fee for the work represented 30 per cent of Craig Gardner's total fee income. This amounted to £12 000 out of a total of £36 000 (this compares very badly with Thomson McLintock of London who in 1933 earned £159 000 in fees).

In terms of social composition Irish accountancy in the post-independence decades was very much a middle class profession. To join an accountancy practice one had to have close contacts with one of the partners; one also had to pay a premium. There were other restrictive features as well: a partner was limited to having at most two apprentices at any one time, and non-graduates, as the bulk of trainees were at this point, had to complete a five year apprenticeship. The premium was quite substantial, somewhere between £150 and 200. This was considerably more than the average industrial wage of the time (in the late 1920s this was around £120 a year). These features effectively ensured that the profession remained middle class. Craig Gardner did not abolish the premium practice until 1957, shortly after this they began to move towards a graduate recruitment policy (Farmar, 1988: 130).

One last characteristic of this era is the lack of innovation or new accounting techniques within Irish accountancy. The USA and Britain had significantly contributed to the technical side of the profession. These contributions had come about due to the merger booms that had taken place within both countries and the advent of the holding company and later on the multi-divisional corporation. In Ireland these organisational structures did not emerge until well into the 1960s and by that time the technical issues had been resolved by others. Because of the small nature of Irish industry the audit was often carried out after the practice had prepared the accounts i.e. there were few rigorous internal audits and few industrial accountants. This meant that the audit technique developed slowly. When the Irish economy did begin to expand rapidly in the 1960s it was largely on account of foreign investment. These foreign multinationals required that their audits be performed to the same standards as the audit of their head office. This meant that Irish accountants implemented non-Irish standards, although the accounts were adapted to the local tax framework. The creation of international links with British and American practices further consolidated this process.

As with most areas of the Irish economy in the 1960s the accountancy profession blossomed. The state moved towards a policy of attracting foreign direct investment at a time when international capital was highly mobile (Kennedy and Dowling, 1975). The change in the economic environment led to new tax legislation, new company formations, increased mergers, increased audits – both from new indigenous firms and from foreign subsidiaries and so forth. All of this activity led to increased work for accountants and to increased numbers of accountants. Between 1964 and 1969 Craig Gardner's fee income doubled from £256 000 to £571 000 (Farmar, 1988: 205–7). The large practices began to reorganise and offer new services. Tax departments grew rapidly, computers were introduced, management consultancy services were initiated for the first time, the post of manager was created within the practices and so forth. (although it must be remembered that this growth had its origins in a very small base). In 1962 of Dublin's 116 accountancy firms only Craig Gardner had ten partners and a mere five other practices had five partners or more (Robinson, 1983: 234). Having stated this, it is reasonable to say that with the sustained industrial and economic growth, these practices began to move in the direction that their British counterparts had already taken.

It was also at this time that mergers began to take place. These amalgamations were both local and international. Many of these mergers clashed with one another, for example Kennedy, Crowley and Co. (Ireland's second largest accountancy firm) formed a separate partnership with the international firm Arthur Young. In 1972 they merged with Stokes, Pim and Co. (Ireland's third largest practice) to form Stokes, Kennedy, Crowley (this was then, and still is, the largest practice). However, a difficulty arose in that Stokes, Pim and Co. had links with the international firm Peat Marwick Mitchell. Thus the new firm had two international links and as a result in 1978 Arthur Young severed its connections with Stokes, Kennedy, Crowley. There was a degree of chopping and changing like this throughout the 1960s and 1970s. Mergers similar to this became widespread both at a national and an international level (for a chronological discussion of these events; see Robinson, 1983). What is noticeable about the mergers with the international firms is the rapid succession with which they occurred. This was perhaps unavoidable in light of the tendency for these firms to expand abroad partly as a reaction to similar moves by rivals (Robinson, 1983: 239).

These international mergers appear to have been instigated by the British or American firms. Both Cooper Bros and Price Waterhouse approached Craig Gardner and proposed a merger. The firm merged with Price Waterhouse possibly because they had dealings with one another in the past. These advances by the international practices reflect the fact that they wanted offices in all the regions that their multinational clients had established sites. Since 1958 Ireland had been attracting substantial numbers of foreign firms, many of these were American in origin and although the overtures came from UK practices this is merely because the UK and US firms had links anyway. The exact nature of these international links appear to be very hard to establish, both for myself and for other authors (see Robinson, 1983; Bohdanowicz, 1984).

Despite these restrictions, the practices appear to operate under a federal structure within which the Irish firm has a great deal of autonomy. When Cooper Bros approached Craig Gardner about the possibility of a merger the terms were quite generous. Craig Gardner would receive 90 per cent of fees from work referred to it by the newly created international firm, it would pay 2.5 per cent of the fee to the firm referring the work, 2.5 per cent of the fee would be kept by the partners of the newly merged firm, and 5 per cent of the fee would be kept by the new firm for its own purposes (Farmar, 1988: 208). Effectively there would be two firms, an indigenous Craig Gardner and an international Craig Gardner/Cooper Bros. This latter firm would derive its fees as described whereas the former firm would be a wholly Irish concern. Craig Gardner rejected this offer and instead merged with Price Waterhouse. The details of this merger are not public knowledge; however, it is unlikely that Craig Gardner gave away substantially more power to its foreign associates when the Price Waterhouse link up took place. To qualify this somewhat, when international amalgamations took place the newly created firm's partnership was usually made up of 50 per cent Irish partners and 50 per cent UK partners, thus some autonomy was obviously conceded. As will be highlighted later on, over the course of the past thirty years this loose federal structure appears to

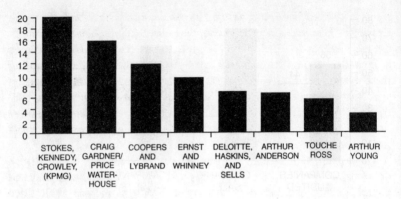

Source: McCurdy, 1988: 11.

Figure 2.4   Title ranking of the Irish Big Eight by fee income, Ir£m

progressing towards a more centralised form. Whatever the exact structure may be, the fact remains that these mergers swiftly put the Big Six at the top of the Irish accountancy league table (see Figure 2.4). In comparison with this the remaining top 25 firms divided a paltry £10 m pounds between them (Fitzgerald, 1987).

ACCOUNTANCY TODAY

As has hopefully been explained, historically there emerged a small number of dominant practices. Throughout the 1980s this concentration increased. In 1982 the Big Nine, as they were then, controlled the vast majority of international audit appointments (see Figure 2.5). Thus internationally there is now a massive gap between the Big Six and the other practices. In 1982 roughly two-thirds of the top 10 000 companies used the Big Nine as their auditors. With the concentration that has taken place since then this supremacy has increased. Within this overall situation if one restricts the inspection to the top 250 international audits the power of the largest practices increases to such a degree that they control 78 per cent of these portfolios (Leyshon *et al.*, 1987a: 10). This dominance translates into greater fee income and greater staff numbers. The fee income of the Big Nine was at least twice that of the remaining top twenty international practices in 1985. They also, on average, employed 2.5 times as many staff, that is 25 000 people as opposed to less than 10 000 for the non-Big Nine firms. These large practices are now massive organisations in their own right (see Table 2.1).

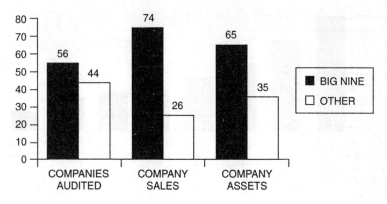

Source: Leyshon *et al.*, 1987a: Table 3.

Figure 2.5   The Big Nine's share of the world's leading international company audits, 1982, per cent

Since Table 2.1 was compiled Arthur Young and Ernst and Whinney (placed second and sixth respectively) have merged, as have Deloittes, Haskins, Sells and Touche Ross (fifth and thirteenth respectively); Klynveld Main Geordler and Peat Marwick Mitchell (tenth and eleventh) also merged. One consequence of this merger process has been that Table 2.1 has altered somewhat.

Table 2.1   The resources of the top thirteen international accountancy firms, 1982

	No. of Partners	*No. of Offices*	*Revenue*
			US$m
Arthur Andersen	1993	165	973
Arthur Young	1964	247	750
Binder Dijker Otte	920	236	N/A
Coopers and Lybrand	2282	429	998
Deloittes, Haskins, Sells	2149	411	800
Ernst and Whinney	1528	314	706
Fox Moore International	N/A	120	N/A
Grant Thornton	1206	286	N/A
Howarth and Howarth	711	127	N/A
Klynveld Main Geordler	2308	369	850
Peat Marwick Mitchell	2197	344	979
Price Waterhouse	1728	345	850
Touche Ross	2054	394	700

Source: Daniels *et al.* ,1986: Table 5.10.

Table 2.2   Five year growth comparisons amongst the top fifteen UK practices

	Fee Income (£m) 1985	1989	Fee Growth per cent	Staff Growth per cent
Peat Marwick Mitchell	132	316	140	49
Coopers and Lybrand	94	225	139	45
Price Waterhouse	85	222	162	64
Deloitte, Haskins, Sells	82	189	130	28
Ernst and Whinney	70	148	112	24
Arthur Andersen	47	144	206	73
Touche Ross	59	142	138	57
Arthur Young	64	135	112	41
BDO Binder Hamlyn	48	89	87	221
Grant Thornton	49	86	76	13
Spicer and Oppenheim	34	83	145	36
Pannell, Kerr, Foster	28	63	127	51
Stoy Hayward	16	48	199	86
Clark Whitehall	21	41	99	25
Robson Rhodes	14	29	109	N/A

Source: Jones, 1989: 13.

Throughout the 1980s, within the UK at least, much of the growth that has taken place amongst the large accountancy practices has been disproportionately concentrated in the Big Six (see Table 2.2).

Whereas all the top eight firms had a fees growth rate of at least 112 per cent over the five year period only three of the remaining seven did – see Table 2.2 (or if you examine the top twenty firms only five of the remaining twelve had). The practices in the lower half of Table 2.2 also tended to expand their staff numbers more rapidly than the Big Eight despite their weaker fee income growth.

Another noticeable trend that occurred in the 1980s has been the stagnation, and even decline, of the audit as a part of total fee income. This is not to say that the audit is unimportant, merely that the growth areas are in producer services such as management consultancy; the audit still provides about 45 per cent of the fees (Leyshon *et al.*, 1987a: Table 5). The comparative figures for Ireland are somewhat similar, although the audit appears to be more important (possibly reflecting the fact that Ireland's multinationals buy at least some of their consultancy services and other services from their home country, see later).

These growth areas are more likely to be control orientated and to be more closely related to organisational strategy, structuring etc. both of

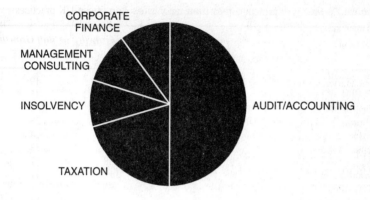

CORPORATE FINANCE

MANAGEMENT CONSULTING

INSOLVENCY

AUDIT/ACCOUNTING

TAXATION

Source: McCurdy, 1988: 75.

Figure 2.6　An analysis of Ireland's Big Eight fee income by function, 1988

which, it would appear safe to assume on the basis of Chapter 1's discussions, have become more important in the 1980s. These figures concerning the audit have led Leyshon *et al.* to comment that the audit is in decline. The fact is that the growth areas lie elsewhere. Because of this fact practices may move back to the situation they were in when they originally formed. During the 1850–90 period accountants acted as advisors and administrators in areas such as insolvency and bankruptcy. In the 1990s, with the audit stagnant, they will increasingly be involved in other areas, although because of the prestige the profession has now, accountants will more likely become 'trouble-shooters' in positions of power and status. There may even be evidence to suggest a similar process is occurring in Sweden today. Jönsson (1991) has highlighted how in the past decade or so accountants have argued for flexibility in costing practices; and are increasingly listened to. Is this evidence of the increased importance of financial control under Flexible Accumulation?

The two trends briefly highlighted above, concentration and a changing market, have had a very perceptible impact upon the profession. In the UK and Ireland, as we shall examine later, the thrust of this impact has been towards polarisation. The profession today is very divided in terms of practice size, client size, and skill (Leyshon *et al.*, 1987a: i). To exaggerate the position somewhat, there are now two types of practice; a small number of large multinational practices serving large national and global clients. At the other extreme, there are a great many small practices serving individuals and small organisations with a limited array of services in a local market (see Davis *et al.*, 1993). As stated, this is a bit of a simplification as it could possibly be argued that there is a third group. This third group is comprised of large medium practices that may have some international connections. There is currently a debate as to whether or not these practices can survive in the present accountancy environment. Writers such as Macaskill (1989) and Fitzgerald (1987) feel that the gap between this second tier of firms and the Big Six can be bridged. However, the over-whelming weight of evidence appears to be against them (McCann, 1988; Counsell, 1988; Jones, 1989; Leyshon *et al.*, 1987a; Briston, 1989).

The other form in which polarisation is taking place concerns the area of skill. The new growth areas within accountancy require a different type of skill to that needed in the past. The more traditional areas, such as the audit (see Chapter 3), are more routine and possibly under some threat of auto-mation (at least in part).

A degree of labour polarisation is developing between the highly qual-ified professionals who concentrate on special tasks and problems, and the heavily computerised support staff with a decreasing need for less skilled junior professionals whose routine work (for example audit) is becoming increasingly automated. (Leyshon *et al.*, 1987a: i)

Notwithstanding these comments, I believe this is not where the major difficulty lies. The early training of an accountant has always been, to some extent routine but, as shall be addressed in Chapter 3, the junior staffs' audit training is the foundation stone upon which their careers are built. The audit training gives them the mobility to move into highly qualified and sought after jobs. As such this routine training has been, and I believe will continue to be, a vital part in the training of the Big Six accountant.

The problem of skill polarisation comes from a different quarter. It relates to practice, and thus client, size. Big Six accountants work in organ-isations that are fundamentally different to those that an accountant in a small practice works in. This means that they get contrasting types of expo-sure and training. It is this factor that goes on to shape the future career of a chartered accountant. The polarisation is not one of an intra-firm skill hier-archy but rather one of two, quite separate, groups of accountants with *very different* skills (see Chapter 3). The polarisation, as regards skill, is hori-zontal not vertical (other factors as we shall examine in Chapter 4 have led to the creation of a hierarchy).

The other feature of growth that emerged in the 1980s and is worth exam-ining concerns London. Leyshon *et al.* (1989) have put forward the sugges-tion that London may be declining in overall influence and that the provincial cities are gaining ground on the capital. They highlight for example the fact that between 1974 and 1984 the percentage of total financial and producer service employment located in London fell from 63 per cent to 59.5 per cent (Leyshon *et al.*, 1989: 12). This decline came about because in many regional cities producer services employment grew at a faster rate than London (London itself did experience some expansion). Nonetheless, what is noticeable about this changing employment structure is the fact that, in relative terms, the older industrial cities and second league financial centres, such as Leeds, Liverpool, and Manchester, declined quite substantially. Thus the growth, by and large, took place in the traditionally smaller centres like Bristol (although Edinburgh did increase quite markedly, this may be connected to North Sea oil). What was taking place, therefore, may simply have been a reshuffle amongst the 'also rans'.

The other aspect to this growth is the fact that it was generally the south that did better, indicating the greater dynamism of the region. There was also a tendency for the regional cities to become more specialised, at least in the 1974–81 period. Thus for example, in Sheffield the percentage of financial service workers in Banking and Bill Discounting increased from 35.9 per cent to 52.6 per cent (Leyshon *et al.*, 1989: 22). It is not unreasonable to assume that many of these jobs were quite routine and part-time as areas of banking have become deskilled throughout the 1980s (Rajan, 1987). This trend towards specialisation lessened somewhat between 1981 and 1984, but it is still important.

Leyshon *et al.* put forward three reasons for this producer service growth. The fact that fewer services are provided in-house today, the fact that advances in communications technology have lessened the importance of location, and the fact that London shed much of the work that was orientated towards the national economy and concentrated on providing services for the world market. This latter feature can be criticised as it would seem to imply that internationally orientated, that is non-local market firms, such as the Big Six, would continue to base themselves in London; if this is the case then London's dominance is possibly even greater today (this argument would be in line with the work of Sassen; see Chapter 1).

However, there are a number of difficulties with this thesis (many of these Leyshon *et al.* highlight). Much of the growth, especially in places like Bristol, may be simply labour intensive work that is shifted to a location where office space is cheaper. These provincial cities also operate in a local market rather than trade internationally thus the long term benefit to the region may be limited. As well as these qualifiers, the fact remains that London's decline has been relatively insignificant – from 63 per cent to 60 per cent: it is still by far the most dominant city in the UK. One last feature is that many of the more successful producer service firms are

operating in areas that have not, as yet, undergone concentration for example Glaswegian legal practices. These same Scottish law firms are now
considering expansion into London, which Leyshon *et al.* (1989: 34)
appear to view as a 'progressive' thing. However, history, and hopefully
this chapter, indicates that when Scottish accountancy practices made this
move 70 or 80 years ago they became London firms. This same process
may very well happen in other areas of the producer services in the future.

It is my contention that it is too optimistic to argue that there is to be a
significant decentralisation of power away from London, at least as regards
accountants. In 1986 three of the leading accountancy firms in the UK had,
on average, 71.4 per cent of their partners based in London. In comparison
with this the next highest figure, Glasgow, was a mere 9.9 per cent
(Leyshon *et al.*, 1987a: Table 21). These firms also tend to locate roughly
half their staff in London. Added to these points is the fact that the top
twenty practices control 75 per cent of the audit appointments in every
region of Britain, thus enabling London to directly dominate other regions
through these organisations. London is also by far the most important
region for audit appointments, followed by the South East (see Figure 2.7).
Within accountancy in terms of partners' votes, staff, fee income, and
client location, London has by far the loudest voice.

Therefore, although Leyshon *et al.* (1989) are right to argue that the
growth of producer services in provincial areas brings advantages, for
instance they are highly embedded within the regional economy and they
have a higher degree of autonomy than many manufacturing concerns, it is
still too early and too optimistic to suggest that 'the south has gone north'.

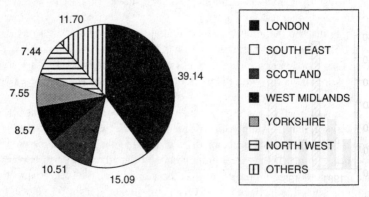

Source: Bohdanowicz, 1984: ix.

Figure 2.7   Distribution of audits by area, per cent

The last area to be examined in this section concerns the issue of international control. In the post-war period the dominant country within international accountancy appears to have been the USA. This trend towards the US entails a loss of power by the UK practices as the bulk of the Big Six firms have their roots in Britain (Leyshon *et al.*, 1987a: 9). There has been very little research carried out to date on the international control processes of the Big Six. This may reflect the reluctance of these practices to divulge any information about themselves (Bohdanowicz, 1984; Stevens, 1984; Robinson, 1988). However, evidence of US prowess may be gleaned from the fact that the American firms are the greatest earners, the largest employers, and have the highest number of offices (see Figures 2.8, 2.9 and 2.10).

The other noticeable trait within this overall picture is that the US practices have the largest number of partners (see Leyshon *et al.*, 1987b: Figures 3, 4, 5). On top of this growth in size has come increased power and influence (Leyshon *et al.*, 1987b: 11).

But this influence is not as cut and dried as one would assume. As can be seen from Figures 2.8 and 2.9 there is some evidence that US power is sagging. This is further reinforced by the process whereby, in relative terms, the number of offices operating in the USA is declining as a percentage of the overall total within some firms. In the past few years the real growth areas for office expansion have been Europe and Asia (Leyshon *et al.*, 1987b: Figure 2). Despite these general trends, Arthur Andersen's US practice has increased its contribution for total firm fee income, up from 69 per cent to 75 per cent between 1981 and 1985 (Leyshon *et al.*, 1987b: Table 9). This is, however, an anomaly and may simply reflect the fact that Andersen's has always been a particularly US dominated firm.

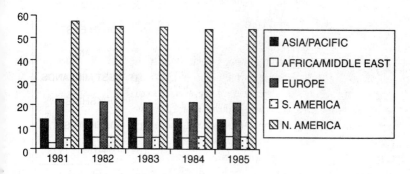

Source: Leyshon *et al.*, 1987b: Table 7.

Figure 2.8   Peat Marwick Mitchell: chargeable hours by region, 1981–5, per cent

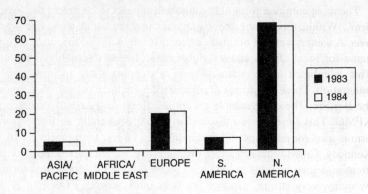

Source: Leyshon *et al.*, 1987b: Table 8.

Figure 2.9   Arthur Andersen: chargeable hours by region, 1983 and 1984, per cent

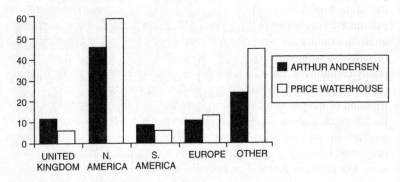

Source: Leyshon *et al.*, 1987b: Table 10.

Figure 2.10   1984/85 world firm staff by region for two of the Big Eight, per cent

As already mentioned the inner workings of these firms remain relatively unknown. Because they are partnerships and have expanded globally, largely through mergers, they are less concentrated than limited companies. In recent decades there has been a move towards a more centralised organisation than has historically been the case, although within the Big Six there is a good deal of variance around the issue of centralisation. The most centralised firm is Arthur Andersen. This practice was started in Chicago and internationalised via takeovers or through starting a practice organically. It opted for a centralised structure in the 1950s when it began to sever all links with other firms. Andersen's is quite unusual as regards its corporate structure.

The most common form of organisation appears to be that of the 'world firm'. Within this arrangement practices use the same name the world over. A weaker version of this is where a strong national firm uses its own name for local clients and its global name for its international custom. This 'combined name' status may be a stepping stone towards greater integration. These two forms of organisation are the most common among the Big Six. The other notable exception, along with Arthur Andersen, is KPMG. This firm uses an associated structure whereby an international firm is used for purposes of coordination, the largest Irish practice Stokes, Kennedy, Crowley is a member of this group. KPMG seem to allow the greatest degree of freedom, possibly reflecting the fact that it was formed by many, very strong, national practices quite recently (Leyshon *et al.*, 1987b: 17).

The large firms seem to be moving more and more in the direction of a 'world firm' structure. In all of these structures common accounting standards are used. These standards are mainly devised in the USA, reflecting the strength of American practices. The local firm is usually subject to an examination every two or three years whereby, a foreign partner or partners arrive to examine the work that has been carried out by the indigenous firm (discussion with partner). Other aspects of these 'world firms' are the policy committees. Each national practice has a number of representatives on these committees; however, the number depends upon the overall contribution of the practice to the firm. As a result of this, these bodies mirror the dominance of the USA. The committees plan and coordinate strategy, put forward proposals for merger, diversification and other similar global decisions. In many ways they reflect what is good for the powerful practices. For example it would be virtually impossible for the Irish partners to convince the firm that a merger should be pursued if it was not beneficial to say, the US practice. How then do these international structures affect the operations of an Irish Big Six practice?

IRISH ACCOUNTANCY'S ERODING AUTONOMY – A NEW FORM OF CENTRALISATION WITHIN PRODUCER SERVICES?

Much of what follows is based on research carried out by the author or, in the section on cross-border trading, the author, Evan Davis, and John Kay (see Davis *et al.*, 1993).

The most noticeable feature about the organisational structure of the international accountancy firms has been the degree of autonomy they have allowed local practices. Because of the tendency within accountancy to devolve power downwards, the Irish partners are allowed run the Irish practices as independent fiefdoms in all matters Irish, provided they adhere to the firm's international standards. Thus the Irish partners decide who will be promoted to partnership, how many partners they need, etc. They alone are responsible for decisions on whether or not to reject clients, buy local practices, use advertising and so on. Anything concerning Ireland is solely the responsibility of the Irish partners unless they choose to consult the international firm. The reason for this is that the Irish partnership is completely owned by the Irish partners. The international link is created through a second partnership which is made up of Irish and international partners. This latter point is not true for Arthur Andersen.

> Yes I mean it is a large practice owned by the Irish partners. Its auton-
> omous except that we would have, particularly in the audit area, there is
> a X way of auditing and a X standard which we have to apply and we'd
> be subject to review every two years by another country to make sure we
> apply the standards correctly. There are other things we have to conform
> to for example we are banned internationally from holding shares in any
> clients. (Stephen Flanagan, Big Six Partner)

So apart from certain standards of behaviour and rules for conducting business these practices are largely independent. However, the standards, technical and otherwise, tend to come from abroad, principally the USA and the UK.

> part of it would be that we have free access to any technical material that
> comes through the UK or is used in the UK because the regimes are so
> similar. (Stephen Flanagan, Big Six Partner)

When dealing with any matters that are not purely Irish this autonomy is restricted. As highlighted the international partnerships have increasingly come under the domination of London and New York firms. Today it is from the USA that the bulk of the suggestions for mergers emanate.

Before these mergers take place a vote is held amongst the partners world-wide. However, because the US partners form a very large minority of the world-wide membership they can, to a large extent, dictate the outcome. The Irish partners on the other hand make up such a small minority of the international firm that their voice largely goes unheard. It is almost impossible for the Irish firm to initiate an international merger and when one, which has been proposed by a larger 'core' practice, is endorsed they must for all practical purposes go along with it.

It wasn't something that was realistically considered [opting out of a newly merged international firm]. Because to us we already had the tie with X, it was very beneficial and we wanted to stay with it. No it would not have been economic suicide to opt out in the strict sense of the term. I should point out that what we call referred work, i.e. work that comes from outside of this country only amounts to 15 per cent of our business. In other words 85 per cent is indigenous or from Irish companies ... so in that strict sense it wouldn't have been economic suicide but it wasn't seriously considered. It would not have made sense from a medium or long term point of view. Economically fine from the 85 per cent of the Irish business but in terms of cutting ourselves off from international developments, opportunities to send our staff overseas to gain the benefits of professional standards and that, it would have been suicide. (Peter O'Neill, Big Six Director)

Kenneth Byrne a partner in a different Big Six firm suggested that opting out of a merger would

have a consequence, you see many of the audit arrangements that these firms do would have an international connection. Some firms are very heavily dependent on introduced work from their international networks and there would be a danger of losing that work if they didn't go into these mergers.

Thus the economic pressures for conforming with international firm policy are enormous. This fact is further emphasised when one examines the degree to which some Big Six practices are dependent on referred work (see Figure 2.11).

When one considers that at the very least up to 15 per cent of a firm's business could be lost to a rival by refusing to partake in an international merger it is not surprising that few firms take this option. Many of these foreign clients would leave because they are looking for firms that could provide them with international standards in the long term and for firms that can provide them with a single world-wide audit technique. These two requirements can only be met by an international practice.

Are these international connections a good or bad thing for the Irish firm and Ireland? The answer is mixed, for the firms themselves they are good. They bring the firms referred work, they have increased the standards within Irish accountancy and introduced new technology, thus bringing the Irish practices up to an international level. They leave the operation of the Irish practice in the hands of indigenous people, they provide locations to which

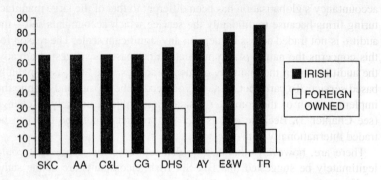

Notes
SKC = Stokes, Kennedy, Crowley/KPMG, AA = Arthur Andersen, C&L = Coopers
and Lybrand, CG = Craig Gardner/Price Waterhouse, DHS = Deloilte, Haskins,
Sells, AY = Arthur Young, E&W = Ernst and Whinney, TR = Touche Ross.

Source: McCurdy, 1988: 74.

Figure 2.11   Nationality of clients amongst the Big Eight in Ireland in 1988, per cent

Irish accountants can be sent to gain international experience (see Chapter 5), they provide expertise to the Irish firms if they ever run into any difficulties and so on. These are all positive things from the firm's point of view.

If one asks the same question about the impact they have had upon Irish society, the answer is less cut and dry. These connections do have certain advantages. It could be argued that the standard of the professional community within the producer services sector is higher now than it would have been if they had not arrived. The producer services are becoming increasingly important as a factor in the locational decisions of business (Gillespie and Green, 1987). As a consequence of this it is possible that through their own firms and through the people who have trained with them and since moved on these practices have added to Ireland's attractiveness as a location for industry.

However, their influence has not been totally positive. There are two possible ways in which these international firms have been negative. The first one is through the creation of an internal international labour market, this market enables the major practices to fill labour shortages in a particular region with accountants from another place. They have also facilitated in the creation of a spatially based international hierarchy within accountancy (see Chapter 5 for a more detailed discussion of these issues).

The second manner in which the Big Six have damaged Ireland concerns the way international trading takes place within accountancy. The nature of accountancy's globalisation has been different to that of the large manufacturing firms because traditionally the service which accountants sell – the audit – is not traded across borders on any significant scale. The reason for this concerns the nature of the product. In the past, as suggested already, the audit has been the mainstay of most practices. The audit is a spatially based service. To carry out an audit you need to be on site and despite the implementation of the computer assisted audit this is unlikely to change (see Chapter 3). Because of this fact the product is not one that can be traded internationally with ease.

There are, however, other factors that reinforce this process. It could legitimately be suggested that Big Six Irish accountants are of the same quality and standards as their British counterparts and yet they are a lot cheaper to hire (see Figure 2.12). Despite the lower costs per hour Irish firms have not been able to penetrate the UK audit market because of two factors. The audit is a service that can only be performed on location, hence the Irish firm would incur extra costs which would offset its competitive advantage (see Davis *et al.*, 1993: Table 6.2). The purchase of expert services is also increasingly affected by reputation. Because the HQs of multinational firms are unaware of the standards of local i.e. non-international professional firms, they are reluctant to buy services from them. At the same time a firm that has a 'good' reputation can use this with increasing effectiveness to penetrate new markets (see Davis *et al.*, 1993 for a more detailed analysis of this argument). Such a reputation is gained in the core states where most of the multinationals originate from. These two factors limit the exporting of accountancy services in the traditional sense and encourage the growth of international practices via merger rather than

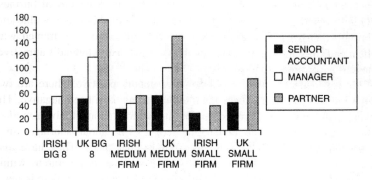

Source: Davis *et al.*, 1993: Table 6.1.

Figure 2.12   Accountants' fees per hours, £ local

organic expansion. Mergers give a firm a local office without expensive start up costs, and they give an international firm local people with contacts amongst the local business community. They also give the local practice a good reputation which it can then use when seeking 'non-local' work. However, the nature of the merger agreement is restrictive. These agreements mean that an Irish Big Six practice cannot compete in the same market as one of its international associates; to trade internationally would entail breaking away from the global practice, and as highlighted earlier this is simply not an option for the Irish firms.

Secondly, the limited international trading which takes place within accountancy is of a negative nature from Ireland's point of view. This trading is located within the growth areas of the profession as opposed to auditing. These areas are less spatially specific than auditing due to their specialised nature. These twin features – highly specialised and geographical mobility – mean these services are exported from particular regions i.e. global cities. The changing nature of trade in accountancy would in part explain the different character of partner specialism within the leading UK accountancy practices by region. Leyshon *et al.* (1987a: Table 23) have highlighted that in the South East region of England of the partners in the Big Eight 14 per cent are in management consultancy and 12 per cent in general practice, whereas, in the more peripheral areas of the South West and Wales the figures are 4 per cent and 54 per cent and 0 per cent and 55 per cent respectively. This would lead one to assume that any management consulting skills required by clients in Wales, and indeed some from Ireland, would be supplied by outside.

How is this negative? It is negative because the spatial organisation of the largest firms ensures that due to agglomeration effects these specialised services are geographically concentrated.This national, and international, trading is all carried out intra-firm. Hence if an Irish Big Six practice requires an expertise that it cannot provide itself, it will employ one of its international affiliates to carry out this service even if another Irish accountancy practice is capable of doing the work. Thus money is moved out of Ireland unnecessarily. The international practice bills the Irish practice and the Irish practice passes on the bill to the client. It is fair to say that business can come into Ireland via a similar process but this is the exception to the rule.

London does engage Dublin from time to time. They'd be inclined to ring here if they've clients seeking to do something in Ireland or clients involved in a particular sector which is well developed here like the agribusiness area. But you'd tend to find the communication more the other way. (Conor Hackett, Big Six Partner)

The benefits and drawbacks of being linked to X international. The benefits are particularly in auditing but there are other areas as well. We feel the way in which we work is up to a professional standard which is partly imposed on us and partly developed by ourselves but this is also related to the resources of X international which we draw upon. Secondly we obviously get a fair bit of work from X worldwide, that would account for a very significant proportion of our fee income throughout the year. The negative side would be that we can't then ourselves go out and compete in other countries. But to reach a stage wherein you'd feel you could go out and compete against X in France or Germany or the UK without the benefits mentioned earlier would never happen. (Stephen Flanagan, Big Six Partner)

Therefore the penetration of Irish accountancy by the large international firms has not been wholly beneficial. The extent to which the merits and demerits of their arrival have affected the future growth and independence of the Irish profession and the Irish economy are beyond the scope of this book but suffice to say there have been positive and negative consequences. The nature of the international structure of large accountancy firms, the importance of reputation as a marketing device, and the increased export orientation of the growing areas within accountancy act as mechanisms through which producer services have become increasingly centralised.

THE ORGANISATION OF THE BIG SIX

Having examined the international structure of the Big Six this penultimate section seeks to briefly describe the internal organisation of an Irish Big Six firm. As will be demonstrated in Chapter 4 there is now an elaborate hierarchy within the Big Six; however, these practices are also broken down into as small a unit as possible thus attempting to keep the benefits of a small firm environment while also being part of a multinational organisation. The most differentiated internal labour market within a Big Six firm is as shown in Figure 2.13. A hierarchy such as that in Figure 2.13 usually comprises part of a division or group within one of the sections that make up a Big Six firm, for instance it would be a section hierarchy within say the audit division. The idea behind using these relatively small groups (see Chapter 3 on the size of an audit team and its management structure) is to maintain a 'small practice' feel to the firm. The overall organisational structure within a complete Big Six practice is highlighted in Figure 2.14. As highlighted,

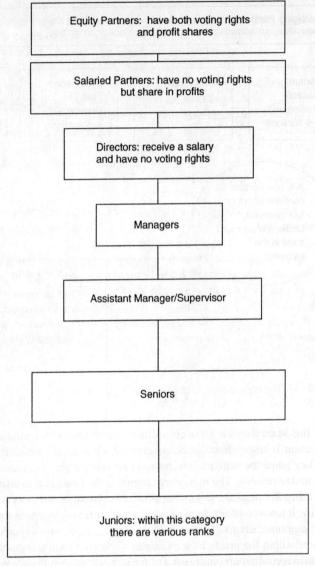

Figure 2.13   The hierarchical structure of a division within an Irish Big Six firm

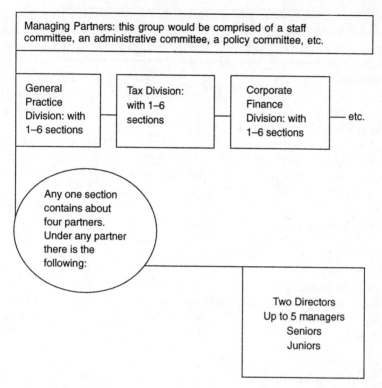

Managing Partners: this group would be comprised of a staff committee, an administrative committee, a policy committee, etc.

General Practice Division: with 1–6 sections

Tax Division: with 1–6 sections

Corporate Finance Division: with 1–6 sections

— etc.

Any one section contains about four partners. Under any partner there is the following:

Two Directors
Up to 5 managers
Seniors
Juniors

Figure 2.14   The organisational structure of an Irish Big Six firm

within the Managing Partners group there are a number of committees. This section is responsible for the overall policy and performance of the firm. They guide the firm, make recommendations for the future and see to its day to day running. The managing committee is the most powerful body within a Big Six practice, somewhat akin to the board of directors within a company. It tends to be made up of people that have been partners for a relatively long time, say five to ten years, and those people who have the largest shares within the practice (see Chapter 4). Within each section there is also a managerial group but this is much more informal. It is comprised of the partners, although they may also seek the advice and opinions of the directors or, where these do not exist, the managers.

Some of these sections will be separate entities rather than legally part of the overall practice. This is because of the rules laid down by the Institute of Chartered Accountants in Ireland (ICAI). The Institute, and indeed many of the Institutes globally, demand that only chartered accountants are made partners within a chartered accountancy practice. The Big Six are, or at least were, chartered accountancy firms. Many of the large practices have sidestepped this rule by creating new partnerships which are not chartered accountancy partnerships, although many of the partners will be chartered accountants. For example one of the Big Six practices has a marketing section, and this section has a number of marketing personnel who are also partners. Under the rules of the ICAI this would not be allowed, so the Big Six practice set up a 'subsidiary' practice that is involved in marketing. All of the partners in the original 'accountancy' practice are also partners in the 'marketing' practice along with one or two marketing people. Theoretically the marketing practice could break away from the overall mother firm but because of the composition of the partnership and the fact that it derives much of its work from the Big Six firm this is an unrealistic proposition. The partners within these two practices all stand on an equal footing as regards voting rights. What has hence emerged is a structure within which there are a number of practices, only one of which is an accountancy practice, with an overall management firm controlling the various activities. Inside this overall structure the hierarchical breakdown is as shown in the General Practice Section of Figure 2.14.

CONCLUSION

Accountancy has achieved a high profile within Anglo–American capitalism for a whole series of historically contingent reasons that did not pertain to states such as Sweden or Germany. Hence accountants have not got some God-given right to manage. Their knowledge and their skills are not the only means of financial organisation. If the rise of accountancy is dependent on certain culturally specific choices then surely other aspects of accounting within the Anglo–American world are also based upon choice and ideology rather than technical necessity; it is this issue that much of what follows addresses. But to return to the content of this chapter suffice to say the historical development of the Anglo–American profession has created a situation that allows a handful of international practices to dominate. These firms are controlled from offices in the major cities of the largest economies, notably the USA.

The spatial progress of accountancy has, to a great extent, been shaped by developments in other economic sectors. As firms in other areas of the economy globalised, the large practices followed suit in order to hold onto clients. The practices internationalised via mergers with indigenous firms. This process was different to the one that took place amongst other organisations. This was largely due to the partnership structure and the reluctance of clients to change accountants. It is because of the importance of the economy to accountancy that many peripheral regions, with underdeveloped economies, have little influence upon the Big Six. The history of Irish accountancy highlights this fact quite nicely.

These developments have left us today with two types of accountancy practice and two types of accountant. There are large multinational practices with close ties to the corporate world and at the other extreme there are small local firms dealing with small companies and individual clients. These firms respectively produce accountants who are groomed for management within large organisations, in practice or industry, or accountants who deal with small clients as advisors or they liaise between individuals and banks, tax officials and so on.

The large practices reflect the power relationships between the core and the periphery. They have acted as a drain from the periphery, Jones (1981) has described how the large London firms have moved people with expert knowledge from Scottish and Northern English offices to London. This further reinforces the agglomeration effects of London. The international firms also prepare people for senior management and have a major impact upon the distribution of income and the control of labour within Anglo–American capitalism. As a result of these roles they hold a pivotal position within the social structure of many states. Because of these features it is important to examine the nature of a Big Six accountant's training and socialisation into the accountancy profession. It is this concern that dominates the rest of this book.

3 Accumulation as an Elite Labour Process within Flexible Accumulation

THEORETICAL PRELIMINARIES

Post-industrial Theory

3 Accountancy as an Elite Labour Process within Flexible Accumulation

In light of the discussion in Chapter 1 concerning the move towards services and the various theories relating to the implications of such a move for the future of work it is insightful to examine accountancy. The purpose of this chapter is to examine auditing as a labour process and to analyse the relevance, or more accurately the irrelevance, of the major theories about work to accountancy. It also seeks to highlight the differences that accountants from different sized practices experience within training. These differences go on to play an important part in the future careers of these people despite their being, to some extent, spurious. The chapter concentrates on auditing because it is through auditing that the bulk of accountants are trained and socialised into the profession.

THEORETICAL FRAMEWORKS

A number of theories have been developed in relation to the future of work and the production process. Each of these has helped to shape the arguments presented in Chapter 1. Because of this they are worth examining. What follows is an analysis of the three most popular theses.

Post-industrial Theory

During the 1960s and 1970s the post-industrial debate commenced. As mentioned in Chapter 1 post-industrial theorists took note of the changing occupational structure within the advanced economies and argued that this was evidence of a move from an 'economising' to a more benign 'socialising' mode. Within this new order knowledge, science, and skill would become the key resources (Bell, 1974). There would be a shift towards a more egalitarian and meritocratic society; education would be made available to all and as such it would act as a passport to social mobility. Class divisions would become increasingly irrelevant as people identified with their occupations rather than their class. The majority of people would work in service employment which would be more rewarding than traditional manufacturing work; alienation would become a thing of the past. In its crudest form skills were to be upgraded and everybody was to become professional. Within such a society investment in labour was considered vital to economic growth (Kerr *et al.*, 1973: 44). Basically, although there are still manual and clerical components to working, the nature of work would change (Bell, 1974: 134).

However, the post-industrialists were very vague about how the content of work would change, except to say that it would become more personal and satisfying. The dynamic force within this new society was to be the professional. These professionals, not the social relations of capitalism, were to fashion the social structure (Bell, 1974: 125). These professional groups would work for the benefit of the whole society. They would not use their monopoly of skills to their own advantage nor would they perform the global functions of capital by helping in the appropriation and realisation of surplus value for one class (see Chapter 6). All of this would happen because the post-industrialists gave the forces of production primacy over the relations within the production process. All industrial societies can become post-industrial and in true modernisation fashion all societies are moving in a linear progression towards a service economy.

In many ways accountants, one would expect, should highlight some of the characteristics of the post-industrial worker. They are highly trained and educated, they have a large degree of control over organisational assets, they, initially at least, work in the service sector, and so on. Thus an examination of the relevance of this theory to the reality of an accountant's training and work should be illuminating. However, before embarking upon a description of the accountant's training some, more general, criticisms of post-industrial theory will be presented.

Needless to say this theory has aroused a great deal of criticism. Why? Largely because it is deemed to have misunderstood the driving force of capitalism. It has been argued that there is little evidence of a shift to a 'socialising' mode (Kumar, 1978). Critics such as Kumar believe that the real driving force is economic, that is the search for profitability, and because post-industrial theory separates the relations from the forces of production it has been accused of technological determinism.

Other criticisms have also been made. Gershuny and Miles have criticised the role it gives to services within the overall economy. They argue that it is a new self-service economy which is emerging and that this economy is based on people serving themselves and as such this form of economic development is leading to renewed manufacturing activity and growth. Thus manufacturing still maintains a central position within their work.

Mandel and other Marxists (see Allen, 1988) believe that services are not that different from manufacturing in terms of controlling the labour process because of the domination of services by capitalists. As a consequence the service sector will undergo a similar process to the one that the manufacturing sector has undergone, and is still undergoing, in terms of ownership, control and so forth.

Finally Kumar and Allen also argue that the service sector does not provide this professional work on the scale the post-industrialists imagine. They state that much of the work in the service sector is poorly paid, non-union, dirty, and in many instances less desirable than work in manufacturing. It is also open to question whether or not many of these 'new professions' are indeed really professional. It can be argued that some groups are merely trying to engage in collective professional mobility for economic reasons rather than any desire to fulfil the traditional Anglo–American idea of the professional which supposedly embraces values such as altruism, impartiality, and/or high moral principles (Kumar, 1978).

Many of these criticisms are valid and have been addressed in Chapter 1's more general theoretical analysis, hence suffice to say that post-industrial theory is not an adequate theory for describing the changes that are taking place both economically and occupationally. It does not describe the situation of certain privileged sections within the service sector, nor does it provide an adequate explanation as to why these groups enjoy the working conditions they do. Fundamentally it ignores the capitalist motive of profitability that lies behind change and the position of groups like accountants within this process (see Chapter 6).

Proletarianisation

The deskilling thesis re-emerged in the early 1970s. It has also been applied to the service sector, having first originated in manufacturing. The general theory proposes that workers are being deskilled, made uniform and therefore interchangeable. This process has the effect of cheapening labour power hence increasing the profit of the capitalist. Deskilling is based on the separation of the conception and execution of tasks, thereby taking as much knowledge of the production process as possible from the worker (Braverman, 1974: 82). This deskilling also increases capitalist control over the worker via a minute division of labour and the embodying of control functions within technology, thus making the worker easily replaceable by weaker and more docile sections of the workforce. This theory comes directly from Marx (Marx, 1976: 545).

As suggested technology, due to the social relations of production, is used to deskill and further subjugate the workforce. This deskilling will spread throughout the manufacturing sector and into services (Braverman, 1974: 83). That no occupation or economic sector is safe from deskilling and Taylorism is also advocated by later deskilling theorists. It has been argued that Taylorism will be put into practice in many of the professions. This has been further facilitated by the advent of microelectronics and information technology (Cooley, 1981). It is not simply the work of those who are employed in traditional industrial areas, such as scientists and technologists, but all professionals even those within the more recently expanded and more 'glamorous' jobs of the service sector. Taylorism will be applied throughout the economy (Hales, 1980: 107).

However, a number of criticisms of the Taylorist thesis have been made (see Wood and Kelly 1988; Gallie 1991). Again it is, to a large extent, technologically determinist. It is correct to argue that technology is often used to deskill workers but this is not an universal application. Many others have shown that the use of technology is influenced by social, historical, organisational and cultural traditions (Wilkinson, 1983: 3). Therefore, simply because technology has deskilled and weakened many of the working class industrial crafts in the past does not mean that middle class professions, especially those that carry out key management functions for capital, will suffer the same fate. Barras has shown that the financial services sector has invested relatively more in technology than either the manufacturing or the public service sectors during the 1970s and early 1980s. These large scale investments in technology have increased productivity (see Chapter 1). This technology, which has been applied to the large accountancy practices, is not seen by the accountants themselves as a threat or a means of deskilling – in fact quite the opposite as we shall see later.

Other criticisms of the deskilling thesis have argued that it ignores the fact that the skilled craft workers, upon which Braverman based his work, distinguished themselves from the rest of the working class thereby helping to fragment it (Gordon *et al.*, 1982). Braverman also implied that deskilling allows the capitalist class total control over the labour process rather than hegemony thus he underestimated the importance of worker resistance (Burawoy, 1988). Added to these criticisms is the fact that Taylorism is not the only school of management thought and control. Others have been used and are quite important, for example the use of internal labour markets, (for a further discussion of all these criticisms see Thompson, 1989). I will argue that the deskilling thesis is an inappropriate theoretical framework for examining accountancy, and most likely the professions in general, even though many have put forward this case (see Oppenheimer, 1973; Hales, 1980; Johnson, 1972, 1986).

At this point I want to turn to a final theory on work – flexible specialisation. Firstly, to allay the fears of the well versed reader, I would like to state that the flexible specialisation arguments have little direct relevance to accountancy as a labour process; however, indirectly flexible specialisation is important for a number of reasons which will be explained along the way.

Flexible Specialisation

The last major global theory which addresses the economic and occupational changes that have taken place and their impact upon the future of work is the flexible specialisation argument. This theory came to the fore with Piore and Sabel's *The Second Industrial Divide* (1984). In this book it is argued that there has been a move away from mass consumption and, as a knock on effect of this, there has been a move away from mass production techniques. Because of this firms have moved towards flexible technology which can produce differentiated goods quickly and easily. This has affected the workforce in that now the worker needs to be polyvalent and knowledgeable. These workers will now work across previous demarcations; they are no longer specialised in one particular activity but are multi-skilled and with a short learning curve can switch from one activity within the firm to another. Again this theory has largely been applied to manufacturing; however, it is global in the sense that it heralds a move away from previous production forms, Fordism, and it is a central plank in the Disorganised Capitalism thesis.

However, as with the other theories there are faults in the Flexible Specialisation argument. Supposedly it is a global theory yet the evidence for it is taken from a small number of regionally specific industries and specific workers (Thompson, 1989: 225). Murray (1988), writing about Italy, has argued that this is only one segment of a general policy of decentralising production. While he accepts that there may be limited benefits, for example to local economies based around a high density of small 'progressive' firms, the overall thrust has been negative. It has led to increased 'putting out' of work to small, non-unionised firms that employ underpaid and increasingly exploited workers. Lovering has also rejected the theory, suggesting instead that the changes in the UK have polarised the workforce into highly skilled, highly rewarded employees and lowly skilled, lowly paid workers. All these workers are differentiated along traditional social lines such as class, race, and gender (Lovering, 1990: 22).

Other criticisms have been levelled at the flexible specialisation theory. It is claimed that it underestimates the flexibility of the Fordist production process, that often the small firms supposed to use this flexible technology cannot afford it, that other systems such as the Just In Time system in Japan are used rather than flexible specialisation, and finally that although flexible specialisation claims to be a global system it very often coexists alongside, and indeed needs, semi-skilled, assembly based, Fordist work (see Thompson, 1989). Despite these faults what the flexible specialisation debate has done is draw attention to the fragmented and unstable nature of the current production environment. Indirectly this thesis is important for accountancy in that this unstable environment led to a growth in self-employment, a growth in the use of subcontracting, the emergence of the flexible firm and other processes. In essence it is the, or one of the, prerequisites for the increasingly differentiated labour market structure of Flexible Accumulation (see Figure 1.1, p. 18) from which accountants have benefited.

If neither post-industrialism, proletarianisation, nor flexible specialisation can explain the nature of the auditing labour process what can? I will argue that the answer to this question entails two parts. It entails a description of exactly what the labour process involves, a factor which is affected by practice size. This description will clearly highlight the irrelevancy of the theories just outlined. The second part to the answer requires an analysis of the way in which this labour process is controlled and, more importantly, the way in which accountants are socialised into becoming 'trustworthy'. This latter feature makes deskilling unnecessary and it makes post-industrial or non-commercial attitudes to work a disadvantage. The rest of this chapter deals with the first part to the answer and Chapter 4 answers the second.

THE NATURE OF AUDITING

Sociology has never been enthusiastic in its examination of the work of accountants. This is partly due to the fact that the service sector, where many of these professionals work, has become a topic of major concern only relatively recently but it is also due to simple neglect by industrial sociologists. As regards accountancy, authors such as Johnson have written about its proletarianisation without actually defining which accountants they are discussing – chartered, certified, management, and so forth, or the nature of an accountant's work and how it is being proletarianised. Instead we are left with a very general argument that is neither really proved nor disproved, merely put forward. In contrast to this I intend to examine the auditing process, especially that labour carried out by trainees and the work it entails. It will be shown that although in the beginning the training is boring, routine and highly standardised, this does not lead to its deskilling nor to the proletarianisation of the chartered accountant.

The following description of an audit is based upon the audit approach of a Big Six firm. This approach by its very nature is less fluid than that of a non-Big Six firm where the demarcation between trainees of different years and between seniors and managers is less rigorous. I have chosen the audit rather than a different section of practice because it is still how 45 per cent of Big Six turnover is generated (see Chapter 2) and it is the section where at least 75 per cent of Irish Big Six accountants are trained (interviews with senior management). It is also argued within the profession that auditing gives an accountant the best insight into how various financial systems are operated and it is auditing which gives an accountant the greatest potential to be a financial or management 'expert'.

> Yes, I think it [auditing] does two things. It gives you a good overview but it also teaches you a certain way of looking at companies, kind of a semi-questioning way which I think is a good thing. It gives you a certain degree of balance. (Stephen Flanagan, Big Six Partner)

Auditing also allows one the facility to specialise in other areas.

> I would discourage people from specialising too early ... you are better off getting a broad training [in auditing] and then making up your mind in light of the aptitudes you have. (Kenneth Byrne, Big Six Partner)

Because 70 per cent of practising accountants are in Big Six firms (deduced from the figures of McCurdy, 1988 and the ICAI, 1988) plus the fact that many of these use this audit training more than any other for gaining entry into managerial posts in industry, I feel it is justified to concentrate on the Big Six audit approach. Other writers have also put great emphasis on the audit and the audit department (Stevens, 1984: 69).

An average sized Big Six audit in Ireland would require about four or five staff to complete it. Ideally out on site there should be a senior accountant and trainees of different years – a first year, second year, and a third year. The senior will normally have qualified or be close to qualifying. Added to these people would be the manager and the partner, both of whom would remain back at the firm's office. The manager and the partner will both have a portfolio of clients and, therefore, a number of audit teams to deal with.

At the beginning of an audit the senior will find out as much information about the client as possible. This will be done by looking at the past audits of the client, which will be held at the office if the client is an old one, talking to staff who dealt with the client previously and other similar techniques. Having done this the next issue is to define the audit scope. The audit scope sets out the parameters of the project by selecting the types of transactions to be looked at. For instance if while carrying out the audit of Marks and Spencer one concentrated on examining the transactions involved in a once off sale of property then the audit would be flawed because this would not be representative of the company's business. Having stated this, these forms of transaction would be noted. It would be embarrassing for a senior if, having completed the audit, he or she was unaware of the fact that a sale was proposed or that any other serious alteration of policy, such as a take-over, was being contemplated by the client management. Although these issues would not alter last year's accounts they may hinder the auditor's ability to give a 'true and fair' account of the company's financial state, at least in the eyes of certain users of such financial statements. In Ireland the audit scope is decided by the audit senior subject to the approval of the manager and partner.

Once the audit scope has been decided then the audit team make an assessment of the reliability of the client's internal controls. This is important as it helps determine how large the sample of transactions examined will need to be. Reliability on internal controls will range from high through to low. Reliability tests come in two forms. Observation tests should be carried out, these are performed by first and possibly second years and include such things as the watching of employees clocking in and out of work and so on. Their purpose is to ensure that controls are effective where there is no documentary evidence to prove it, for example did employee X or Y clock in for X? Compliance tests are carried out by junior staff, examples are checking the addition on documents, ensuring they were signed by the appropriate people, checking that these tests had been done by the client as well, etc. If these tests prove to be reliable then the senior will conclude that errors in the statements are likely to be low. After these tests have been carried out the design of the audit approach is made, this involves deciding on the sample to be taken. If reliability is low there will be a need for more substantive tests to be performed and a different, usually a larger, sample will be taken or in very extreme cases the client may be deemed unauditable. The senior has a very large say in these decisions and is fairly autonomous out on a job although the decision to refuse a client will be taken at a higher level.

The sample is decided by an assessment of the controls with reference to the accounting concept of materiality. This is a term used to judge by how much the accounts can be misstated before they mislead somebody reading them. For example it is improbable that the Ford accounts would be seriously misleading if they were undervalued by £1m. But if they were out by £100m then they might mislead. There is a difficulty with the concept in that different users of financial statements – stockbrokers, bankers and so forth – are looking for different types of information, thus what is material for one may be immaterial for another. There are no hard and fast rules defining materiality because every situation is different and as a result the accountancy practices can only draw up guidelines. Therefore, materiality is still, to some extent, a subjective opinion, although practices are beginning to look at it in a more rigorous way. At all stages in this the senior and the manager would stay in close contact and they would discuss many of the issues that arise. However, it would not be a case of the senior being told what to do, they would both form an opinion on the basis of the information they have gained and the manager would be relying to a large extent for his or her information on the senior.

> He [the manager] will get a comfortable feeling I suspect. It'll come down to some of that, he'll say X or Y is a good guy and you know that he'll do a reasonable job on this thing and if there is anything worrying he'll have found it and told me about it. I mean there is a lot of that kind of reliance in the business, that kind of professional reliance on somebody else who is out there doing the work. (Gabriel Oak, ex-Big Six Senior)

This is far from being deskilled or made interchangeable. Here there is a heavy reliance on the knowledge and skill of subordinates. At the same time because of the constraints on profitability the senior is not completely free to check a company's accounts and ensure that the public interest is being served as he or she is accountable to a superior hence neither is it a case of a post-industrial professional working for the greater good of society (see Chapter 4).

When the sample is taken, checked and verified as being correct then the auditors will produce a report and acknowledge the company's accounts as being accurate. Again these reports are to some extent subjective. How can the auditor predict how much claims against a new drug will cost a chemical company in the next year? He or she can make an estimate based on past experience and knowledge, but that is all. The following month the same auditor may be doing the same thing for a different company with a different set of circumstances. Thus a lot of the situations are in some way unique and much of the expertise is derived from accumulated skill and experience. Auditing is not a 'science' in the sense that an auditor's knowledge is not something that can be codified and reduced to a series of steps that are applied in every circumstance.

> I don't think so [that the audit could be carried out by examining the information away from the client's base]. Certainly one of the philosophies we have in our firm is that you've got to get out and see the client, see the business, see what's happening, see what's happening now as against last year, and we would feel there is a huge or it's very important, that our people's feeling about the company is very important. So no I don't think you could do that. (Stephen Flanagan, Big Six Partner)

THE TASKS INVOLVED ON AN AUDIT

As one would expect, different levels of staff perform different types of functions on an audit. It seems fair to say that there is a progression from routine to harder, more interesting, and more responsible work.

> That's true all right. When you start you do an awful lot of ticking and bashing, totting schedules and cross totting balance sheets. But as you go along then you're more, you delegate all that, but I'd say now the work is probably harder because you're under an awful lot of pressure. I find in here you've jobs and they're all back to back. A job mightn't be 100 per cent finished and you're off stuck in something else and you're called in. But it's definitely much harder than when you start off first, granted it's a lot of mundane work but at least when you've done it its done, whereas here the responsibility carries over and the buck stops with you. (Philip Carey, Big Six Senior)

As hinted in the above quote first year trainees carry out very basic work. They spend time photocopying, checking calculations, checking signatures, reading computer printouts (on a few of the bigger jobs) and so on. This work is aptly called 'totting and ticking' due to the abundance of addition and the verifying of names and other mundane tasks.

> But when you come in here, generally you go in and you do certain tests, its called systems work. You make out a list and make sure they're dealing with their documents right, that they're filing them, that they're totting them correctly … you go through them and you tot them and you see that somebody has signed it, that they've checked it and all this kind

of work and its done right. And that is very tedious. But it can be like the pits, going even looking for the documents they tell you there are the files they're in number or date order and you just have to go through them ... it can be very tedious work. But it improves as you go along, that is first and part of second year. (Charles Darnoy, Big Six Senior)

This work is carried out by all first years irrespective of their educational background. It can be quite disconcerting for trainees and it often appears to them to be quite useless.

> The first years get quite frustrated with their work, partially because they don't see where it ends up, very often because somebody else takes it from them when they've done ten or maybe fifteen tests at some mundane level. (Gabriel Oak, ex-Big Six Senior)

However, even at this stage a first year should be trying to get some idea of what is happening in the client organisation. For instance, if they were working in the wages section first years should have an idea of whether wages are rising or falling as a percentage of total turnover in comparison with last year and so on but despite this the work does not require a great deal of intelligence.

The work takes a significant change for the better when one gets to third year.

> Even within auditing you only spend a year at the more mundane tasks in the sense that you have to learn somewhere and obviously you start doing more interesting stuff. (Cathal Murray, Big Six Assistant Manager)

A third year's work will entail more supervision. They will collect the first year's work and record sheets and make sure that they are accurate and that the work has been carried out. They will also produce schedules indicating all the work that has been done and summarise these highlighting any points that the senior may need to take note of and raise with the client management team. Here again there is a certain degree of responsibility, one must decide what should be highlighted and what should not. The third year will help the first year in deciding how the sample of invoices should be taken and tested and he or she would also carry out tests. All paperwork produced by the various subordinates on the audit is given to the senior.

The senior will spend a lot of time with the client management. He or she will discuss any issues that the client would like taken into account when defining the audit scope. The auditor will recommend some improvements in the internal control system. As stated earlier, they will also discuss any issues that have had or will have an effect upon the client's accounts. The senior will also keep in close contact with the head office and meet with the manager at least once a week.[1] The senior will check all the paperwork that the audit team have compiled and on the basis of this and client discussions produce a summary of the accounts and highlight any points or recommendations that he or she feels are worth mentioning. There is also now a pressure on the senior to produce a good management letter for the client containing some worthwhile suggestions for the future. This is almost akin to management consultancy.

One thing that is noticeable about the audit is the amount of conflict the process involves. While by no means universal there is a significant degree of hostility shown by clients to the auditors.

> Well its repetitive, you know, you're doing the same thing year in and year out. It's very much after the event situations, you're constantly hassling people to do something. An audit is not something that anybody wants but they have no choice in the matter they have to have it and the attitude of the client can be, I mean they can really get that across at all levels. They can take that attitude with the partner and by the time they reach us it's sometimes impossible to deal with them. You are fighting against something that they don't want. I'd prefer to work with people than against them like that. (Jane O'Driscoll, Big Six Senior)

> I think there are two types of client, there are those guys who will actually help you, they'll get you information and see you as a help. Then there is the other who'll think you're there to get them. They'll see you as the enemy ... they wouldn't be aware as to what we're there for, they think we're going to show them up. (Joseph Moore, Big Six Senior)

It is not surprising that this tension exists considering the fact that, despite what Joseph Moore says, there is increasing emphasis put on the recommendations an auditor can make to the client management concerning the possibility of improving their accounting system. This feature is largely a means of justifying the audit fee to the client, thus an element of criticism is part of the process.

> I expect industry would be a bit more personal environment work wise. Us, like we go in and we make our reports and we say this is wrong and that's wrong and then we go off to the next place. (Jean Devoy, Big Six Senior)

This lack of cooperation on the part of certain clients is compounded by the fact that the accountants are under pressure from managers and partners to perform to budget and to improve on last year's audit (see Chapter 4). This can make auditing quite a pressurised and distasteful experience.

Its just, I mean audit work you just get so hassled with and you're under so much pressure when the audit is on and its [the audit], I wouldn't consider it particularly rewarding work to do an audit and I think people just after four years decide I just don't want to do this anymore. You know I've put up with it for four years, I've qualified, I did good work and now I deserve to go on to something a bit more interesting. (Michelle O'Brien, Big Six Senior)

I would say a lot of people do not generally like auditing and they come in here for three or four years and get good experience. Like I mean it does, you begin to see so many different companies, but at the end of the day I don't think a lot of people who qualified with the Big Eight firms as accountants particularly like auditing. (Peter Daniels, Big Six Senior)

I mean if you're in the Big Eight especially, doing pure audit or something ... I don't think you're going to meet anybody who tells you pure audit is a dream, its not and it's only if you see promotion past it that you stay, otherwise by that stage you've usually had your lot of it. (Kathy O'Malley, Big Six Supervisor)

Because the audit is such an important part of practice it lessens practice's appeal. This work element plus other factors, such as the higher rewards to be gained in industry (LSCA, 1990), increases the attraction of industry, resulting in a large number of accountants seeking to leave practice (see Figure 3.1). Only 13.6 per cent of all respondents found practice rewarding enough to feel they would definitely spend the rest of their working lives in it. This high level of dissatisfaction was most noticeable amongst young Big Six accountants. When those still in practice are broken down by age and by the size of organisation they are in the results are quite revealing (Figure 3.2). The figures for accountants under 35 years of age in a small or medium practice must be treated with caution as they refer to only five and eight people respectively.

The Big Six accountants under 35 are the most eager group to leave for industry, only 9.8 per cent of them will definitely stay in practice. This possibly reflects the more rigid and less enjoyable nature of work in the Big Six and also the perceived ease with which the Big Six can enter industry. These

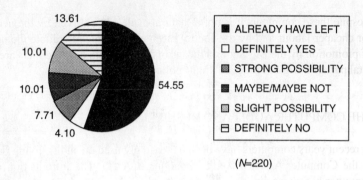

(*N*=220)

Figure 3.1   Have you left or are you intending to leave practice? (%)

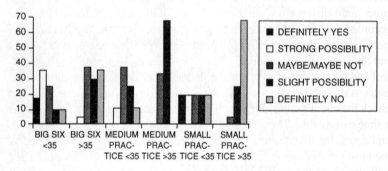

Figure 3.2   Are you intending to leave practice? (%)

features, plus the polyvalent nature of the accountancy labour force and the high demand for accountants, is what gives practice its very high labour turnover. Greenwood *et al.* (1991) estimate that the industry's average labour turnover is 40 per cent every four years. Within my survey, although 62.3 per cent of respondents were trained in a Big Six firm only 26.4 per cent currently work in one, thus 66 per cent of Big Six trained respondents had left the Big Six to go elsewhere. This turnover is not deemed to be a problem, rather it is a vital part of the industry's organisation.

An accountancy firm operates on the principle that people come in for training and go through a cycle ultimately of deciding whether they will remain within the profession or move outside to industry and that is dealt with in a very positive way. Its a natural thing, we'd need all the build-ings on the street if we kept everyone. So its a natural cycle of people moving on all the time. (Conor Hackett, Big Six Partner)

Despite these comments it is not a 'natural cycle'. It is driven by the need for cheaper labour and by the control mechanisms which facilitate the use of promotion by the Big Six as a means of control; both of these facts are a vital part of a Big Six practice's staff policy (see Chapter 4).

THE COMPUTER AUDIT AND DESKILLING

In recent years computers have been increasingly used on audits giving rise to the Computer Assisted Audit Technique (CAAT). The introduction of computer based accounting systems in large organisations led to the use of computer audits by the Big Six. However, this technology has not deskilled accountants. In fact quite the contrary appears to have taken place. A computer audit differs from a traditional audit in that now the transactions are recorded on disk rather than on paper. This has led to the use of computer personnel on some of the larger audits. However, these people do not carry out the audit they are guided by the senior. Hence, the senior is still in control and for reasons of cost it is the senior's job to make sure that the computer staff, who really only gather information for the accountants and check the client's computer reliability controls, are on the audit for as short a time as possible. The computer personnel come to the client's premises and access the mainframe to get the sample that the senior has identified as the most reliable one for gaining an accurate picture of the accounts.[2] They will also check the reliability of the client's computer controls. But it is still up to the traditional audit team to compile the information and reach a judgment on the accounts. At the end of the day the computer people come in during the audit to get information the auditors feel is needed and the auditors then make a judgment on this information. It is not possible for computer staff to carry out the audit, for technical as well as legal reasons.

> You still have to do a certain amount of work before you can get to the stage where you can use a computer, so probably no you wouldn't use the computer that much. (Anne Doyle, Medium Practice Senior)

> No, mainly because its a very subjective business at the end of the day. Computer auditing is critical especially in assessing large firms, particularly in the financial services area where you may need a computer programme to dig out information ... but at the end of the day you're looking at a number of things and you have to use your judgment on these and that's why I think the auditor will always be needed and it is not something that can be automated. (Stephen Flanagan, Big Six Partner)

Therefore, computers cannot be used to deskill the workforce. They have increased the productivity of accountants and enabled more work to be done in less time, thereby increasing profits, but they have not deskilled the work. It is not possible for a computer to deskill people where many of the responses of the worker will be unique. Child (1988) has also argued that where tasks involve a degree of risk and judgment then technology is less likely to deskill. A degree of risk and judgment is very often required in accountancy.[3] Clients change their financial policies from year to year and no two financial policies will be the same. These policies have an impact on a set of accounts which the auditor must take into consideration. The once off sale of assets in six months' time will affect a company's financial standing in the eyes of the users of financial statements which the auditor must verify. It is difficult to see how technology can incorporate this knowledge. Accountants themselves feel that this knowledge cannot be deskilled.

> If computers are to deskill, one has to be sure of what the skill is and in accountancy I don't think that skill can be computerised. I think that skill is the skill an auditor has in knowing where he needs to worry on a particular client and what he needs to worry about and what he doesn't need to worry about ... the sign of a good auditor is the guy who doesn't waste time on things that don't need time wasting. It is a guy who just knows what to look at ... I think it is very much an intuitive thing that comes from experience. (Gabriel Oak, ex-Big Six Senior)

To gain this intuition one has to go through the first and second year and slowly build up a knowledge of a set of accounting systems and the way that they are compiled. Many accountants feel that far from deskilling them computers have given them an extra skill over and above the older generation of accountants.

> Yeah, there is a big difference, I mean I never touched a computer before I came in here literally. In my other firm the nearest they got to a computer was a calculator and a typewriter with memory, now I believe they've gone computerised but not when I was there. I think the top partners were afraid staff would know more than they did at that stage. (Kathy O'Malley, ex-Medium Practice, Big Six Senior)

> In relation to the computers I think what you have is a great number of professional accountants in their mid thirties to late thirties and forties who have missed the skilling of computers and are scared of it. (Gabriel Oak, ex-Big Six Senior)

Hence, unlike the Taylorist thesis would suggest, technology is not always used to deskill and homogenise labour. Its implementation within accountancy has increased the productivity of the labour process as well as increasing the skill of this particular workforce. Wood and Kelly (1988) have highlighted three necessary aspects to the use of technology if it is to be implemented to deskill. First, the labour process must be rendered free from workers' traditions and knowledge second, these must be replaced by 'scientific' knowledge and, third, there has to be a separation of the conception and execution of the task and the use of the managerial monopoly over skill to control the labour process in detail. On all three counts the application of technology to accountancy fails.

Having stated the above there appears to be evidence that technology and accounting technicians or non-graduate accountants may be used to perform the tasks currently carried out by first and second year trainees (Jack, 1992). Jack has suggested that for a series of reasons related to profitability the larger firms are seeking to move away from their traditional policy of hiring large numbers of graduates as trainees and then eliminating their numbers upon the completion of their training (largely via the 'natural wastage' described earlier). The new policy revolves around the idea that the technically simple, indeed rather unskilled, work is passed on to non-graduates and/or computerised hence less graduate trainees are required. These trainees can quickly be employed in the more specialised and more skilled areas of accounting. It is these latter areas that are growing within the profession. These elite workers would then be backed up by a non-graduate, information gathering, rather unskilled, larger group.

This would create two benefits for the firms. Fewer resources would be devoted to training, graduate accountants could be quickly moved into the more specialised and lucrative areas. With the decline of the more mundane aspects of the audit the likelihood of accountants leaving practice because of poor job satisfaction would also decline, hence further lowering the costs of recruitment. Jack never mentions what the role of the audit would be in the training of these elite accountants. I am led to suggest that they will do less of the tedious auditing work but still carry out a good deal of auditing given the role it plays within the teaching of accountancy and its overall importance in allowing one to understand accounting systems. Unfortunately this point is not examined by Jack's newspaper article. Whatever the future of auditing will be within these possible changes the policy will not deskill the chartered accountant, rather the structure of the firm will be altered. A new type of employee, one who will have a different educational and class background to the chartered accountant and one who will fulfil the three deskilling requirements outlined by Wood and Kelly (1988) will be introduced to accountancy practices.

The chartered accountant will not be deskilled because, unlike many other occupational groups, accountants are providers of vital services and information to various managerial elites.[4] It would be unwise to deskill them, thus running the risk of increasing unrest amongst those at the lower end of the profession. As well as these factors there are also other issues involved. The big selling point, amongst the Big Six practices in particular, is the quality of their workforce and the professional nature of their staff. Neu *et al.* (1991) have highlighted the very important role of social factors in accountancy. The issues that are most salient for potential clients are things such as personal contacts, the reputation of the firm, the opinions of other professionals, experience of the firm, its level of 'professionalism' and so on. Many of these features revolve around image or perception rather than direct experience. As a consequence having a deskilled and dissatisfied staff on an audit may damage a practice's reputation. In the long run this would prove more debilitating than beneficial. The authors go on to comment that what is surprising about accountancy is the lack of emphasis on price when the ultimate selection is made by the client. This idea of reputation and 'professionalism' is well understood by the Irish Big Six.

> If we ever lose our reputation for professionalism, integrity, honesty, whatever, then being commercial accounts for nothing. Essentially clients come to us because they want the best professional advice. (Peter O'Neill, Big Six Director)[5]

If the Big Six were to deskill their staff they would lose this selling point, create labour unrest, and suffer from the fact that they would probably lose the ability to attract the type of staff they have hitherto attracted. At present, many trainees simply put up with the first year or two of boredom because they know it will get better. If it did not get better, due to deskilling or for any other reason, most of these would probably leave. Greenwood *et al.* (1991) have commented upon the increased exodus of managers from large accountancy firms after a merger has taken place. Within four years of the merger over half the managers had left. It is therefore not unreasonable to assume that with a significant decline in current job satisfaction or future job satisfaction, due to deskilling, the Big Six could be swamped by a massive outflow of staff. Accountancy could then become an occupation for members of the working class who have not got the same 'respect' for professionalism nor the same ideological commitment to capitalism. In light of Neu *et al.*'s paper it is a moot point whether or not clients would like such homogenised and traditionally 'unprofessional' groups gaining access to such a sensitive position.

The Big Six themselves appear to be aware of this. Thus when they recruit staff they look for middle class traits (see Chapter 4). The features sought are not likely to be found in people straight out of second level education. However, they will be found in graduates and because of the nature of Ireland's education system these graduates will overwhelmingly be middle class (the issue of class will be taken up in greater detail in Chapter 4). Considering these points, in terms of profitability and growth, it is wiser to increase the quality of the workforce, maintain its middle class origins and its ideological belief in capitalism and continue to allow accountants carry out the important functions of capital as they have a traditional commitment to the system. Added to all these advantages are the facts that accountancy has grown rapidly over the past decade and that historically it has had no labour unrest nor militancy to speak of. So why change a winning formula? There is no likelihood of chartered accountancy being proletarianised, nor is there any sign of a separation of the conception and execution of an audit, and due to the sensitive nature of the profession there will be little likelihood of these processes emerging in the future. In the light of this I would suggest that the potential policy changes mentioned earlier are unlikely to be introduced. These comments, however, should not be taken to mean that the issues of profitability and control are unimportant, as we shall see in Chapter 4 nothing could be further from the truth.

FRAGMENTATION AND SPECIALISATION

Within the Big Six there has been a fragmentation of the tasks traditionally done by an accountant. An accountant usually works in one of the main departments within the firm. These are normally auditing, management consultancy, tax, corporate finance, and the small business section. Twenty years ago many of these sections did not exist (Farmar, 1988). It is possible for an accountant to be moved from one section to another when training, if it is convenient for the firm,[6] but after qualifying seniors are expected to specialise. This fragmentation is not due to any policy of deskilling and routinisation on behalf of the management. It is due to the greater knowledge and skill needed when working in an area such as tax, one only has to think of the massively increased number of new tax laws in the past 10 years to accept that it would be extremely difficult for an accountant to be an expert in say tax legislation, auditing and corporate finance!

There are obviously issues of economies of scale and profitability that arise here. It pays the Big Six to break up the labour process in this way and, therefore, be able to offer their clients an expert in tax law rather than a 'jack of all trades'. This reflects the different nature of the markets and the needs of the clients that the Big Six and the small firms have. The Big Six have large multinational and national clients who require specialised information; in these instances time and knowledge mean money. Therefore, a specialist is the quickest and most profitable solution. This is not the same as a fragmentation of tasks required before deskilling takes place. The smaller practices do not have this expertise, rather they subcontract when they need such facilities. It would not pay a small practice to have these experts on the payroll full time.

> I do subcontract in relation to tax. I'd say 80 per cent of the tax can be done but we do subcontract specialised tax areas. We haven't generally subcontracted audits or that unless we are too busy but our real subcontract is related to expertise in tax. We don't subcontract to the Big Eight because they are our bigger clients that are subcontracted and there is a fear that they will be stolen by the Big Eight. We subcontract to two tax specialists, both ex-inspectors of taxes. (John Peters, Small Firm Partner)

> We cultivate relationships with certain specialists and we use them all the time. That is our answer to having a computer department and a secretarial department and so on. We obviously don't have those departments but what we have are sound working relationships with other people, who might be sole practitioners really but sometimes not. (Charles McCabe, Small Firm Partner)

This policy of subcontracting work and circulating it amongst groups of professionals has also been noted by Neu *et al.* (1991) in their work on Canadian accountancy. Fragmentation has led to specialist knowledge; not a standardised but a differentiated labour market. Some of these subcontractors have benefited from this need for specialist knowledge. It is conceivable that many of these workers came from large professional organisations. As one of the quotes above indicates some of these professionals have previously worked for the government and many will undoubtedly have come from the Big Six, where they would have picked up skills such as management consultancy and taxation advice. These people would, to use labour market terminology, be primary external workers (Child, 1988: 243). In many instances they would be the beneficiaries of the move to Flexible Accumulation.

In the area of subcontracting the large multinational practices are unusual. Whereas many of the moves towards subcontracting work in the past decade have been made by large organisations seeking to increase their profitability by shedding labour and by concentrating their efforts on core economic areas which are not subject to severe demand fluctuation (Child, 1988; Murray, 1988), this has not been the case amongst the Big Six. All of the large accountancy practices have been seeking to expand their range of services. They have increasingly been moving into non-accountancy areas such as law, actuarial services, engineering and so on and taking on large numbers of non-accountants, so much so that they are now the largest private employers of lawyers globally (Steven, 1984; Counsell, 1988).

It is possible that the other 50 per cent [non-audit fees] will become more spread. We've taken on marketing people and we've considered, but done nothing about it yet, starting a corporate law department. (Peter O'Neill, Big Six Director)

This somewhat unusual trend stems from the fact that it could prove very dangerous for the large firms to start subcontracting work.[7] Because all the areas of a company's finances are interlinked firms are reluctant to let different organisations examine their financial policy; for example some companies in the same business area will insist upon using different auditors (interviews with senior management). This fear on the part of their clients is one reason why the large practices like to be able to provide a comprehensive range of services. This issue has been an important factor as regards the justification of some recent mergers.

Clearly a merger is generally to improve the range of services you're able to give clients. But the top firms they could always provide any service a firm would need anyway unless there are specific things. A merger is unlikely to enhance that. (Stephen Flanagan, Big Six Partner)

Thus in many ways the large accountancy multinationals are out of step with the move towards the dispersal of production. This characteristic, I would suggest, is further evidence of the fact that accountancy services are sold in a fundamentally different way to manufactured products and, indeed, to many other services. If anything one could argue that the Big Six are also one of the beneficiaries of high skilled subcontracting on behalf of other organisations. This proposition is plausible considering the rapid growth in fee income the Big Six have witnessed in the past decade (see Chapter 2).

Is this differentiated and specialised labour force also flexible? The answer appears to be 'yes'. Accountants are multi-skilled and capable of moving from one section to another with relative ease, although there will be a learning curve involved. This is due to the accountancy training and exams which cover all areas within the profession and give people a good grounding in the basics.

> Most of our people will not specialise until after they've qualified and
> the whole thrust of the Institute is against specialising pre-qualification.
> (Kenneth Byrne, Big Six Partner)

This policy towards a general education is reflected in the attitude of respondents to their training (see Figure 3.3). When the type of training received is cross-tabulated with the size of organisation one trained in there are some noticeable differences. 95 per cent of those trained in a small firm and 100 per cent of those trained in a medium practice felt that their training had been general or too general. In comparison with this only 75 per cent of the Big Six accountants responded as such, 25 per cent felt that their training had been specialised or too specialised (overwhelmingly the former). These results reflect the more rigid nature of the Big Six and the fact that they are organised into quite separate departments. Therefore, the size of organisation one trained with appears to affect the type of training received. However, one must not put undue emphasis on this. This more differentiated training within the Big Six is noted by the seniors but it is not deemed to be too great a problem.

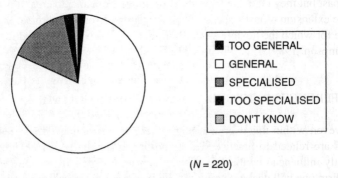

■ TOO GENERAL
□ GENERAL
▨ SPECIALISED
■ TOO SPECIALISED
▨ DON'T KNOW

$(N = 220)$

Figure 3.3   The views of accountants on the type of training they received, (%)

You can I suppose switch, they are all covered in the exams you do. You have tax, auditing, accounts, management services, now we'd do little management services that'd be the sort of thing done by the partners, but apart from that we'd all do the rest. Tax and accounts would go hand in glove, like you do accounts to work out what the tax would be, the majority of the clients who are here are here at the end of the day because they don't want to pay too much tax ... the auditing would be that little bit different because its a bit more specialised. (Mark Wright, Medium Practice Senior)

I think we have the skills but not the training for management consul- tancy, etc. there is nothing stopping us from doing that if we transferred in. They would give us the relevant training or whatever and I would say we'd do just as well at that as we are doing at the moment, you know that's all that's missing. I think we have enough basic experience to be able to move into any of those areas with very little training or whatever. (Jane O'Driscoll, Big Six Senior)

The fact that chartered accountants are so flexible and polyvalent is reflected in the wide variety of manufacturing and service areas that they work in – from chemicals to computer services to textiles and management consultancy – and the fact that within this wide variety of industries they hold a large array of positions – from corporate tax adviser to general man- agement to company secretary (ICAEW, 1988); within my own survey there were large numbers involved in various pursuits (see Chapter 6). It does appear to be a genuine flexibility which occurs within practice. People specialise due to the greater knowledge that is required today as opposed to the past but they maintain their ability to move from area to area. It is not a mere extension of tasks nor is it the fabrication of some superficial knowl- edge for which the flexible specialisation thesis has been criticised for (see Thompson, 1989).

DIFFERENCES IN TRAINING: DAVID VERSUS GOLIATH

However, within this overall scenario there are restrictions. These restric- tions are related to practice size. Exposure to accountancy techniques is greatly influenced by the size of the practice one joins. If one joins a Big Six firm one will deal with large clients, get to see how large firms operate, see how internal control systems within a multi-site operation work and how they can be improved upon, learn to deal with influential business people and make a lot of contacts in the business world. All of this can be done while auditing. Auditing is basically a mechanism whereby you check, criticise, and certify different accounting systems and in the process one gains a knowledge of what is good and what is bad and one makes judgments on diverse business decisions and strategies. Because of the nature of Big Six operations one's knowledge of, say, tax may be good enough for the Institute's examinations, due to study and ICAI courses, but one's actual day to day exposure to such techniques will be quite limited except in so far as they impinge upon the audit.

Accountants in a small practice gain quite a different form of training. The hierarchy of these firms will be less rigid. Partners in small practices would work more closely with trainees, upon qualifying many would become managers straight off, responsibility would come earlier and so forth. Whilst still a trainee many of these small firm accountants would be completing whole jobs on their own. These people deal with clients that run small businesses, many of whom would have no accounting system to talk of. Trainees would perform what are called 'shoebox' jobs. Literally a client would arrive with a box full of receipts and the accountant would collect them together, carry out the book-keeping and prepare a set of accounts, and then fill in the client's tax return. He or she prepares a statement for the inspector of taxes and tries to ensure that the client pays as little tax as possible. This work is more satisfying at an earlier stage than the work of a Big Six trainee because the small firm member completes it him or herself or at least they see what the completion of the work entails. There also appears to be a point to the work, for example money is saved that may have been given 'unnecessarily' to the tax inspector. The smaller firm would produce a different type of accountant. They would receive exposure to far more personal tax, they would deal with small clients, they would be able to put together a set of accounts much more readily. But they would be less exposed, less comfortable with, and thus less suited to auditing large firms or setting up internal controls on an accounting system.

I very much wanted a Big Six firm. I couldn't truly call myself a chartered accountant and have all the experience you'd expect them to have, which is mainly good audit experience, and small firms just don't carry out the extensive audit. (Conor Hackett, Big Six Partner, ex-Small Firm)

I would definitely think that you would go into a large office you specialise in an area and most of the intake guys seem to specialise in auditing. Whereas you go into a smaller office you prepare accounts, you do audits, you do tax work, you take the job right through, you meet the client and as such you probably come out as better overall accountant

but if you're in a larger office you come out as a better specialised auditor and there is a difference. (John Peters, Small Practice Partner)

The difference is one of exposure and experience. It is not that smaller
accountants can never do what the Big Six accountants do, they can.
Accountants from smaller practices, in order to gain this exposure, join a
Big Six firm upon qualifying and after a short learning period seem to be as
capable as the people who have always been there; Conor Hackett quoted
on p. 100 is now a Big Six partner and amongst the survey respondents
21 per cent of accountants who trained with a small practice are now in the
Big Six.[8] The same is the case when a Big Six person moves to a small
practice.

   Given that the two groups, Big Six and non-Big Six, receive different
forms of exposure and that the Big Six receive experience that is more
orientated towards large organisations one could be forgiven for thinking
that this allows the Big Six greater mobility into industry. However, on this
issue there appears to be some confusion. When respondents were asked
which accountants were the best equipped to join industry the results were
as in Figure 3.4. As can be seen in Figure 3.4 the medium practices poll the
highest, some 10 per cent ahead of the Big Six, whilst the small practices
are overwhelmingly viewed negatively, scoring a mere 2.3 per cent. The
relatively high polling of the medium firm was evident across both the Big
Six and the medium practices. The same cannot be said for the Big Six
however (see Figure 3.5).

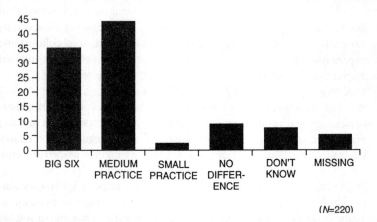

(N=220)

Figure 3.4   Which group of accountants are the best equipped to join industry? (%)

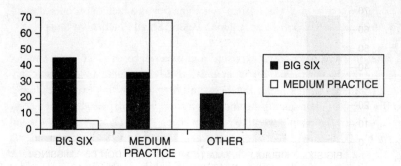

Figure 3.5   Which group of accountants are best equipped to join industry, by practice size? (%)

As Figure 3.5 demonstrates only 44 per cent (60 respondents) of the Big Six trained staff felt they had the best training and were the best equipped for industry, a further 36.5 per cent (46 respondents) felt that the medium practices trained the best accountants for industry. In comparison with this, of the accountants trained in the medium practices 68 per cent (17 respondents) felt they were the most suitable accountants for industry, whereas only 8 per cent (2 respondents) thought that the Big Six were. The category 'Other' is made up of small practices, missing values and 'don't knows'. Although the medium percentages are based on a very low number of responses they are, I believe, made valid by the surprising level of support given to a medium practice training by the Big Six accountants, as Brendan O'Reilly commented:

> Having seen both sides of it at this stage you certainly get very good experience in auditing with the Big Eight. You get exposed to industrial experience, you get into large organisations that have the state of the art accountancy systems and they're very well up in technical matters in accountancy. But on the other side of it in a small organisation, in small firms when you are training you get the hang of how a set of accounts comes together much quicker. You go through your training contract in a bigger firm and never really know how a set of accounts are put together. I know myself having done that, having completed the three years myself it was probably about three months of a learning curve in here before I really knew how a set of accounts hung together and getting into the nitty gritty as opposed to having everything presented to you on an audit. There is a big difference and I think the ideal at the end of it all is to train in a medium sized company. (Brendan O'Reilly, ex-Big Six, Medium Practice manager)

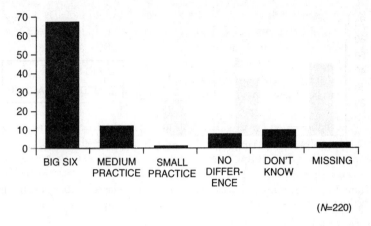

(N=220)

Figure 3.6   Which group finds it easier to join industry? (%)

Despite this level of support for the view that the medium practices produce the most suitable all round accountant, when asked which accountants find it easier to join industry the Big Six accountants overwhelmingly fared better (see Figure 3.6). Despite the positive showing of the medium practice in terms of skills needed for joining large scale industry they have a relatively poor showing in terms of ability to join industry. This was evident across both the Big Six and Medium practice groups (see Figure 3.7). 75.2 per cent (103 respondents) of the Big Six trained accountants felt it was easier for the Big Six to join industry, only 8.8 per cent (12 respondents) of them thought that medium practice accountants could enter industry easier. Of the accountants trained in a medium practice 58.9 per cent

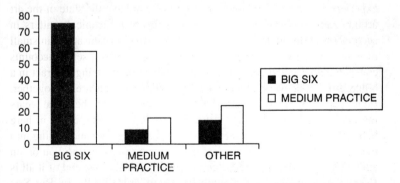

Figure 3.7   Which group finds it easier to join industry, by practice size? (%)

(33 respondents) felt the Big Six found it easier to join industry and only 17.9 per cent (10 respondents) felt that they could join industry more easily than their Big Six counterparts. Once again the category 'Other' is a mixed bag. The real losers within this situation appear to be the accountants trained in small practices, see Figures 3.4 and 3.6. A training in a small firm appears to be largely suited to staying within the area of small practice.

> Its probably easier for Big Eight staff to join industry because you've got a little better knowledge of the big overall spread of things. If you're a firm say like Bachelors or something like that well they've got foreign exchange stuff to do and so on in many areas. You wouldn't see that in a small practice where as you would see it in a big one. Things like that you'd have a better overall view of how a company was run. (Brian Riordan, Big Six Senior)

> The benefit of having trained in a large firm is people will say 'yeah that's a SKC [Ireland's KPMG branch] person, Cooper's person, a Craig Gardner's person and so on. The Finance Directors who are recruiting people have an understanding of the level of a person from a large firm … and you can take a lot of things as given and if you interview them and get on with them then you hire them. A fellow from a small firm has a lot more things to prove. Nobody can really say what standard you can expect from somebody trained in Joe Bloggs and Co. because you don't know if Joe Bloggs and Co. is good, bad, or indifferent. (Conor Hackett, Big Six Partner)

> Obviously easier [to join industry] for Big Eight. There is much more awareness of the type of firm they come from on the one hand and there has always been and continues to be a leakage especially to the larger companies which are audited by the Big Eight firms from the people who carried out that audit. It is quite a normal practice. (Shane Donovan, Small Practice Manager)

This dominance is not as great as one would have reasonably expected considering that 62.3 per cent of the sample trained with a Big Six firm, nor is it as great as the above three quotes would lead one to believe (see Figure 3.8).

As already indicated there is a strong feeling that the medium sized firms give the best all round training, they scored 38.2 per cent in Figure 3.8.

> I'd say if you were in a medium, a large medium firm you would get a better training. The better auditor, Big Eight would give you the better auditor, so it depends on what sphere you're looking for. But industry

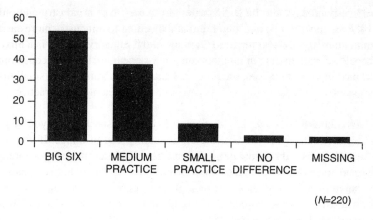

(*N*=220)

Figure 3.8   Which size practice is the best to train with? (%)

has a very big snob factor in that they see a Big Eight name they'll think, that's why I came here after I qualified, they'd see the Big Eight name and they will presume Big Eight people are better. There is also the thing that in the Big Eight you're going to get, depending what jobs you're put on, but if you're put on the very big audits, you're going to get exposure to a lot of different ways of management and different ways of accounting structures, different ways of accounts that can be produced from computer systems. You're not going to get that from a big medium firm. The small firm all you're going to do is small, what they call 'shoebox' jobs ... but if you get into a big medium firm you're going to have to do your stint on 'shoeboxes' because of the slack season and you're going to have to do audits but you're not going to get the very big audits. (Cathy O'Malley, Big Six Supervisor, ex-medium practice)

Thus the medium firms appear to give one a better grounding in more aspects of accountancy (see also Brendan O'Reilly quote on p. 102). However, arguments in favour of the Big Six entering industry are very similar to those presented in Chapter 2 about the buying of, or more accurately not buying of, accountancy services from local practices by multinational firms who appear to rely on a practice's reputation. Much therefore relies on image and perception rather than actual technical know how.

The size of firm and the type of client dealt with determines the exposure, the experience one receives and the perceived relevance of one's training. However, this training is still flexible enough to allow one a lot of mobility from one position to the next provided one has not specialised in a particular area for too long (this does not occur up until about the age of 30). This flexibility is not, however, as a result of a shift from one form of production process (Fordism) to another (Flexible Specialisation); accountants have been mobile in terms of the size of practice or the type of industry they work in for a long time (Chapter 2).

CONCLUSION

Many of the theories about work and control are inadequate when one applies them to accountancy. Are accountants professionals in the traditional sense of the term – displaying all the virtues of altruism, impartiality and so forth thereby providing us with an example of future post-industrial work? This proposition, I am afraid, has got to be rejected. Accountants play a very important role within the capitalist production process, they help to realise surplus value and legitimate the actions of the capitalist class on the basis of costs and efficiency, hence they are not part of some overall trend towards Bell's 'socialising' mode (Chapter 4). Many of the privileges they enjoy derive from the fact that they perform such functions which in turn makes them immune from proletarianisation and a devaluation of their labour (Chapter 6).

Another aspect of being a professional is that one is expected to have control over one's own labour process (Freidson, 1973: 56). As we shall see in Chapter 4 on the basis of this the Big Six accountant fails. If one accepts Freidson's arguments then it cannot be legitimately argued that accountants are a 'professional' group. Again I would suggest that such a proposition has to be rejected.

How, then, should we examine the work of the accountant? If accountancy is not catered for by the main arguments about the future of work and the control of work, how can it be explained? Accountancy must be explained through examining the roles of mobility and control. Chapter 4 highlights how the work of the accountant is very tightly monitored, however, this supervision is acceptable because those who successfully complete the obstacle course are duly rewarded with organisational power. This is fundamentally different to working class jobs wherein mobility, if it is offered at all, is very limited. Likewise it is somewhat different to the control mechanisms 'public service' professionals endure because the controls to which accountants are subject to revolve around the issue of commercialisation. The success one experiences within the profession is largely determined by non-technical factors, thus relying on social and/or commercial issues; in essence, like so much about accountancy, success relies on reputation, image and perception. It is to a discussion of these issues that we now turn.

4 Flexible Accumulation and the Emergence of the 'Commercialised Professional'

If, as Chapter 3 suggested, accountancy is not moving towards some post-industrial occupational utopia, nor is it being deskilled, nor is it a profession in the sense that individual accountants control their own work situation, nor is the profession objective, then how are these accountants monitored? The purpose of this chapter is to highlight the way in which practices ensure that employees perform according to the wishes of the firm.

However, this chapter has another, possibly more important, point to make. It argues that the nature of this socialisation and control has altered in the past twenty years in order to facilitate the controlling role accountants exercise within the emerging Flexible Accumulation regime. The chapter suggests that the changes highlighted in Chapter 1 and the increased emphasis within accountancy on 'commercial' issues are linked. All of this has led to a questioning of the role of accountancy within capitalism.

This questioning is typified by the fact that the public spirited role of the professional has become a contentious issue within both academic and popular debate. There appears over the past decade or so to have been a fundamental shift away from a public interest orientation towards a more commercial, or at least more blatantly commercial, role. This shift has not been uniform nor indeed universal, it appears to be concentrated within those professions that operate in the private sector. Accountancy has been particularly affected and there is increasing evidence that the legal profession has also moved towards commercialisation, albeit to a lesser extent. This commercialisation has led to a crisis within the accountancy profession. Austin Mitchell MP accused the profession of colluding with senior management into deceiving shareholders and the taxpayer (Mitchell, 1992). Ian McNeil (1992), head of the Institute of Chartered Accountants in England and Wales (ICAEW), replied to these criticisms in the *Observer* newspaper by stating that it was the job of senior management and not the auditors to find fraud and by reaffirming the public interest spirit of the profession as being of paramount importance. A similar debate has taken place in Ireland with John Callaghan, ex head of Ireland's largest accountancy practice, putting forward a similar argument to McNeil's in the *Irish Times* (1992). These arguments surely miss the point – if large scale fraud is taking place it will involve senior management as it is they and not shop-floor workers who have access to the apparatus and the knowledge to perpetrate the crime! In Ireland a Commission was established to examine the state of financial reporting and auditing within the country in the light of major business scandals and the loss of confidence of both the business community and the public in accountancy. An equivalent loss of confidence has emerged in the USA where the majority of people now believe that auditors bend the rules to suit their clients (McHugh and Stamp, 1992).

CRISIS IN ACCOUNTANCY – THE BACKDROP TO THE 'COMMERCIALISED PROFESSIONAL'

Why has this crisis arisen now? I believe it is due to the changing nature of the profession over the past fifteen years. I am assuming that there has always been a tension between the 'commercial' segment – tax department, management services department, corporate finance department – and the 'public orientated' audit segment. This is difficult to prove because despite the important role of accountants within Anglo–Saxon capitalism and particularly within senior management there is a tremendous paucity of sociological evidence on the profession. My contention is that the commercial sector has firmly tipped the balance of power in their favour and that this is reflected in and has shaped the socialisation and control processes that accountants within practice experience. I am not suggesting that there was a golden past in accountancy wherein the profession was public spirited, altruistic and so on. What is being suggested is that in the light of the recent changes within the profession there has been a significantly increased emphasis on profit and on being commercial.

What has this shift entailed? Over the last decade there has been a dramatic change in the ideology of the Anglo–Saxon countries within which accountancy is strong. This has largely entailed a move towards an 'enterprise culture' (Keat and Abercrombie, 1991). Within this new cultural environment the commercial enterprise is paramount in a way that previously had not been the case and the consumer-producer relationship has changed. The consumer is now both sovereign and active, in direct opposition to what existed previously wherein the consumer was a passive receiver of goods and services. This change means that in order to be successful, that is commercial, one must give the consumer what he or she requires. This process is evident in industries such as publishing (Abercrombie, 1991), design (Whitely, 1991) and personnel management (Collinson *et al.*, 1990), all of which have rejected any non-commercial criterion in a way which is in contrast to their history.

At a more 'professional' level accountancy and law have also been altered. Both now shape their services to suit the needs and demands of their clients (see Galanter, 1983 and Cain, 1983 for a discussion of this within legal practice). Because these clients are made up of accountants, lawyers or very well informed middle class business people, they are very active and know exactly what they want from the professions and as such they merely get the professional firms to translate these needs into an accountancy or legal meta-language.

I think that [client tells the professional what s/he wants] it depends on the client, it's true for a lot of them. In addition many of the clients have moved as much as they can in-house, especially in tax – we see much less of the client's work there than we did [in the 1980s – interview conducted in late 1993]. So they're really only looking at the advice side of it so they've become more specific. So yes they already know, at least to a degree what they are looking for that's true of many clients. (Frank Rogers, US Big Six Manager)

This dominance by the consumer means that Johnson's (1972, 1977) belief that what distinguishes professionals from other workers is their dominance of the producer–consumer relationship has to be rejected or else we must accept the notion that large elements of the accountancy and legal professions are not really professional. This is not the case in a profession such as medicine. Peschel and Peschel (1986) give a long list of doctor–patient interactions wherein the most noticeable feature of the relationship is the latter's dependence, fear, and ignorance. A doctor appears to manipulate this relationship by being objective and scientific hence implying that there is one correct answer to the problem. There is also evidence that doctors are increasing their control of this producer – consumer interaction (Porter, 1990). In contrast, in accountancy or at least its 'commercial' areas there are various routes to the end result – a higher rate of profitability. The issue of which route to take or the parameters within which the subject is debated are laid down by the consumer.

Moving away from the cultural changes to the related area of economic change we find that accountancy has also been radically altered. There has been a major reorganisation of capital within the last twenty years. This has led to increased buying in of services and to the increased use of flexible strategies by management (see Chapter 1). Elite professional workers have benefited from this process (Hakim, 1990). One group of such workers has been the accountancy profession. The major accountancy firms have expanded their product range, their geographical spread, their labour force, and their profit margins quite dramatically in the 1980s (Leyshon *et al.*, 1987b). As a result of this the audit market has remained, and is forecast to remain, stagnant while areas such as tax, corporate finance, management consultancy and so on grow. Similar processes have taken place within law (Stanley, 1991).

These cultural and economic changes have left their imprint upon the profession. Functionalists portray professions as homogeneous communities unambiguously sharing the same values, interests, world views, etc. This is not the case. There are always a number of different segments within a profession, which share different and sometimes conflicting values (Strauss, 1975). Within accountancy such segments also exist, for example the major firms versus the small firms, the industry based accountants versus those in practice, the commercialists versus the professionals, to name but a few. It is the latter conflict that is the one of interest to us. There are a number of dimensions upon which these segments disagree. What follows is based on the imaginary creation of ideal types.

- *Sense of a mission*: The new growth areas feel that it is important to give sound managerial advice, to be profitable, and to work vigorously for one's client to fulfil their needs (see O'Neill quotes on pp. 121,122,132). In comparison with this the public spirited segment stress the need to serve the public (McNeil, 1992).
- *Work activities*: The way in which work is experienced in accountancy often depends upon what one is doing, for example many accountants and clients view auditing as a waste of resources whereas providing tax minimalisation skills or working in industry is seen in a positive light

in the end as well you don't really feel like you're fulfilling anything. All you're doing is fulfilling a legal requirement. You're not actually, there is very little benefit to the client all he is doing, like he has to do it by law whereas maybe if you're in industry you'd feel money is actually being made and you're helping to make it. You're actually doing something that is real as opposed to just going in there and annoying someone for two or three weeks and giving them a whopping bill at the end of it. (Jean Devoy, Big Six Senior)

it [the audit] is very much an after the event situation. You're constantly hassling people to do something. An audit is not something that anybody wants but they have no choice in the matter. They have to have it and the attitude of the client can be, I mean they can really get it across at all levels, they can take that attitude with the partner down and by the time they reach us it's sometimes impossible to deal with them. (Jane O'Driscoll, Big Six Senior)

There is very little sense of worth in the quotes above. The audit is not seen by these accountants as a public crusade to ensure fair play, it is merely an expensive exercise in futility.[1]

● *Client relationships*: As has been stated specialisms within accountancy have different types of relationships with clients. The auditors appear to be a nuisance to the client whereas those in other areas such as tax are seen as experts bought in by management to increase profitability. The auditors have tried to move down this commercial road somewhat by presenting the management with a management letter. This letter is suppose to indicate possible improvements to the accounting and account-ability systems, it is written at the end of the audit to make it appear worthwhile and is a recent phenomenon (see Chapter 3).

On all of the above three issues there appears to be a divergence between the two groups. In the 1990s the commercial segment is in the ascendancy. Again I would like to reaffirm that I am not suggesting that it was always otherwise. There is very little analysis of the profession in the past; however, Hastings and Hinings (1970) highlight some differences in the values of the practising and industry based accountants 25 years ago – these could poss-ibly be loosely divided into the two groups I term 'public spirited' and 'com-mercialised' professionals. It would also seem reasonable to assume that during the 1970s the professional ethic would have been under less severe attack. What the changes of the past decade have meant is that there has been a decisive shift in terms of prestige and status towards those commercial areas like management consultancy, corporate finance and so on and away from the public spirited, or at least the ambiguously commercial, audit. There is also evidence that a similar process has taken place within law. For exam-ple the large law firms have no public orientated departments such as family law, civil liberties and so forth. All of their departments are in areas such as corporate law, litigation, employment law, etc. Galanter (1983) has argued that the closer a specialism is related to altruism in law the less status it has.

These changes have meant that accountancy has been commercialised to a great extent and that this process has infiltrated the audit departments. Hence accountants are now trained and work in very profit orientated environments to an extent that did not exist in the past (Farmar, 1988). One consequence of this is that they are controlled in a way that is different to that of other professionals such as doctors, academics and so on. It is this issue that is the concern of the rest of the chapter.

SUPERVISION OF MIDDLE CLASS LABOUR

The chapter operates on two premises: first, that labour control is a managerial problem within practice and second, that there is a distinction between technical and social competence. An explanation of these assumptions is obviously required.

Control within accountancy practice is a managerial problem on a number of grounds. As will be highlighted throughout the chapter being a professional does not mean being a disinterested provider of services, accountancy is now very profit orientated and by its very nature this implies a coordination of the labour process at a hitherto undeveloped scale (see Marx, 1976). It also requires a means of ensuring that labour performs its duties adequately. Within accountancy these features are further complicated by the fact that the firms are viable mainly through the use of articled or apprenticed labour. This need to control labour is made difficult within accountancy by the fact that at the beginning of one's training the work involved is both repetitive and boring (see Chapter 3). To combat this many juniors engage in activities similar to Burawoy's 'games' (see Harper, 1989). In effect trainees 'lark about' and as such need supervision. Added to this is the fact that these apprentices need to appear 'professional' when dealing with clients. This demands some form of standardisation, both in terms of product and behaviour, which in turn gives rise to a managerial problem. The aim of these firms is to increase their profitability. In order to achieve this they are presented with the problem of organising and maximising the performance of labour. To do this there is a need for control. Why? Because these organisations are social arrangements and due to the hierarchal structure within accountancy the juniors at the lower end of the hierarchy will not have the same interest in increasing profitability and expending their labour power to the degree demanded by the partners. Accountancy practices must control labour to guarantee a maximum return. To ensure this within accountancy entails a variety of control mechanisms. These control mechanisms tend to be quite successful at encouraging a hierarchical consensus rather than a 'them and us' situation.

The idea that middle class workers who help supervise the labour processes of others are themselves a managerial problem is not new. Marx,

Braverman, and Edwards have all suggested that white collar work would increasingly come under scrutiny as a labour process. Murray and Knights (1990: 169) have also argued that managers experience tensions within the production process because they are engaged in a labour process of their own on top of supervising the labour processes of their subordinates. In the light of this supposed contradiction it is interesting to look at accountants and to examine how they are controlled and how they, as workers, react to this control. The fact that accountants go on to make up an important section of management within industry subsequent to their time in practice provides an added incentive to examine the control procedures they themselves experienced.

The second premise upon which this chapter operates is one which distinguishes between technical and social competence. By 'technical' what is meant is the actual physical performing of the work itself, that is the defining of the audit scope, assessing the reliability of internal controls and so on. The idea of social competence is broken down further throughout this chapter. Fundamentally there are two aspects to the notion of 'social competence'. The first is general social ability, for example clothes one wears, ability to communicate, level of general education, attitudes to work, level of promotional ambition and so on. The second is what I call 'commercial ability'; this latter feature relates to one's capacity to reach the 'right' conclusions as laid down by management, the ability to control budgets, etc. in short the ability to generate profit. Throughout the chapter the two are somewhat artificially separated, for example one's ability to communicate will obviously affect one's ability as an accountant because the job entails assessing and analysing information. Having stated this, the two areas, although they overlap, are not interchangeable as we shall see. Within the chapter it is argued that this social competence, in both its forms, is as important as technical skill when promotion is being offered. This is a well established argument within sociology (see Edwards, 1979; Offe, 1976; Crompton and Sanderson, 1990; Jenkins, 1986; Collinson *et al.*, 1990).

The chapter is divided up into a number of different sections. The first section will briefly examine how the Institute's education programmes instil a meritocratic ideology. The second examines how the prospect of promotion is used to create an atmosphere of competitive individualism amongst staff, and how this leads to certain standards of behaviour. The third' will apply Offe's (1976) theory of task continuous and task discontinuous control mechanisms to practice. The fourth, looks at the growth of internal labour markets and their role within the firm. The fifth will then look at the issues of pay, budgets and the technical management of accountancy. The sixth, will examine control of the labour process out 'on site'. The seventh section will then look at the formal assessment and promotional procedures. The final section will highlight the formal and informal sanctions at work within accountancy.

INSTITUTE EDUCATION

It has been argued that accountancy has both an ideological and a control function. Accountancy has been used to increase the control of management over labour by making sections within industry more 'accountable' (Hopper and Armstrong, 1991). Because of these features it has had a very important social effect. However, this effect has often gone unnoticed or at the very least it has not been commented upon because it is deemed to be above dispute (Tinker, 1985: xv). Why has accountancy not examined its own ideological and political role? Largely because accountancy is influenced by one, very right wing, theory of economics – marginalist economic thought. This gives primacy to the individual be it a person or a company. One consequence of this is that the impact of an accounting decision upon the larger society has very often been played down. Although accountancy is beginning to move away from this narrow view via the implementation of things such as the social audit, it is still very much at the centre of the profession (Tinker, 1985: 82). This ideology is at the heart of how accountants view things such as profitability, assets and so forth. By doing this they also have a large impact upon issues such as dividend price, share price, wages, etc. – in effect the distribution of income.

This value system is instilled into new recruits through a variety of mechanisms. These mechanisms include screening, limiting the profession to the middle class, and the education of accountants. This education system favours rote learning over discursive educational values. Institute exams are seen as an obstacle to be overcome rather than as a means of enlightenment.

> Up to Part Three its definitely learning by rote. Its like college exams you know your stuff and you go in and write it all down. (Barbara Wilkinson, Senior Big Six)

Power (1989) has argued that the ICAEW's exams and training are seen by employers as character building and as a commitment to business values rather than as a means of passing on the critical skills necessary for the profession. To put it simply they are viewed as an investment by the individual in the future, a future that will, as a result, be too expensive to jeopardise by uncooperative behaviour. One academic accountant reinforced this viewpoint. He suggested that the work and the night time studying combined to bring about a 'pressure cooker effect'. If one survived three or four years of this pressure one would be deemed to be motivated. The learning process is based very much on formula. The emphasis is on scoring with unambiguous points. This is further reinforced by the fact that to fail your exams will badly damage your career. Power also argues that for groups such as accountants the large amounts of time spent studying by oneself encourages an attitude of self-interest.[2] Added to this is the fact that the time a trainee spends studying or working narrows their frame of reference to accountants. Hastings and Hinings (1970) echoed these sentiments over 20 years ago. They suggested that an accountant's training led him or her to be cautious, exact, professionally exclusive, rationalistic, to quantify complex problems, and finally to be anti-theoretical. All of these factors lead to a situation whereby people, who had most likely accepted that reward is down to individual effort anyway, believe it is the individual that counts. In accepting this they enter into competition with one another and to put it rather crudely competition leads to conformity. They are uncritical, individualistic, and meritocratic during their professional education. Lovell (1992) also highlights how the professional education and, indeed university degrees, in accounting are too technical and mere rule learning as opposed to teaching people to think. This leads these accountancy students towards exercising a great deal of self-discipline. They also bring these qualities to their places of work which in itself is not unusual for middle class workers (Thompson, 1989). This is not to say that the accountancy practices themselves have no control mechanisms. On the contrary, they operate an abundance of them.

PROMOTION

The first control mechanism is screening. At the selection process practices can pick candidates that will be controllable. This is possibly one factor in explaining why the Big Six have moved towards recruiting graduates rather than school-leavers. This is despite the fact that 60 per cent of degree holders within the sample stated they made no current use of their degree. Presumably graduates will be more middle class, professional in outlook and appearance, and therefore less difficult. Jenkins (1986) has argued that the most important feature within recruitment is to employ somebody who will be easy to control, will take orders and will fit in with the existing workforce. Within the area of professional work it is most likely that the middle class will fulfil these functions hence recruitment directly from the universities. Jenkins also suggests that even though at a formal level candidates may have the same qualifications, that is both are equally 'suitable' to use Jenkins' terminology, a whole range of informal criteria will be used to select someone who is viewed as more 'acceptable', i.e. fits into the world view of the selector as a responsible employee. This process works to the disadvantage of ethnic minorities in Jenkins' research. I would suggest that the informal criterion within accountancy recruitment works to the disadvantage of the working class graduate. The fact that the large practices will recruit people with a 'non-relevant' degree merely highlights the importance attached to issues of acceptability rather than suitability.

> As far as we're concerned we're not overly worried about the background of the person – the educational background of the person. We're not overly concerned if they've studied zoology or accounting and finance. What we're looking for are the qualities in the person rather than the academic course they've taken. We'd be looking for characteristics like intelligence, well read, high degree of motivation, articulate people who are capable of mixing, that are not loners. People who would be able to work in a team, people with a level of maturity and independence and obviously people who have a track record of achievement as well – academic and other things. (John O'Grady, Big Six Personnel Partner)

All of the above are social not technical criterion. They are all traits which the middle class would obviously fulfil a lot easier than people from a working class background. Jenkins (1986) and Collinson *et al.* (1990) have demonstrated how the use of social criteria reinforces the stereotypical images recruiters have of ethnic minorities and women. Both accept that the same processes exist when these are applied to the working class. There is no reason to assume that the situation would be any different within accountancy, and as we shall see later on it is not. As further evidence of the discriminatory nature of the selection process in professional areas see McGovern (1992). He describes the selection process for engineers and chemists in Irish electronics and pharmaceutical firms. The qualities sought bear an uncanny resemblance to the sought after qualities in accountancy. Despite this both Stanley (1991) and Galanter (1983) argue that law, which as stated is undergoing similar changes as accountancy, has become more meritocratic, however, neither really elaborates on this point.

After the selection process the first thing communicated to the new recruits is the fact that someday they may make it to partner level. Thus promotion for those who are 'good' is stressed and indeed it does occur. Causer and Jones (1990) have highlighted that promotion is used in similar ways within electronic engineering. Rapid promotion prospects in electronics firms are stressed for three reasons: it enables firms to recruit new graduates, it socialises new graduates into the firm by emphasising the incentives for complying with managerial expectations and, it allows an early linking of both the technical and the managerial functions within the organisation. As a result of this employees at the age of 23 or 24 are given control responsibilities.

Equivalent processes are at work within accountancy. Because of the decentralised nature of international accountancy practices the partners of the Irish branch are free to promote whoever they want.[3] Even for people who do not want a career within practice there is the attraction of becoming a manager before leaving to join industry – having been a manager would obviously increase one's mobility. These features lead to competitive individualism and hence to certain standards of behaviour. Many of these standards are social and include things such as the type of suit one wears, the haircut one has, the condition of the car one drives and so on

> There's a lot of that, you know the actual impression you create. There was actually a recent case of where a client actually rang up a manager and asked to have a guy taken off a job because the staff were complaining. The guy had a really bad B.O. problem, it really is bad. That's the sort of thing like presentation. (Paul Devine, Big Six Senior)

> The thing with juniors is that the work they're doing its basically, it would be, its the most boring work and probably the easiest so therefore there is very little room for major error so unless they did something dreadful socially it's very hard [to make a major mistake out on a job]. There used to be a guy here who wore a white suit a few years ago, he stayed as a junior for about three years. They even gave him a suit allowance. (Jonathan Andrews, Big Six Senior)

As these comments suggest the Big Six firms encourage social conformity. This conformity is not peculiar to accountancy, it also occurs in other professional areas. Moore and Moore (1991) have argued that law firms in the UK should ensure that employees are aware of the standards of dress and so forth expected of them. Staff would be pulled up on these issues and one conformed or forfeited the chance of promotion. Somewhat similarly, Knights and Morgan give an account of control within an insurance salesforce.

Here we can see in vivid profile the individualising and normalising effects of this power exercised by management for it stimulates the individual pursuit of sales returns but imposes a standard mode of behaviour since no deviants are going to gain entry to the 'club' merely by virtue of sales success. (Knights and Morgan, 1990: 377)

Within accountancy partners have the sole say in who becomes a member of their 'club' and who does not. It is fair to comment that technically partners are very good; however, to make partner one needs more than just good technical accounting skills.

Consequently, such things as personal manner were another way an individual could display keenness and worthiness of promotion (alongside such things as accounting skill, not addressed here). And indeed this is what ambitious seniors were told, either informally or formally. In effect promotions pressure increased an individual's willingness to adopt the appropriate methods of presentation. (Harper, 1989: 155)

This selection process on the basis of social skill and conformity took place at an early stage and was understood by all.

I had a bit of difficulty with the exams so there wasn't any chance I was going to reach partnership in X. They do tend to discriminate very early on with people that they think will make it and people they don't. Even if they don't say it you get the vibes as to which group you belong to. (Brendan O'Reilly, ex-Big 6, Medium Practice Manager)

As we shall see the things in which conformity was sought concerned areas such as presentation, the ability not to antagonise clients, capability to reach the right conclusions (these were set down by management), ability to uphold the practice's 'good name' and so on. A large part of an accountant's training concerns these issues. Conformity is encouraged from early on because conformity may well be rewarded and even if it is not there are plenty of positions out in industry that are as well, or perhaps better, paid. These controls are internalised in much the same way as Offe's normative controls.

OFFE'S CONTROL MECHANISMS

Accountancy appears to fit into Offe's task continuous and task discontinuous control sequence (see Offe, 1976). Offe argues that there is a move within capitalism from a task continuous status organisation to a task discontinuous status organisation. The former organisation is one whereby control is maintained by the use of specific technical rules and regulations which everybody knows are needed for adequate functional performance. Within this scenario your superiors are more qualified or expert in your particular field than you are – they are technically more competent. In these organisations hierarchical differentiation must be relatively undeveloped, allowing direct communication and direct supervision of execution. Actors must be close to each other in rank and perform the same functions. The use of supervisors who are technically more expert provides management with two main advantages. Firstly, it makes it a lot more difficult for employees to perform their work in a technically bad or sloppy way and secondly, it can make control more acceptable to subordinates as control appears as part of the technical division of labour. This latter point is especially the case when the junior is a trainee. The staff may even view supervision in a positive light because they can still learn from their superiors. As a result it is more likely that control will not be thought of as a negative sanction which is required because the employee is not trusted. Accountancy fulfils some but not all of these conditions. For instance, seniors out on site are in direct supervision of trainees but nobody directly supervises the senior, managers are back at the head office.

A task discontinuous organisation operates in a fundamentally different way. Control in this form of organisation is not based on technical rules and regulations (although these do have a role) but upon other normative orientations. The hierarchical structure of the organisation is the main reason for this change. A person's superior does not have a more expert knowledge of the technical rules and regulations of the job, in fact he or she may well have less knowledge of the job than the worker. In this case, because control via technical rules is weakened, due to the fact that the superior may not be aware of the technical rules or, to extend the Offe thesis, may not be there to directly supervise the worker even though the supervisor may be technically as expert, a new internal control mechanism is required. Normative controls fulfil this function. They ensure that when a worker has to use discretion and make a decision he or she will make the 'right' one. Some of these normative controls are used by accountants. A fact of which accountants are aware.

To a certain extent we supervise ourselves. (Greg Walsh, Big Six Senior)

However, the situation is different to the one Offe describes in that an accountant's superiors within practice are also accountants and, probably, technically better. Thus practices are not dependent on either form of control but use a combination of the two. However, within practice the higher up the hierarchy one proceeds the greater adoption of the 'right' normative orientations one must have. To be technically a good accountant is necessary for promotion to partner level but on its own it is not enough. For promotion within practice one needs extra-functional orientations such as loyalty to those in charge, the acceptance and adoption of organisational culture and so on, hence the development of paternalist relations between those tipped for promotion and senior partners (see Harper, 1989; Dirsmith and Covaleski, 1985). This mentoring process also exists in legal firms (Moore and Moore, 1991).

There are a number of ways by which a person can show loyalty to a practice. The use of the system whereby one buys into the partnership and receives the same amount back when one leaves is a means of expressing loyalty or commitment to the practice, as well as increasing the firm's resources. Buying into a practice is not required by all the Big Six firms but of the four that the author visited three had procedures for 'buying in'. Most large partnerships are made up of equity and salaried partners (see Figure 2.13, p. 72). The latter do not own any of the business but they receive a large salary and have voting rights although they do not share in the profits of the firm. Hence in many ways it is a 'normal' promotion. All the partners interviewed were very reluctant to talk about how one becomes an equity partner. None would tell me how much it would cost to do so, they would not even suggest a rough 'ballpark' figure.

There is a graduated scale amongst equity partners and, as a result, not all partners own the same amount of the partnership. One buys in at the minimum amount of equity that a partner is permitted to own.[4] Over the course of time one may be asked, or one may ask, to re-introduce money into the partnership, thus increasing one's stake. This naturally results in partners receiving different profit shares. As regards these purchases the practices generally seem to provide loan facilities to potential partners if the individual concerned cannot raise the finance required. The exact nature of much of these procedures is unknown to the staff of these firms. For example Philip Carey, a senior in a Big Six practice, felt one had to come up with the total sum of money required when buying into the firm completely on one's own

> Well you'd have to buy your way in and if you don't have the bucks you won't get it, its as simple as that ... there is no way you'd save those kind of bucks.

Another means of expressing loyalty and commitment is to bring clients with you.

I think to become a partner in an established organisation you have to have a portfolio of clients with you and as such it's more difficult today. (John Peters, Small Practice Partner)

From my experience it is really very good people that become partners in Big Eight firms. Anyone who makes partner in the Big Eight, unless they are exceptionally good altogether, will have to work really hard all the way along. They'll really have to plug their corner very much, by getting good results, achieving budgets and I suppose at the end of the day making profits for the partners they're working for while trying to build up their own reputation. It is a bit of a rat race. (Brendan O'Reilly, ex-Big Six, Medium Practice Manager)

If one cannot make this commitment or refuses to, then partnership will be withdrawn. As outlined by Philip Carey's ignorance of the 'buying in' process partnership is a somewhat intangible thing.

Partnership is an unusual thing, because you can have a large number of bright people but there may be no vacancy at partnership level and the people who are promoted are – one, very good people . But you have to be technically good, an able person in your profession. But aside from that you have got to have a good personality, you've got to get clients if you're going to be a partner. And you've got to have a bit of cash or some sort of equity or the ability to borrow it. (Robert Murray, Big Six Assistant Manager)

Thus technical, financial, and social issues play a part in promotion. One needs to have the resources and contacts that partnership work requires as much of this work entails the search for new business.

We actively go out and seek new work and we try to get our people out and we do public profile things and jobs so we're known. (Stephen Flanagan, Big Six Partner)

One, I suppose, and one should never ignore it, a firm like ours is a commercial organisation and the bottom line is that. In other words unless an individual is going to be able to contribute to enlarging the cake they really have little or no chance ... first of all the individual must contribute to the profitability of the business. In part that is bringing in business but essentially profitability is based upon the ability to serve existing clients well. (Peter O'Neill, Big Six Director)

In terms of qualities the first is profitability and it is hard to distinguish it from the first but the next is to be technically very good. At the end of the day in a professional field you're providing top quality advice. Increasingly I think we're going to be looking for non-technical skills in picking partners. I think we'll be concentrating more and more on social skills, in people skills and this is not just me as a personnel professional trying to express my desired candidate but I think there is an increasing awareness that the skills, the strengths, getting the best out of the firm will come from using our prime resource, which is people. (Peter O'Neill Big Six Director)

One has to be willing to make these resources available to the practice. Not all technically good accountants will have these extra necessities and, therefore, they will not make partner. The above two features, bringing clients with one and buying into the partnership, distinguish accountancy and indeed law from most of the other professions working in a commercial environment, for example engineers and chemists (McGovern, 1992). In engineering and chemistry there are avenues within say R&D by which the 'technical boffins' can gain promotion to very high levels. This is not the case in accountancy because of its somewhat unusual organisational structure and the almost entrepreneurial way in which partners are supposed to operate. Partners must actively court new business rather than make a technical breakthrough and then expect others to exploit its potential profitability. Within other professions such as medicine or academia the issue of profitability would play an even less important role. This is not to say that there are no social factors involved in the promotional procedures experienced by academics or doctors or indeed by the 'technical boffin' in engineering and chemistry; rather it implies that these social issues would be different and less directly commercial in nature.

The possession of knowledge and ability directly related to performance is still necessary, but now the category of normative rules becomes a further functional precondition for participation in the work process. (Offe, 976: 31)

Hence, although Offe's theory is open to some criticism, for instance, it may not be accurate to say that all sections of the workforce are moving from a task continuous to a task discontinuous status hierarchy, for example it does not appear to apply to the skilled trades in the building industry (Scase and Goffee, 1982). The theory also needs to be extended in that accountancy practices combine both control strategies and they, potentially at least, make use of a financial regulation as well as the technical and nor-mative ones outlined by Offe. Having accepted these qualifications it is a very useful concept to use for accountants. Technically, all trainees, seniors, and managers have their work judged. Work is examined and passed up the hierarchy to be examined again by somebody more compe-tent. The senior's work is rigorously scrutinised by the manager and then less rigorously graded by the partner; at this stage the senior is judged on technical know how. However, the other features of accountancy controls are normative. These are used to appraise all the accountants who are tech-nically good and to decide who is to be promoted and who is not. The train-ees and seniors are conscious of this and alter accordingly. Lastly, the financial proviso within the promotion to partnership could prove crucial in times of difficulty, for example when the practice requires a capital inflow. All of this implies that promotion to partnership is a nebulous thing within which an infinite number of questions may have to be considered. For example there are often subjective issues involved, such as do the partners like the candidate? And there are other external factors that have nothing to do with the candidate at all. These external factors cover a wide variety of things such as do the partners want to keep tight control? Is the firm expanding? Does the partnership need money? Thus there are no guaran-tees of partnership and in most cases people are dealing with an unknown quantity. This is quite different, at least at an official level, to the way in which promotion takes place in bureaucratic organisations (Edwards, 1979) and in middle class clerical work (Stewart *et al.*, 1980). The issues surrounding who gets promotion will be addressed later on.

INTERNAL LABOUR MARKETS

The internal labour markets (ILM) that have arisen in the Big Six are another form of control. Again the ILM is not a feature that is unique to accountancy practices nor, indeed, to the service sector (see Edwards, 1979; Burawoy, 1979 who have written in depth about ILMs in the manu-facturing sector). The use of ILMs creates a situation whereby people have an incentive to stay and mobility is encouraged within the firm rather than between organisations. This use of ILMs has only been partially applied in the accountancy practices. These ILMs are partial for very good reasons. There is a lot of mobility out of practice because the Big Six simply cannot promote everyone and it would be too expensive for them to use three or four fully qualified seniors on a job when only one is needed (see the Conor Hackett quote in Chapter 3, p. 90). Theoretically the ILM helps a practice to keep its 'brightest and best'. The people who are not the 'brightest and best' are happy to leave because their ambitions will be better fulfilled in other organisations. The people who leave take status and experience from the Big Six and the Big Six are happy to let them go, having got relatively cheap labour out of them for three or four years. Trainee accountants make up the largest group within a Big Six office. Their salary is quite low in comparison with their fully qualified counterparts. The reason for this is quite simple; they are apprentices and have little option but to accept a low salary during their training. On the other hand McGovern (1992) has demonstrated how graduates in engineering and pharmaceuticals receive regular and relatively large increases in pay during the first year or two with a firm despite the fact that they are still being trained. The reason for this stems from the fact that the firms are seeking to maintain a gap between their unionised technicians and their non-unionised, graduate–professional scientists. When a graduate first joins a firm he or she is paid less than a technician and the employers feel that this situation will be tolerated by the graduates for a relatively short period, hence the pay increases. The fact that these industries are unionised and, to some extent, bureaucratic forces the firms into doing this. Accountancy and law because they do not suffer the 'scourge' of trade unionism and because they are more individualised and commercial do not have to indulge their trainees like this, leading McManus (1992) to ask whether or not they were exploited. Once the trainees reach the promised land of qualification their salary rises quite dramatically, by as much as 20–30 per cent within a year of qualifying. The reason for this is again quite simple: the demand for qualified accountants puts these individuals into quite a powerful position on the labour market. This is true for all Big Six practices and is recognised by the accountants themselves.

> I think that coming out of here our CV is going to be better. Number one its a Big Eight firm and number two the clients are fairly prestigious. So it helps both ways and I do think that is an advantage over somebody coming out of a smaller firm. (Jane O'Driscoll, Big Six Senior)

The ILMs perform their job quite well. Before the stage where a senior decides to leave s/he will have directed his or her energy towards competition with other seniors in the hope that s/he (and not other seniors) will gain promotion. This thus directs conflict horizontally and when promotion is granted the general view is that the 'best' person won.

These internal markets are well established and, indeed, in recent years they have been expanding in the Big Six. In the smaller practices the various levels are trainee, senior, manager, and partner. People are normally a senior for a short period of time. Some medium firms make seniors into managers within a year of qualifying. Smaller firms again have maybe one manager and a handful of seniors. But in the Big Six the hierarchy is a lot more differentiated (Figure 2.13, p. 72). The various levels are trainee, senior, supervisor or assistant manager, manager, executive or director or senior manager, salaried partner, and equity partner. Not all of the Big Six have these levels but they appear to be at least moving in this direction. This increasingly differentiated hierarchy serves the purpose of encouraging *some* people to stay by granting promotion. There is evidence that in the USA the major law firms are also moving down this road (Galanter, 1983). In many instances the increased responsibility that one expects with promotion is more imaginary than real, but nonetheless it does distinguish and separate people.

> You get a few more thousand a year and you get the name supervisor but you're doing the same thing as a senior. (Jean Devoy, Big Six Senior)

However, not only do you get a few extra thousand but you are also made aware of the fact that of the people you came into the firm with only three or four of you are supervisors and, therefore in competition for the post of manager. This increases your chances of becoming a manager, making you try harder. Because these people are normally ambitious they will probably stay to gain that extra promotion (and the one after that). Even in the situation where they are made a salaried partner they will try to become equity partners.

> Its a prestige, status thing. They might be getting paid that little bit better. I would call partnership equity partnership, the other isn't really partnership at all. (Robert Murray, Big Six Assistant Manager)

There are two reasons as to why the Big Six are moving towards an increasingly hierarchical ILM One is simply the fact that these organisations are becoming very large, Stokes, Kennedy, Crowley now employs over 700 staff in Ireland (including non-accountants). The recent merger boom means that these firms are going to get even larger, more impersonal and, therefore, run the risk of alienating staff.

> I think for actually training them as well, like this place is getting too big. There are people here like that you'll never meet, like socially its bad, its just getting too big and people are making less and less effort

because you could be talking to someone today and they could be left tomorrow. So I think this place has reached the largest now that it can possibly reach. If it gets any larger its going to get inefficient because there are going to be too many people ... it has damaged staff morale already. (Jean Devoy, Big Six Senior)

However, if one views oneself as a supervisor or a manager then the group to which you feel attached to is not so large and hence less impersonal. This may lessen the damaging effect on staff morale and encourage those, whom the partners want, to stay on.

The second reason for this differentiation is also due to this need to hold on to quality staff. Because of the fact that the audit market is stagnant and the growth areas, such as management consultancy and corporate finance are more experience based, it is vital for a large practice to offer some form of incentive to hold on to the more qualified people. This diversification into other areas will incorporate the use of non-accountants and may lead practices further down Offe's discontinuous status path. There is also evidence that law firms are also undergoing this diversification process (Counsell, 1988). Without these qualified staff the Big Six will find it increasingly difficult to operate in these growth markets. One way of holding on to these people is by promotion and by increasing the number of levels within the firm. This will mean that if a person does not make it to equity partner he or she will at least have achieved a high position within the hierarchy and the benefits that go with this, he or she will also have spent so long doing this that it would be hard for them to move into industry. In many ways this hierarchy is a control mechanism in that if you do not fulfil the requirements you will not go up the ladder. But it is also a response. It is a response to the fact that with the changing market and the new demands from clients practices had to do something to lessen the exodus of accountants.

> Yeah this is true but it is not just management consultancy there are other areas particularly tax and other financial advice areas. Certainly a year ago we, in structuring our salary levels, were very conscious of the need to hold onto the guys you're exactly talking about, who were qualified with no exam commitments and who we feel are good and who we want to retain and we were finding it very difficult. (Stephen Flanagan, Big Six Partner)

Accountants were not prepared to remain as seniors or managers in large numbers and opted for work in industry. The fact that industry provides competition for the practices in terms of recruitment allows these workers to exert a greater pressure on their employers than some other professionals whose labour is less in demand on the labour market, for example doctors, academics, civil servants and so forth. It is an example of how workers influence control strategies.

> If he waits till over 40 and he hasn't been made a partner he'll more than likely never be made one ... I think if they reach 40 it's getting critical and they must go into industry. A new managerial level – executives like in SKC – will need to be created for people who stay in practice as not enough room for partners and not enough room for new firms exists. (Gabriel Oak, ex-Big Six Senior)

This internal market differs from Edward's bureaucratic control in that there are not clearly defined rules nor is there as much emphasis on issues like seniority. One may do everything correct and still not become a partner. Practices are very secretive about what qualities make a partner and even if one has all of these there are still no guarantees.

> Because it is a partnership and it requires a majority vote nobody can guarantee you that you'll be made a partner. (Stephen Flanagan, Big Six Partner)

The existence of relatively high levels of mobility, both vertically and horizontally, is maintained even at partnership level. It is not that unusual for a partner in a large firm to give up partnership and join industry (having been headhunted). Neither is a move like this frowned upon by those left in practice. This distinguishes accountancy from certain other professions. For example Paterson (1983) has shown how judges are very reluctant to leave the bench and if they do it is deemed unacceptable conduct by their colleagues. Accountants can also be distinguished in another way. The salary levels within practice are solely determined by the market value put on accountants. This is unlike industries that have been unionised wherein the presence of the unions puts upward pressure on the salary levels of all the non-unionised professionals within these industries. Likewise the dominant firms in electronics and pharmaceuticals pay their staff over the odds in order to keep them from moving to more satisfying but less well paid jobs. This problem has not existed for practices in the past despite the fact that practice pays less than other areas (LSCA, 1990) largely because, I would suggest, the importance of the audit meant that the firms could survive by using apprentice labour. The Stephen Flanagan quote on p. 126 implies that

this ability to pay relatively low wages may be receding and that accountancy firms, like their engineering and chemical counterparts, may be forced
to pay above the odds.

BUDGETS, PAY AND THE TECHNICAL MANAGEMENT OF ACCOUNTING

There are other, more technical, means of control. Accountants are supervised quite tightly. All work is examined by a manager and a partner. This
is facilitated by the fact that when a work team is out on a job they must
record on paper everything they have done. This paperwork is examined by
the senior to make sure it is all in order and then it is handed over to the
manager. The manager goes over the work in detail and if it is correct it
will be passed on to the partner. The partner will also examine it although
this examination will normally be more superficial.

> There is a comprehensive technical and training function which defines
> the standards, these are implemented by review sources. So the manager
> will review the work of the senior and the partner would review the work
> that is carried out by the managers and there are matters of professional
> judgment that are the prerogative of the partner. If there are difficulties
> that affect the opinion of the firm or are of interest to a partner then there
> are procedures where more than one partner can consider that. (Tim
> Madden, Big Six Manager)

This type of supervision is not just used in the Big Six but in all practices.
Because the partners are liable for work done it is in the partners' interest
to examine things. In many ways this checking by the partner is a formal
arrangement merely to allow him or her to 'sign off' the books, legally
only a partner can do this. It is not the same as a manager's scrutinising
of the senior's work. The manager will be very competent technically and
as a consequence of this his or her work will not need to be 'judged' as he
or she can be trusted not to get it wrong. This trust would be undermined
by a detailed technical examination of the manager's work. Because of
these issues the final partner analysis of the work is quite brief and
largely a formality. However, it is still fair to say that unlike the traditional image of the professional these managers are not in full control of
their work.

Another feature of how the work is tightly controlled is the area of budgets. Budgets and, therefore, the amount of time available for a job, are

decided by the manager. The senior, when doing the preliminary work on the audit, puts in a draft budget and this is accepted or rejected by his or her superior. There is a strong pressure to do the audit with less resources every year and to come in under budget and make more profit. This pressure affects the manager in particular although it also has an affect upon the seniors. If one makes the practice money and is, therefore, a good asset promotion is more likely. Thus there is an incentive to come in under budget, however, if one does so one makes it harder for those following

> Well it depends on your personality and how strong you are to force it. Budgets here are the exact same as they are in industry you're going to build slack into your own. Not unless you're extraordinarily ambitious and want to do it say in two weeks and bust yourself. If you do a job in two weeks this year and it was four weeks last year, for the guy coming along next year he is going to have to do it in two weeks as well. (Philip Carey, Big Six Senior)

This pressure to come in under budget leads to a situation wherein staff often do not record all the time they have spent on a job hence bringing the cost down through unpaid labour. This 'eating time' as it is known will affect those employees who have to do the job the following year. If the person coming up next year does not do it in the same time then s/he will look poor in comparison to the person gone before.

> It [eating time] is one of those problems that is really hard to identify and really hard to stamp out because some people don't do it and other people do do it but even then they do it for different reasons. It is definitely something we hate. I always hated it. Following anybody who had eaten time is horrible because suddenly you look like an idiot, maybe I am an idiot but you just couldn't win. (John Barnes, US Big Six Senior Manager)

Despite the comments of John Barnes, which may lead one to think that eating time was an isolated occurrence, the practice appears to be quite widespread and institutionalised

> It's the thing that I detest about my job and it's the thing that's going to drive me ultimately from public accounting. It's the constant pressure to do things in less time and although we have what is supposedly an iron clad rule which requires all our staff people to put all of their time on their time sheets they quickly learn that thats not going to help their

careers at all, so our staff don't put all their time on their time sheets. Managers more or less explicitly encourage them not to do so, although I try very much to encourage all my staff to do so but I don't put all my time on my time sheet. The net effect is that then my numbers don't look as good as other managers and so I don't come out as well when it comes time for raises, my realisation isn't as good. But if you don't put the time down you're just killing yourself or whoever has the client next year who has to match your time. (Frank Rogers, US Big Six Manager)

However, it is more important for managers to be able to control budgets than seniors. Managers are the people really held responsible for making the money once the partners have attracted the clients. They are suppose to know which people to assign, how many people to assign, and how much to charge so that a profit can be made without the fees appearing exorbitant. If managers cannot do this then partners question their suitability for partnership. The key feature in proving your capability if you are a manager is not to run over budget.

No, I think a lot of talk [about budgets] is a little bit over stated. My own experience was that a lot of jobs went over budget and you know from experience and being there to what extent you could run over budget … I wouldn't say that it's true that the firms monitor in any serious way the performance of their seniors against budget. I think probably managers are evaluated against budget more than seniors. They'd be evaluated in terms of getting yours fees in on time, but yeah if there was a serious overrun that couldn't be recovered it is the manager who would take quite a bit of the stick on that rather than the senior. (Gabriel Oak, ex-Big Six Senior)

Hence seniors can overrun to a certain extent possibly because managers have already 'built slack' into the budget.

You just explain why you're over but usually as you're going through I'd ring up and say like its not going to be done on time due to whatever. Usually it's fine. (Anne Doyle, Medium Practice Senior)

Managers cannot afford this luxury. They could not go to partners with consistent shortfalls on budgets. However, when talking about budgets the partners, not surprisingly, play down their importance in order to maintain the image of carrying out a comprehensive job.

They [budgets] would be one of our concerns but on the Green Forms or the Six Monthly Forms [these are employee assessment forms] budgets are never mentioned but every job has certain things to be done and the person responsible for the job is accountable for the budget. But it's not wrong to say that most jobs would tend to go over budget slightly. In most cases it probably isn' t the fault of the manager, very often it's a case that more work had to be done. Certainly if a senior was consistently over budget and we felt it was unreasonable we would question his ability to manage but it's not a major problem. What would be a lot more important would be his ability to reach the proper conclusion and get along with clients and be able to get the right information. (Stephen Flanagan, Big Six Partner)

Despite the comments of Stephen Flanagan the seniors feel somewhat differently about budgets.

Yeah managers are constantly monitoring budgets and costs. You know if you're getting so much time and you're going over it they do notice. (Paul Devine, Big Six Senior)

Budgets will have a trickle down effect. A manager will be more favourably disposed to a senior who comes in under budget and will, therefore, support him or her when the candidates for promotion are put forward. Budgets also have an impact upon the quality of the work and many would say it makes the work more 'unprofessional'. Practices, however, are in business to make a profit and only those who make money for them, i.e. tightly control their budget, will be promoted. The Cohen Commission in the USA found the same (Stevens, 1984: 87). This process effectively puts everyone under some pressure.

In response to these pressures senior management in large accountancy practices have begun to alter the idea of what it is to be a 'professional'. They have shifted this idea away from the old notion of somebody who performs a task for the 'public good' towards the concept of somebody doing their job well or expertly. To do your job well implies that the customer, i.e. the person who pays for the work, is content. Hence these large practices reject the idea that they should discover fraudulent activity if it is taking place within a firm, they are thus increasingly reluctant to perform their 'public watchdog' role (Humphrey *et al.*, 1991). This has expressed itself amongst the management of accountancy practices in the need to be commercial (see Peter O'Neill quote on p. 121). Professional now means the same as being a professional manager or a professional footballer and so on, one does a good job for one's employer or client.

There is not a great deal of movement of clients and we'd argue that the best source of new work is to do your existing work well. The best way of getting new work is to have a reputation of doing work well, giving good advice, being technically sound, commercially aware or whatever. (Peter O'Neill, Big Six Director)

Clients are looking for the best advice plus the qualities of discretion and non-public interest on behalf of the practices. As stated earlier these are vital qualities that a trainee must learn. These 'professional' qualities are used for the benefit of the client not the public. Commercialism now depends upon these professional traits been exercised for the benefit of the customer. This altered professionalism has emerged in a number of sectors within the producer services. Savage *et al.* (1988) have argued that there is an increasingly fragmented service class developing. This fractured service class should be divided into two groups, the traditional public service or large bureaucratic service class member, and the new 'professional entrepreneur'. This latter group has emerged with the restructuring that has taken place within the advanced economies in the past fifteen years or so.

These people exhibit a number of noticeable traits. They are paid an individualised, differential salary which is related to their work performance, hence they are not simply trusted in the same way that the traditional service class worker is (see pp. 147–50). These professionals are very often trained in a large firm or bureaucracy which they leave upon qualification. After qualifying they engage in a great deal of inter-organisational movement. This feature can be witnessed within Irish accountancy. Despite the fact that the Big Six trained 70 per cent of Irish accountants they employed only 26 per cent of the sampled population. A second trait amongst these professional entrepreneurs is the high level of new firm and spin-off growth. 20 per cent of the total accountancy sample stated that they would establish their own practice. This trend is reinforced by the fact that the number of Irish practices almost doubled throughout the 1980s, up from 400 to 700 (Fitzgerald, 1987). Savage *et al.* also suggest that the areas where these new professionals work are characterised by the twin processes of concentration and small firm growth, with the medium firms suffering in the resultant squeeze. This has been a noticeable trend within Irish accountancy over the past decade (McCann, 1988) and it is emerging within law (Stanley, 1991). These new service workers step straight into the service class upon completion of their third level education as opposed to the more traditional route of working one's way up the organisational ladder.[5] Again this trend is nicely highlighted by Irish accountants, as we shall see later. Finally it has been suggested that if these people are spatially mobile it tends to be when they are quite young as opposed to being mobile throughout the course of their working lives. Again there is evidence of this within Irish accountancy (Hanlon, 1991). This is in marked contrast to the traditional professional. Parkhouse (1991: 105) has estimated that on average doctors move three times during their careers and that if one simply looks at male doctors 7 per cent of men move six times or more.

This move towards commercialised professionalism is part of a more general change within the labour market. It represents a sectoral move in favour of the post-industrial occupations that comprise large numbers of small firms and self-employed people (see Chapter 1). It also appears to be evidence of a move towards the flexible firm which now buys in services as opposed to providing them in-house. As a result of this change certain professionals now need to be competitive on the market. This led to radical changes within accountancy throughout the 1980s This period witnessed the introduction of advertising for the first time this century, diversification into new services and new market areas, the intensification of the debate about whether or not the partnership structure should be dropped in favour of a limited company format and so on. The move towards the flexible firm wherein 'expert' services, amongst other things, are bought in is only possible if the 'experts' act in the buyer's interest and not in the interest of the public. As stated accountancy is not the only commercialised profession, law firms were undergoing similar processes (Counsell, 1988). One nice example of this commercialism is the fact that within industries like engineering and chemicals the nature of the product is dependent on R&D and the more bureaucratic structure of the firms insulates the R&D department, to a limited extent, from the market. This allows for failure to be tolerated (McGovern, 1992). The same cannot be said for accountancy or law. All the departments in accountancy practices sell their services directly on the market and hence they are highly exposed to this market. This means that a failure directly damages a practice's reputation because it implies that the firm did not give 'sound commercial advice'. As such, failures are not tolerated.

It is premature to say that this is a universal trend. For example self-employment growth in Europe has been restricted to Ireland, the UK, Italy and Belgium during the 1970–85 period (Steinmetz and Wright, 1989). There is also evidence to suggest that the UK is somewhat unusual in its quite widespread adoption of the flexible firm management strategy (Hakim, 1990). However, it is in the light of these changes that the emergence of the 'commercialised professional' and the control processes that they are subject to should be understood. It is most unlikely that traditional public service professionals such as doctors, academics, civil servants and so on would be commercialised or controlled in the same way despite the partial encroachment of the market on their work.

WORK OUT ON SITE

How are employees controlled out of the office and what can go wrong? Quite obviously budgets are a control mechanism giving the audit team a specified time to carry out their work. Control is in the hands of the senior when the audit team are out on site. It is his or her responsibility to see that the work is done well, on time and that the practice's image is maintained or improved. If the senior 'messes up' it can put an end to his or her career with the firm. Again the legal profession appears to be the same, one mistake in law can permanently blight a young person's career (Chambers, 1986). They must ensure that their subordinates are also good, this involves both teaching and management skills.

> One of the main problems with the juniors is that they just don't know what to do. They've never stepped inside an accounts department, they've never encountered that type of situation before, they've never had to ask client staff for information, they've never had to respond to information received, they don't know how to put information together on a piece of paper and for the first couple of months it's really a mundane exercise until you develop some experience. A junior grade in here has to do that for twelve to eighteen months and for the first six months they need a lot of supervision but as time goes on they'd need less as they'd be doing the same work. (Jonathan Andrews, Big Six Senior)

Thus there has to be a substantial degree of teaching by the seniors to ensure that the junior can 'respond to information received' and so forth

> Initially yes, I would think it's half and half, teaching initially and after that then managing. (Paul Devine, Big Six Senior)

This presents a dilemma for the practices as their people must appear to be professional and yet there is a lot of on the job training for people that, at least in the beginning, know very little about the work. Technically a junior's work is deemed to be simple hence it is the personal appearances and social factors that can damage a junior's promotion prospects as these affect the practice's image.

Secondly, to behave continuously in a very unprofessional way for instance if you came in every day not wearing a tie or didn't come in properly dressed ... and if people advised you on this and you still didn't well obviously come the end of the year you don't really fit in. Clients wouldn't know what we're sending out to them and it's just not working out. It sounds like a petty thing but as a firm we have to show a professional image to the outside world. (Conor Hackett, Big Six Partner)

In the light of the discussion in Chapter 2 concerning the importance of reputation in accountancy it is easy to see why image is so important. These image factors are the ones that most worry seniors. When recounting instances or possible future instances of things going wrong on a job many talked about social things, for example staff wearing awful suits, having B.O., or getting drunk when out with a client rather than anything technical.

I suppose the most embarrassing situation would be something like if you went out on a Friday night for a few drinks after the audit was over and the junior because he was inexperienced got absolutely pissed and threw up everywhere or ran off at the mouth that would be embarrassing. (Jonathan Andrews, Big Six Senior)

The shift towards recruiting graduates rather than non-graduates is, at least partly, to lessen the likelihood of these immaturity based occurrences taking place. However, recruiting graduates by no means eliminates them entirely. One ex-senior told me of a graduate who was quickly labelled a 'plonker'. This was because he showed a lack of tact by asking a partner on the welcoming day for the new recruits how much it would cost to buy into the partnership. Another thing that the junior is warned not to do is to hassle the client for information or make a nuisance of him or herself by constantly quizzing client staff.

A junior can never really hassle anyone that much for information. He wouldn't be looking for vital information and if he can't get it he'd come to the senior who'd sort things out. It wouldn't be right for a junior to persistently be searching out for information. It's not something you'd encounter much because if a junior can't get it he'll come to the senior and tell him. (Jonathan Andrews, Big Six Senior)

However, juniors do not always come and tell the senior immediately. An accountant recounted to the author how he was told to check the amount of outstanding debts for the firm and when he asked the client staff for the documentation concerning debts they told him, they had no debts only accounts receivable information (these are the same thing). He proceeded to wander around the office doing nothing for three hours before plucking up the courage to tell the senior he could not find any debts. The senior asked him, had he not checked the accounts receivable files and when the junior admitted he thought they were separate things the senior informed him 'what an idiot he was'. This incident is not an isolated one.

> It will happen that if they can't get information or don't know what information to get they'll sit there and be too afraid to ask but you'll just have to watch out for it. (Paul Devine, Big Six Senior)

These occasions are embarrassing for the practice because the trainees appear to be unprofessional and more like what they really are, trainees. This appears to be quite unique to accountancy amongst professional workers. Other professions do not appear to send out four or five people on a job only one of whom is qualified. For example, project teams in engineering sometimes comprise of workers who are technically more expert than the managers of the team in specific areas. Managers may even learn from their involvement in such teams.[6] In other instances where large numbers of trainees are used, for example engineering, they appear to be based back at the firm's factory and are thus hidden from the clients (McGovern, 1992). The only comparable profession to accountancy in this incidence appears to be medicine. Peschel and Peschel (1986) highlight how young doctors or interns look after patients who may be very seriously ill and try to convince these patients that they are in good hands even though the hands are inexperienced and shaking. In one account they describe how a young intern having left medical school did not know how to fill in a death certificate despite the fact that of the group present he, as a doctor, was the only one legally capable of doing so.

As with engineers (see Causer and Jones, 1990) control is made easier because of the collegial nature of the small group on an audit. Seniors are in an unusual position because they may be away from Dublin on an audit for a fortnight living with people of their own age and yet they must get the job done to a certain standard whilst getting on with those they have to live with.

> here we go out on a job, we could be left alone for two or three weeks and you could have four people working for you and basically you've got to keep them busy, make sure they're not making a fool of them-

selves in front of the client, make sure all the work is done on time and at the same time is done well but you can't set yourself up as a manageress as you're one of them. (Jean Devoy, Big Six Senior)

Having stated this the management of an audit team is not perceived as being too difficult because being a small group there is a lot of close contact between the staff.

> The senior is constantly monitoring the juniors' work, they're constantly talking about this and that. I'd say nearly every hour you'd have a chat and you don't really need, basically you know how its going. (Paul Devine, Big Six Senior)

This does not mean that juniors are unable to cut corners. This cutting of corners by juniors is very difficult to detect because it is usually with work that is relatively unimportant.

> I suppose so if you've been asked to inspect twenty invoices and if the first say sixteen are correct I suppose there may be times when if you're behind you'll take it that they're all okay. Something like that is no risk. (Jonathan Andrews, Big Six Senior)

The seniors, however, cannot afford this luxury because much of their work is based on forming opinions and if a senior is unable to form the correct opinions his or her future career is put in jeopardy.

> For seniors no, there is very little scope for cutting corners at the senior level. (Jonathan Andrews, Big Six Senior)

So what distinguishes one junior from another if the work they do is routine and of relatively little consequence? One is obviously speed and efficiency, some juniors simply perform the job quicker. However, because of the relative lack of importance attached to the work carried out by trainees there are a lot of social factors involved. For example seniors talked of 'general friendliness, a laugh, whatever'.

> Well say you're down the country if you get on with people you can have a laugh. You want some guy you can go for a pint with, not someone who'll go up to the room and study ... I mean if you think about it what else will you do down the country (Paul Devine, Big Six Senior).

FORMAL ASSESSMENT AND PROMOTIONAL PROCESSES

The formal assessment procedures within the Big Six are detailed and rigorous. What follows is based upon the policies of one practice. However, although there was some variation between the practices as regards formal assessment they were remarkably similar. They usually involve four processes; continuous assessment, quarterly appraisal, six monthly evaluation, and finally a yearly assessment.

- *Continuous assessment*: After every assignment a report about an individual is compiled by his or her immediate supervisor. These reports cover a wide variety of areas: technical competence, capacity to get on with clients and colleagues, ability to relate to the client's needs and cope with pressure, facility at conveying findings on paper and to be analytical, ability to follow and give instructions and so on. These reports are largely written up by people on the audit with you and hence they evaluate your social skill. Managers appear to get their information for seniors on the audit from the written documents, their own experience of the interaction between the manager and senior on that particular audit, and they also rely on informal networks such as conversations with juniors, client comments or complaints, and their knowledge of previous work.[7] The individual discusses the report with his or her supervisors and agrees or disagrees with the findings, these comments are noted. The person then signs the report and a copy of it goes into the person's file. These reports are then used as the basis for discussion when the employee meets with a counsellor at the quarterly evaluation.
- *Quarterly appraisal*: All staff, from trainees through to managers, undergo this process. The staff meet, individually, with a professional counsellor who discusses their attitude to work, their strong and weak points, how they can improve and so forth. They are then partly judged at the six monthly meeting on how they have reacted to these criticisms.
- *Six monthly evaluation*: Every six months individuals meet with their immediate managers and partners to consider the person's performance since the quarterly appraisal. These meetings really examine the person's character and technical skills. Very often at these meetings, although this is firm specific, a pay review will take place.
- *Yearly assessment*: This is the longest meeting and it takes place between the partner in charge of an individual's group and the employee. It covers areas such as the person's role within the firm,

their future with the practice, the requirements they feel the firm should fulfil for them and so on. For managers in particular this meeting is carried out on the basis of the evidence of the other assessment procedures and a self-evaluation paper which they complete. This evaluation paper contains details of how they view their last year's performance, together with their goals and objectives for the forthcoming year and, in less detail, for the next two to five years. The partner concerned will discuss with the individual their self-evaluation and map out how the firm saw his or her performance and potential.

Many of these appraisal mechanisms are used in the legal profession. Moore and Moore (1991) suggest that three employee reviews should be held: 1 a performance review assessing an individual's job performance and ways of improving it, 2 a reward review, and 3 a potential review within which the firm would map out how they saw the individual's future with them and vice versa. The areas to be assessed within this overall process are: (1) technical competence, (2) problem-solving abilities, (3) motivation and enthusiasm, (4) interpersonal skills, (5) client care skills, (6) overall assessment. These areas are very closely related to the technical and normative skills required by accountants. Another similarity is the fact that the employee fills in a form which refers to the following: (1) the employee's main achievements, (2) the difficulties they have experienced, (3) the areas in which they need to improve, (4) their training needs, (5) their career development objectives. Again this is very similar to the self-evaluation processes that managers undergo within accountancy and quite dissimilar to other professions such as medicine or academia.[8] Even whilst training young academics are subject to quite arbitrary and in some instances relatively few controls. There is no real standardisation within academia as to such mundane issues like how many meetings a research student should have with his or her supervisor or how often they should present written or oral work and so forth. Control is largely down to the proclivities of the individual supervisor.

Promotional Processes: When promotions are being granted there are also a number of processes. The movement from a junior to a senior is largely automatic and it is based upon time served. When a person is being promoted from a senior to a supervisor or assistant manager it is decided by the partners of the particular section that he or she works in. Sometimes, depending upon the firm, their decision has to be ratified by the staff committee (which is made up solely of partners) but this is merely a formality.

If an individual is being made a manager normally he or she is recommended by the partners immediately in charge of the relevant section and then this decision is put to a vote amongst all partners. This vote requires a two-thirds majority for the recommendation to be endorsed.

As would be expected the promotion to partner level is quite a detailed affair. Most firms appear to have two lists of potential partners made out and circulated to all the partners. These lists are updated as needs be. One list contains a series of names who are imminent potential partners if and when a vacancy arises. The second list is made up of people who are partner possibilities in the longer term, sometimes even recently qualified seniors could be on this file. The people on both catalogues are totally unaware that their names have been put forward. The idea behind these lists is that partners who would normally not work with the individuals concerned are aware of them and can assess them when their paths cross at functions, special jobs and so on. If a vacancy does arise a person is forwarded from the shortlist of immediate prospects and a vote is taken. Depending upon the firm this vote may require a 75 per cent majority or a 90 per cent majority. However, in reality the vote is usually unanimous. This is because the partners from all over the country meet biannually to analyse these lists, amongst other things, thus those people that are doubtful are quickly written off.

When one examines the differences between partners and managers it gives an indication of what the 'suitable' candidate for partnership is like. Features such as education and class have a major role to play in identifying the 'ideal' partner. As one would expect accountancy in Ireland is a middle class profession. However, it is the dominance of the upper middle class which is the most striking feature about accountancy. The class backgrounds of the surveyed population are highlighted in Figure 4.1. Of those accountants surveyed only 10 per cent had fathers who were manual workers of any

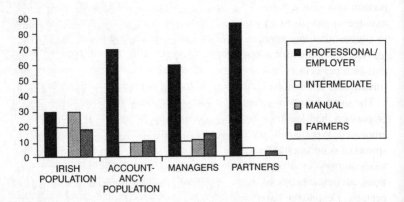

Figure 4.1   The occupational background of fathers within Ireland (%)

description. In comparison with this manual workers made up 29 per cent of the total working population in Ireland in 1985. A similar picture emerges when intermediate non-manual workers are examined. They comprise 22 per cent of the Irish labour force but only 10.5 per cent of the population surveyed. Those people from farming backgrounds have been left out of this analysis. This is due to the difficulty of placing them within an appropriate class when the farm size is not given, as happens within the survey – farmers make up 17.5 per cent of the Irish labour force and 11.2 per cent of the sample. This means that 68.6 per cent of those accountants surveyed had fathers who worked either as self-employed/employers or professional/managerial. This compares with only 29 per cent of the Irish workforce.

What is even more striking about this imbalance is the extent to which elite backgrounds dominate within practice (see Figure 4.1). Of those accountants who had reached the position of manager or assistant manager within practice 61.7 per cent had fathers who were professional/managerial or employer/self-employed. Although this is lower than the corresponding figure for the total survey population an analysis of the managerial group is nevertheless revealing. If one breaks their parental background down further one discovers that 12.5 per cent of them had a father who worked as a director or company secretary, etc. and a further 12.5 per cent of them had a father who was also an accountant. This is despite the fact that in 1990 accountants made up 1.32 per cent of the total working population and this figure was up from 0.32 per cent in 1971 (Corcoran *et al.*, 1992), this latter figure being the more realistic one given that the sample's fathers would have been working in the 1960s and/or 1970s.[9] The corresponding figures for the total accountancy population were 10.3 per cent with fathers who were company directors, etc. and 9.4 per cent with fathers who were accountants. These figures are slightly lower but not enough to assert that managers came from a particularly elite strata. In fact the evidence appears to suggest that managers come from backgrounds that are no more nor no less exclusive than for accountancy in general. This is reinforced by the fact that 11.6 per cent of managers had fathers who were manual workers and a further 10.5 per cent had fathers who worked in intermediate positions.

The same, however, cannot be said of partnership. A massive 86.8 per cent of partners had fathers who were professional/managerial or employer/self-employed. What is also noticeable within partnership is that there is a greater spread of occupational backgrounds amongst their fathers, for example directors, company secretaries and so forth make up 9.5 per cent of paternal occupations, accountants 9.5 per cent, engineers 7.1 per cent, army officers 7.1 per cent, etc. Despite this diversity there is still a higher concentration of elite backgrounds to be found within partnership – 86.8 per cent of their fathers were elite workers as opposed to 68.6 per cent for the accountancy population as a whole. What is also very striking is the poor showing of the manual working class, not one partner had a father from this occupational background. Thus although the numbers involved within the partner subgroup are small ($n = 42$) and should be treated with a degree of caution, it appears reasonable to assume that your class background, and indeed your position within the middle class, has a significant impact upon whether or not one makes it to partner level.

This social exclusiveness is currently being reinforced via the use of third level education. A degree is now more or less a prerequisite before joining a large accountancy practice. Yet the actual relevance of a degree is open to question, of those sampled with third level education only 33 per cent felt that they made current use of their university training. Wickham (1989) and McGovern (1992) both suggest that the same is true for engineering and pharmaceuticals. Added to this is the fact that 28 per cent of these graduates had a degree in a non-business subject. Figure 4.2 highlights the educational qualifications of the total population and our managerial and partner subgroups. The reason for the slightly lower educational attainment for partners is due to the fact that they are on average slightly older than the other populations. If one breaks the partners into two groups, plus or minus 40 years of age, one finds that some 80 per cent of those under 40 have a university education. The corresponding figure for those over 40 is 55 per cent. Hence educational attainment is of growing importance. Managers under 40 are not as well educated on average as their counterparts in partnership, only 67 per cent of managers have a degree (the number of managers over 40 is too small to be of any significance). Hence third level education appears to be playing a greater role than previously in determining who makes it to partner level, despite the fact that it has been

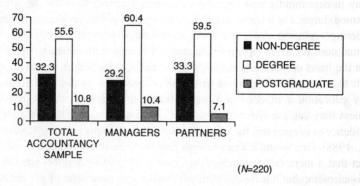

(*N*=220)

Figure 4.2   Education levels within accountancy (%)

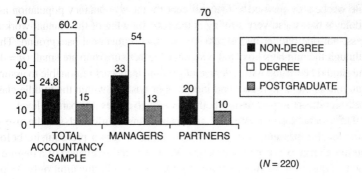

Figure 4.3   Educational levels of accountants under 40 (%)

criticised for being a replica of the professional exams (Lovell, 1992). For the total accountancy population under 40, 75 per cent have a university degree. Thus managers are less well educated than their colleagues and partners are slightly better educated (see Figure 4.3).

When compared with the Irish population as a whole accountants are exceptionally well educated – only 19 per cent of the Irish school population reached third level in 1980/1. As one would expect these were overwhelmingly middle class, with 50 per cent of upper middle class boys and 35 per cent of upper middle class girls attending further education. This compared with 4 per cent and 7 per cent respectively from the semi-skilled and unskilled manual working class (Breen *et al.*, 1990: 132). All of this suggests that the service class is becoming more and more closed. Educational qualifications are the key mechanism for sealing off access to the service class. Even within this class education appears to have an important role to play in determining how high a person rises. In the light of the work performed during one's training and the fact that some firms appear to be considering replacing graduates with non-graduates it would seem that the actual need for a degree within accountancy is non-existent (see Chapter 3). On the basis of what was stated earlier about acceptability it would appear safe to assume that even where a member of the working class with a university education applies for a job within accountancy they will be refused unless they can present a convincing middle class image. There is a lot of evidence to suggest that the UK has experienced a similar process (Savage *et al.*, 1988). One would legitimately suspect that gender also plays a role. The fact that a mere eight women were either managers or partners reinforces this suspicion but it leaves us with too small a subgroup to be of any statistical relevance. Females made up 10.8 per cent of the sample population.

The evidence concerning the differences between partners and managers indicates that to make it to the very top of the promotional ladder it is of great help if one is a male, from an upper middle class professional/ managerial or employer/self-employed background and possesses a university education. This is not surprising as it is this group that would most likely have the necessary business contacts required by a partnership seeking new business. Without all of these credentials one faces an uphill struggle. The gaps in terms of class background and education between partners and managers are quite large, suggesting that practices use these social criteria when promoting people from management to partnership level. These social criteria embrace areas such as club membership, public profile, world view, contacts and so forth. This ensures that the practice is dominated by an elite upper middle class fraction.

This regular and detailed monitoring and assessment of staff means that people know exactly how they should behave and what errors they need to rectify. If they do not do so they are quickly dealt with. There are a number of measures both formal and informal that are meted out to 'unsuitable' employees.

FORMAL AND INFORMAL SANCTIONS

For every level of employee within the firm there is a minimum and a maximum salary, people are given a salary within this range depending on their performance. This is one of the mechanisms whereby people are informed how they stand in the competition for promotion. This means of individualising payment is another way of controlling staff by dividing them (see Burawoy, 1979). This system is deliberately used to isolate and ostracise those that the firm do not want or those who they feel will not improve.

> They won't ask you to leave in any direct way but while everyone else is getting a 10 per cent annual increase you'll get 2 per cent or your manager will call you in on the half yearly assessment and his comments on you won't be very positive. (Gabriel Oak, ex-Big Six Senior)

There is very little point in disagreeing with the pay award despite the supposed two-way nature of assessment discussions and because of the individualised nature of the firms other accountants will most likely view the award as just and hence there will be very little possibility of collective protest.

If you disagree with it, you're only wasting your time disagreeing with it. If you disagree with it its not going to change it. If you disagree with it and you're qualified you'll probably leave … the only sanction you have is to go. (Philip Carey, Big Six Senior)

This isolating strategy is not used solely within accountancy practices. As already stated it is part of the more general move towards the 'commercialised professional'. Causer and Jones have highlighted that the same mechanisms are operated amongst electronic engineers as does McGovern (1992) and Knights and Morgan highlight how poor sales staff in the insurance industry suffer a similar fate –

presumably the cynics and "wankers" will be ostracised and pressured sufficiently to make them either leave or change. (Knights and Morgan, 1990: 377)

Accountancy practices are at least consistent in their use of social and peer pressure. Partners who do not function adequately seem to suffer from isolation as well (Stevens, 1984: 25). On the removal of partners Stephen Flanagan a Big Six Partner commented

I doubt if a partner could be sacked using that term but he can be encouraged to leave.

This social pressure has a strong impact and helps to ensure conformity. No accountant wants to be viewed worse than his or her colleagues by the firm nor do they want this to become public knowledge – which is usually what happens. To avoid this they give greater effort and commitment.

For the people who are not wanted by the practice or are simply bad trainees it is unlikely that they will be sacked directly. Normally the person leaves of their own accord or they are told they have so much time to look for another job. There are no quick redundancies.

Yeah I think part of it is if you were to be sacked as an accountant your career would be ruined. Yeah I think they just have that more gentlemanly way of doing it. There is no doubt that everybody knows people are sacked in the way that they leave. (Gabriel Oak, ex-Big Six Senior)

This more 'gentlemanly' way of doing things ensures that there are no large scale grievances. These would cause disruption and the fact that they do not occur reflects the ethos, organisational culture, and class issues that accountancy entails. It also serves the purpose of not alienating people who may be in a position to act as a future client. By so doing the Big Six can develop strong alumni links.

> Alumni. These people left hopefully with a good taste in their mouth and keeping in touch with them, what they're doing, where they are and that is essential to grow your business because you'll be sitting there you know having a sandwich with them or a drink or something and you'll start talking and the next thing you know you can help them with something. So you know it's essential. (Tom Wallace, US Big Six Manager)

If an accountant is still in the training stage then the practice has a legally binding contract to allow the trainee finish his or her training. However, if the trainee is bad there will be consequences. The most likely, and potentially most damaging, is that seniors will not want the trainee out on a job with them. These trainees tend to spend a lot of time in the office doing small bits and pieces for everybody and a lot of administrative type work.

> Well you don't put them on jobs, you keep them in the office all the time if they're not suitable to go out. But most people, they're strenuous interviews here so they don't leave much to chance. (Anne Doyle, Medium Practice Senior)

> I've never heard of anybody being let go unless they were out of articles. I think that the only thing that could happen to you is that you wouldn't be asked out on jobs ... or you'd get loaded with all the horrible little jobs. (Barbara Wilkinson, Big Six Senior)

The fact that one would get very poor on the job training would severely limit one's chances of passing the examinations; these are difficult enough anyway, the ICAEW has roughly a 40 per cent failure rate for those sitting exams for the first time (ICAEW, 1988) and the ICAI's failure rate is 30 per cent (ICAI, 1989). Added to these issues are the facts that your pay would be less than your colleagues and that there is a social stigma attached to being 'bad'. It is thus not surprising that many would leave.

> I think that the person will be unhappy as well as the company, so it will get to both and you'll have a chat with you manager or partner to see if you'd carry on. (James Dywer, Medium Practice Senior)

Hence the practices have developed sophisticated ways of isolating staff that are deemed 'undesirable' and dealing with them without encouraging collective protest.

PUBLIC VERSUS PRIVATE PROFESSIONALISM

As highlighted there are an array of control mechanisms within the Big Six. Accountants use a lot of self-supervision and at the same time are quite heavily monitored. There is also the use of an internal labour market (ILM) within which accountants can achieve rapid promotion. Even if this avenue is closed off to them they have enough mobility to achieve an equally high position outside of practice. People who will be in some way disruptive or are not capable of doing the job are quickly spotted and pressure from above and their peers, or at least a noticeable lack of support from their peers, will be applied in order to force them out. These control mechanisms are quite different to those applied to other sections of the workforce. Unlike the management of manufacturing industries in the UK and the USA where distrust of shopfloor workers is common (see Wilkinson, 1983) these practices have more confidence in their employees and leave decisions to them to a much greater extent. This is partly due to the nature of the work but it is also due to reasons of class and ideology. These accountants are mostly upper middle class and they have a commitment to and a belief in individualism. If they fail to get on in a firm it is perceived as their failure and not a failure of the firm. It is widely believed that once qualified everyone is on an equal footing and thus all it takes is effort and one will succeed. This effort of course brings in more profit for the firm.

> Not when you get into the firm because when you join a firm we all have the same level of experience whether I've done a business degree or you've done a science degree, we both know nothing about going out to clients. (Greg Walsh, Big Six Senior)

At the same time these professionals are to be distinguished from professionals that work in the public service or even in many of the large scale, private firms. This latter group are often subjected to something like Edwards' bureaucratic control. Quite often they develop firm specific skills thus restricting their movement on the labour market (see Child, 1982 for an examination of this as regards scientists). Failing this, more often than not there is a limited market in the private sector for their skills. In 1982 for example 82.6 per cent of those doctors who qualified in 1977 worked in the public sector (Parkhouse, 1991: Table 8.4), a similar process can be high-lighted in Ireland, between 1971–90 the percentage of professional health workers employed in the medical service itself, which is heavily dependent on the public purse, increased from 72 per cent to 77 per cent of all such employees (Corcoran *et al.*, 1992: 70). As a result of these features this group has not undergone the same degree of commercialisation.

This process of change has, however, altered the accountancy profession within practice. There has been evidence that accountants within industry have had little difficulty in dropping their 'professional' ethos for a more managerial outlook (Hastings and Hinings, 1970; Child, 1982). Child suggested that within industry they were concerned about issues such as achievement, recognition, and advancement rather than the supposedly more professional concern of control over their own labour process. At this stage in the chapter it is apparent that an accountant does not have total control over the labour process in practice. They are also, like their indus-trial counterparts, concerned more with issues of promotion, pay and so on (see Figure 4.4). Promotion in practice is based around the issue of profit-ability as it is in all other areas of private sector capitalism. The fundamen-tally opposing doctrines of professionalism, with its concern for the labour process, and managerial ideology, with its belief that control of the labour process is solely the prerogative of those in charge, no longer exists within these 'commercialised professions'. Managerialism has swept the day.

How has this change been achieved in key areas of the producer services? Some of the occupations concerned have had a long tradition of profession-alism within the Anglo–American world, for example accountancy, law, and so forth. It is my contention that this shift has been relatively painless due to two factors, the labour market position of many of these workers, and the traditions of the professions concerned. Let us take the first point first. There

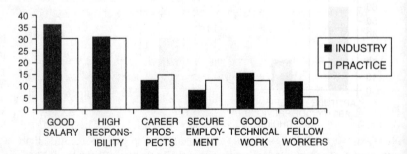

Figure 4.4   First and second future job attractions for Irish accountants (%)

has been a large increase in the opportunities for many of these workers due to the restructuring of capital that has taken place since the 1970s. This brought with it the move towards the flexible firm and a growth in demand for producer services, both of which have been well documented (see Chapter 1). This growth meant that these professionals could take advantage of the labour market and achieve high pay, high levels of responsibility, and/or self-employment quite easily.

The second point is that for some of these professions the degree of antagonism between their professional outlook and that of managers was not that great in the first place. Hastings and Hinings highlighted this second point as regards accountants over 20 years ago. Child (1982) also points to this fact in the case of engineers. He documents how engineers are only partially labour process orientated. Thus they can move into senior management given the opportunity. Child found that scientists on the other hand have greater difficulty as their professional ethos runs deeper and they can feel restricted in private firms as they may not be able to publish findings and so on. Thus for them control and autonomy are issues of greater concern. The same would appear to be the case with chemistry and engineering despite Child's work. In these areas many people appear to still hold on to some professional ideals in the sense that although they are quite prepared to submit to the idea of profitability, satisfaction from the actual labour process is still important to them (McGovern, 1992). Doctors are also concerned with these labour process issues. Figure 4.5 shows the factors highlighted by doctors regarding a number of variables that would influence decisions made about their career. Respondents were allowed indicate more than one variable (Parkhouse, 1991: Table 3.21).

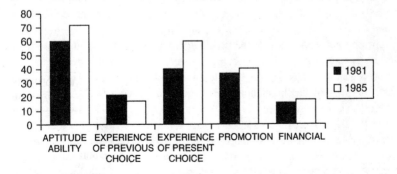

Figure 4.5   Importance of various factors to the future career decisions of the 1974 doctors' qualifying class (%)

The top three factors are ones that could be considered 'technical' in some broad sense and as such approximate the good technical work variable in Figure 4.4. The overall point is that doctors are much more labour process orientated than accountants. Accountants in practice are not labour process orientated, possibly because many of them view practice as a passport to other things such as gaining degrees of organisational power.

> I never wanted to do auditing ... like everyone else I saw the ACA as a qualification to move on to what I really wanted to do which in my case is investment. (Mark Dawson, Big Six Senior)

CONCLUSION

This movement towards commercialisation is a general trend of the past decade. However, which professions it affects depends upon market changes, capital restructuring, and the traditions of those professions concerned. On the basis of this it is unlikely to affect professions such as medicine, academia and so on in the same way as it has affected accountancy and law. These alterations have brought great benefits to those at this elite spectrum of the labour market. The fundamental reason why certain professions have benefited relates to the issue of control. The effected professions allow capital greater control which is a basic requirement within the Flexible Accumulation regime. These 'controllers' are themselves subject to monitoring. This comes in the form of the increased 'need to be commercial'. I would suggest the accountancy profession has responded to this challenge by socialising its trainees in a way that is different to the socialisation procedures experienced by accountants under the more consensual Fordist regime. Today the emphasis is very firmly on being commercial and on performing a service for the customer rather than on being public spirited on behalf of either the public or the state. As I have already stated, these practices have always been interested in and sought after profit. The difference today is possibly as ideologically driven as it is economic. Maybe all that has happened is that these firms have finally ditched any pretence to their being public spirited in light of the ideological shift of the 1980s. There may of course be an economic motive for this ideological shift as the source of new work has changed and become more commercially based. Because of the lack of research in this area one can only surmise as to which is the more important factor, the ideological or the economic change. I would suggest a combination of the two. However, the overall point still stands, there has been a significant alteration. The service class now appears to be more closed than in the past and it has fragmented to the benefit of those in private producer services. These changes help to explain the polarisation of society written about in Chapter 1. These issues are further developed in Chapter 6. However, before addressing them it is important to examine the role of emigration within Irish accountancy. In some respects emigration is a control mechanism which is exploited by the Big Six. It is with this aspect of Irish accountancy that Chapter 5 is concerned.

5 Accountancy and the International Division of Labour

This chapter addresses the issue of internationalisation and its affect upon the Irish economy, in particular the Irish accountancy profession. Capital has internationalised on an unprecedented scale since World War II (Armstrong *et al.*, 1984). This globalisation was led by manufacturing firms largely seeking to penetrate protected markets (Lipietz, 1987). These firms later developed global production lines, international product markets, and international labour markets. Service firms, such as the Big Six, have followed the manufacturers down this road. This move, on behalf of service corporations, was partly client driven (see Jones, 1981 and Winsbury, 1977 for the case of accountancy and Maycock, 1986 for the case of banking) and partly due to the fact that these service firms were also chasing new markets and new areas of profitability. There is some evidence to prove that from the middle of the 1980s the latter factors are of growing importance (see Chapter 1). Certain service companies, including the Big Six, have likewise created international labour markets. These markets have different international structures to their manufacturing counterparts, albeit that the outcome is the same: the periphery loses qualified professionals to the core.

Before moving on to the substantive issues addressed in Chapter 5 a brief outline of the chapter's structure will prove worthwhile. The chapter is divided up into nine sections. The first four sections examine the nature of the world economy and how it has impacted upon Ireland both historically and contemporaneously. The next four sections examine how the globalisation of the Big Six has affected the nature of Irish accountancy and the accountancy labour market; in particular they examine why it is that this market has developed an international aspect. These sections also seek to analyse the similarities and dissimilarities between Irish accountants who emigrate and those who stay. The final section draws some conclusions.

CAPITAL'S INTERNATIONALISATION

The post-war globalisation of capital led to the formation of dependent industrialisation in the periphery. The periphery had previously been characterised by the exporting of raw materials and labour to the core. The foreign direct investment (FDI), which was initiated at a hitherto unheard of scale in the post-1945 period, was driven by the desire of western multi-nationals to get passed the tariff barriers protecting peripheral markets. This investment led to the creation of what has been termed a New International Division of Labour (NIDL). This NIDL entails the division of the produc-tion process into three separate parts. These are, the conception of the prod-uct, the skilled manual work required for the production of the item, and, the low skilled, labour intensive work required. These three processes are spa-tially divorced. Needless to say the low skilled, labour intensive areas of production are located in the periphery where labour is cheapest (for a more in-depth analysis of this NIDL see Lipietz, 1986, 1987 and Cohen, 1987). Lipietz (1987) has suggested that this NIDL was largely a chance discovery on the part of capital which had initially located in the periphery in search of markets and in the hope of halting the declining profitability which was brought on by a whole series of factors back in the core.

This penetration by manufacturing of the periphery was exploitative in the sense that the multinationals took advantage of cheap labour and enforced, or sought to enforce, working conditions often reminiscent of capitalism in the core a century previous (Ehrenreich, 1984). Samir Amin (1980) maintains that the periphery is super-exploited through a whole range of mechanisms which in turn allow capital 'buy off' the labour force in the core and that this super-exploitation is now necessary for the repro-duction of the global capitalist system. While accepting these points this penetration was not without its benefits. It led to what Lipietz (1987) calls Peripheral Fordism. This entails the creation of a sizable middle class and the presence of an autonomous local capital base; Korea would be perhaps the best example. The impact of this industrialisation, however, should not be overstated, Asia's Gang of Four plus Brazil and India account for 70 per cent of the South's manufactures, yet the South produces a mere 3–4 per cent of all the manufactured commodities consumed in the North (Lipietz, 1987: 95). Added to this is the fact that the NIDL is concentrated in a relatively small number of industries (Thrift, 1988).

The investment by core multinationals in the Less Developed Countries (LDCs) is only one aspect to the internationalisation of capital and, it could be suggested, a relatively minor one considering that these countries supply only 9 per cent of the total multinational labour force (Thrift, 1988: 32). The bulk of the investment by multinationals has been within the OECD. Multinationals have sought to trade and invest within the core (Lipietz, 1987). They have invested in underdeveloped regions of the core to exploit the advantages of cheap labour and easier labour control in light of the growing militancy of core labour forces in the post-war era, especially the 1960s and 1970s (Cohen, 1987; Lipietz, 1987). This process was partially responsible for the investment within the United States in the Southern and Sunbelt regions and away from the Northeast. It has been suggested that peripheral areas of Europe also benefited from these developments (Seers *et al.*, 1979).

IRELAND AND THE GLOBAL ECONOMY

Under the Old International Division of Labour Ireland performed the role of a typical peripheral state. Before independence in 1922 Ireland had altered its economic base a number of times in response to the economic needs of Britain. Hence prior to the 1660s Ireland was the largest exporter of sheep and cattle in the world. With the introduction of the UK Cattle Acts in the 1660s Ireland switched to tillage because its largest market, England, was closed off. When Britain began to industrialise and require cattle products in the 1800s the Cattle Acts were repealed and Ireland turned back to cattle production with disastrous consequences for a whole cottier class that had survived via tillage production on rented land. These people were driven off the land and swelled the ranks of emigrants. They emigrated because Irish industry had been wiped out by its larger British competitors in the free trade environment that emerged out of the Act of Union between Britain and Ireland in 1801. All of this meant that between 1871 and 1926 those employed in agriculture declined by 19 per cent and the numbers employed in industry dropped by 43 per cent (for a more detailed discussion of the pre-independence Irish economy see Cullen, 1972 and Crotty, 1986).

In post-independent Ireland very little changed until the 1960s. Prior to then the economy was still largely agricultural. Ireland exported cattle, other agricultural products, and people to Britain. For the most part the Irish state pursued protectionist policies in the belief that they would stimulate industrial development. These economic practices met with some limited success. However, the industrial base that emerged was weak and made up of small inefficient and unproductive firms trying to provide too many products to too small a market (Crotty, 1986).

As with the pre-independence era one of the most noticeable features of this time was emigration. Emigration, which was driven by economic factors (Jackson, 1963), continued throughout the 1920s and 1930s. The primary destination in the post-1930s was Britain. The heavy dependence upon agriculture, and cattle goods in particular, had led to a social structure that forced many abroad. This social structure centred around property ownership and the family farm. The farm was past on to the eldest son and other members of the family either stayed on as 'relatives assisting' or went overseas. Some admittedly did take up work in Dublin or other cities, but these were a minority. These features led to a massive haemorrhage of people from the country in the 1950s. Some 400 000 left the country throughout the course of that decade (Jackson, 1963).

The popular image of the Irish migrant of this time is one of a single, unskilled, rural migrant going to either the USA or the UK. To a large extent this is accurate. Between 1876 and 1921 84 per cent of all Irish migrants went to the USA (Drudy, 1985: 72). There are two very significant reasons for this. One, the USA was easily entered, especially for English speaking migrants and the second, more important reason, was that the booming US core acted as a magnet for labour. In the post-war era Britain fulfilled this magnetic role. In the interim the USA introduced restrictions upon entry plus the Depression dampened the demand for labour (Drudy, 1985). During and after World War II Britain required labour; this fact, plus the inhospitable conditions at home, ensured that the Irish migrated to the UK core in search of work and a better standard of living (Hannan, 1970; Jackson, 1963, 1986). Conditions at the core thus exerted a tremendous influence upon the migration decisions of the Irish.

What is often underplayed in the analysis of pre-1958 emigration is the exodus of the middle class. Skilled and professional people left Ireland in large numbers (Drudy, 1985: 2). Blessing (1985) has suggested that throughout the 1800–1920 period an average of 25 per cent of migrants were skilled. These fell from a high of 75 per cent in 1820 to a low of 9 per cent in 1900. In 1920 he estimates that some 40 per cent of the migrants were skilled; within this 40 per cent 8 per cent were professional, 26 per cent were skilled manual, and a further 6 per cent were farmers (Blessing, 1985: 19–20) Hence merchants, artisans, and professionals had a significant role to play in the Irish migration of this time. These people had been driven out of Ireland by the nature of the Irish economy and the attraction of career opportunities abroad. Even in the 1950s when the unskilled, uneducated, rural labourer was the 'typical' migrant there was still a notable minority of skilled people leaving. The 10 per cent of migrants going to the USA in the 1950s were largely middle class and thus, one suspects, reasonably educated (Drudy, 1986) and of Irish males working in Britain in 1971 11 per cent were self-employed, 3 per cent were professional, 9 per cent were intermediate, 7 per cent were skilled non-manual, and 34 per cent were skilled manual workers (Jackson, 1986: 130). This fact is often forgotten, particularly by the media, when comparisons between emigration today and emigration before industrialisation are made. Irish migrants have not been solely made up of unskilled people nor has Irish emigration been a completely Irish affair, developments internationally have always played a significant role.

It is in the light of this global influence that the changes which took place in Ireland towards the end of the 1950s should be examined. The global economy was moving towards greater free trade, sustained economic growth, industrial concentration, and there was also a renewed wave of and indeed growth in foreign direct investment (Perrons, 1981). Ireland could not have brought about the changes that took place after 1958 on its own; a pool of internationally mobile investment was required. The policy shift away from protectionism to 'industrialisation by invitation' stimulated the most sustained period of economic growth that the country had ever witnessed (Breen *et al.*, 1990). Industrial output and employment grew, agricultural output grew whilst agricultural employment fell, markets were diversified both spatially and in terms of products, GDP and living standards grew and so on (Kennedy and Dowling, 1975; Fitzpatrick and Kelly, 1985). This economic prosperity came at a price. Ireland remained a semi-peripheral country although the nature of this peripherality altered. The Irish state lost much of its autonomy and room for manoeuvre. Ireland became less dependent upon the British market and agricultural products; however, it became more dependent upon its integration with foreign capital and upon maintaining an 'attractive' investment opportunity for this capital. The necessity of attracting foreign multinationals in order to create employment meant that large financial packages were offered and low capital taxes maintained.

The penetration of foreign capital brought with it a number of economic difficulties. The multinationals tended to locate in the more modern, technologically sophisticated, and growing areas of the economy whilst indigenous industry was largely in the traditional, mature sectors; these indigenous firms tended to be less efficient and less export orientated than their multinational counterparts. There were few linkages between the two sectors in comparison with more advanced countries (see Telesis Consultancy Group, 1982 and Culliton *et al.*, 1992 for a further examination of these features). The economy thus exhibited a high degree of dualism – a feature characteristic of peripheral economies (Seers *et al.*, 1979). Ireland also failed to attract the most skilled aspects of production. For example, in the electronics industry the firms lacked significant R&D or marketing facilities. These electronic firms also tend to employ more operatives or assembly workers than their UK or US counterparts (Wickham and Murray, 1987: 7).[1] However, having stated this they employ more skilled people than similar firms in the Newly Industrialising Countries (NICs). It could thus be said that within the global production process Ireland's foreign investors have seen fit to locate medium skilled work here (Telesis Consultancy Group, 1982; Culliton, 1992; Wickham and Murray, 1987; O'Malley, 1987). Thus the NIDL that emerged in the 1960s and beyond brought investment and work to Ireland but it did not bring the highly skilled work that would facilitate self-sustaining growth.

As the crisis within global capitalism deepened in the 1970s and 1980s Ireland's fortunes took a serious downturn; new manufacturing jobs came largely from foreign owned firms (who now controlled 35 per cent of manufacturing employees), and Ireland had amassed a large national debt through borrowing in order to pay for industrial development and for a welfare state that the industrial planners of the 1950s had not envisaged creating so soon (Breen *et al.*, 1990). As recession bit deeper unemployment rose due both to job losses and the fact that the labour force increased by 46 000 in the 1980–89 period (Tansey, 1990). These disadvantages were reinforced by the fact that the market for mobile capital became increasingly competitive as many strong industrial economies also sought foreign investors (de Jonquieres, 1986). Within this overall situation net emigration once again became a feature of Irish society for the first time in almost twenty years.

The expansion of capital into the periphery on the scale that took place after 1945 led to a new international order. Areas that had previously simply exported raw materials and people to the core were integrated into the global production process in order to increase the profitability of multinationals headquartered at the centre. Products were divided up into different component parts and each component could be produced in a different geographical location. This allowed multinationals both to reap the advantages of economies of scale and to penetrate protected markets. For the first time an international production line was created, the marketplace became global on an unprecedented scale and the labour market, as we shall see, was globalised. Ireland was part of this process; Ireland developed an industrial base which was heavily dependent upon foreign investors; within the international skill hierarchy that had emerged Ireland was located about midway between the core and the NICs; Ireland had more skilled workers than the Southern periphery but less than the advanced economies. These processes have radically altered Ireland over the past thirty years. They have brought great benefits in terms of improved living standards.

However, in some ways the changes have been more imaginary than real. There is more large scale structural unemployment today. Unemployment has risen by over 200 per cent since 1971 (Corcoran *et al.*, 1992), within this certain sections of the Irish population are still harder hit than others, for example the semi-skilled manual and the unskilled manual industrial workforce experienced an unemployment level of 21.8 per cent and 45.6 per cent respectively in 1926, in 1981 these figures were 20.0 per cent and 49.4 per cent (Breen *et al.*, 1990: 145). Emigration has once again emerged as an issue, a net figure of some 177 000 people leaving the state between 1981 and 1989, causing the total population to decline from 1987 (Tansey, 1990).

Considering the fact that there are similar structural weaknesses within the Irish economy of today and the one before 1958 has Irish emigration altered its shape? The answer has to be, to use Breen *et al.*'s phrase, 'continuity within change'. Irish emigration has been subject to some form of public relations exercise over the course of the 1980s (Hanlon, 1992). Many have tried to present it in a positive light by suggesting that migrants now go abroad, gain professional experience, and then return to put this experience to use. Hence emigration benefits Ireland. As has been mentioned, in the pre-1958 waves of emigration a middle class exodus was present although often underplayed. It appears safe to say that this form of migration accounted for between 10 per cent and 25 per cent of all migrants. If this is accepted the stress which has been placed upon recent middle class migration has been unwarranted. A dichotomy appears to have emerged, it stresses the unskilled nature of the pre-1958 migrant and the supposed highly skilled and highly educated nature of the 1980s migrant.

IRISH EMIGRATION IN THE 1980S

Irish emigration rose dramatically in the 1980s. During the 1970s there was a net immigration of 100 000 people (Tansey, 1990). However, even throughout the prosperous 1970s 60 000 people under 34 years of age emigrated (Drudy, 1986).[2] Emigration arose as a major difficulty in the 1980s largely for economic reasons. Between 1981 and 1990 the gross migratory outflow was 360 000 or an average of almost 40 000 per annum. This was offset by an inflow of 150 000 leading to a net emigration of 208 000 (NESC, 1991). The two primary forces behind this were large scale job losses and a rapidly expanding labour supply (Tansey, 1990). This meant that many people were faced with the stark choice of unemployment or emigration. In contrast to the glossy image some would like to put on Irish emigration, King and Shuttleworth (1988) argue that the vast majority of migrants were the 'urban and rural poor'; NESC (1991: 160) have reinforced this by stating that 40 per cent of their migrant sample left because of unemployment.

Despite the fact that the bulk of migrants are working class I am going to concentrate upon professional/graduate migration as this highlights many of the weaknesses inherent within Ireland's policy of 'industrialisation by invitation'. Graduates made up a mere 3.6 per cent of all migrants in 1986, down from 7.9 per cent in 1984 (Shuttleworth and Kockel, 1990). This figure underestimates middle class migration as the figures for graduates are derived from a survey of graduates carried out by the Higher Education Authority (HEA) one year after their qualification. As such, this figure only accounts for those who have emigrated within a year of leaving university and is therefore unrepresentative of the true emigration figure. NESC (1991: 87) suggest that those with a third level qualification only made up 6–7 per cent of the emigrants in 1988–9. This rather low percentage is despite the fact that professional and/or graduate emigration rates increased quite dramatically over the course of the 1980s. The rate of emigration amongst graduates rose from 5 per cent in 1982 to a high of 19.9 per cent in 1988 and has since declined to 13.1 per cent in 1990 (HEA, 1991: 8).[3] Within this overall picture private services, where accountancy practices are based, had the highest emigration rate amongst those who found employment. In 1990 some 44.6 per cent of private services graduate employees worked overseas (HEA, 1991: 9). As one would expect emigration rates varied by discipline. Engineering graduates have traditionally been the most likely ones to emigrate. In 1990 35.5 per cent of these left the country reflecting the 'milk rounds' carried out by overseas multinationals at Irish universities although on its own this is too simplistic an explanation (Shuttleworth and Kockel, 1990). The other disciplines that suffer from high emigration rates are Arts and Social Sciences (29.9 per cent), Science (25.8 per cent) and Commerce and Business Studies (21.8 per cent) (HEA, 1991: Table F).

One good example of the increase in professional migration is the emigration of Irish accountants. Irish accountants have always been employed overseas. In 1911 14 per cent of the ICAI's members worked abroad. Throughout the 1911–80 period the emigration rate fluctuated around the 15 per cent mark (ICAI, 1911–80). However, during the course of the 1980s this figure rose from 14 per cent in 1982 to 22 per cent in 1990 (ICAI, 1982–90). The education system in Ireland is class based (see Chapter 6) hence it is safe to assume that the bulk of these graduates have middle class origins. This increased outflow of graduates and professionals is reflected in the changing occupational structure of the Irish in Britain. NESC (1991: 184) have highlighted the fact that the Irish have undergone a substantial upward shift in occupational attainment, although they are also more polarised in class terms today. These high rates of emigration can also be found amongst those who have stable employment in quite lucrative jobs (Wickham, 1989; Hanlon, 1991; Sterne, 1987). It is this issue that the rest of this chapter will address.

As with previous cycles of emigration the majority of migrants are economic migrants. NESC (1991: 14) highlighted that 86 per cent of migrants
gave the search for employment as their reason for migrating. However, on
its own this economic explanation is inadequate. There are social factors
concerning issues such as status of occupation, career development, over-
certification and so on involved. Although these social factors have an economic undertone they are not solely economic based.

It is the argument of this chapter that the nature of Ireland's industrialisation process has an in-built mechanism which leads to professional
migration. As has been mentioned Ireland has a relatively low skilled
industrial base. Despite this fact Ireland devoted 6.2 per cent of its GNP
to the education sector, a figure higher than virtually all other EC states
(O'Rourke, 1988). The situation whereby a low skilled economy, with
structural unemployment on a large scale and a history of emigration,
devotes relatively more resources to education than more developed
states is not unusual. Dore (1976) has written about this quite extensively
although he was concerned with countries such as Sri Lanka when he put
forward his views on over-certification (for an in-depth analysis of this
problem see Dore, 1976; Simmons, 1980; Watson, 1982; Irizarry, 1980;
Adams, 1971). Education is a double edged sword. Todaro (1980) has
noted that the greater the exposure a person has to education the greater
their propensity to migrate. Hence during the wave of emigration that
swept Ireland in the 1980s it is not surprising that those with the greatest
exposure to education, the middle class, have been the most willing to
emigrate (see Figure 5.1).

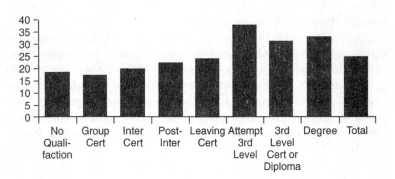

Source: NESC, 1991: Table A6.4.

Figure 5.1   Percentage of 1981/2 second level school leavers who emigrated by
1987, according to level of educational qualification

Again on its own education, like purely economic answers, does not explain middle class migration. NESC (1991) have suggested a mere 12 per cent of their survey left upon completion of their full-time education but some 42 per cent left a job to emigrate. It is this factor that is of the greatest interest in the middle class migrant's move abroad. It indicates that these people are in some way unhappy, either in terms of their jobs or, more broadly, in terms of the Irish lifestyle, culture, way of living and so forth. The evidence appears to suggest the former rather than the latter. Of a sample of respondents based in Ireland but with definite plans to go overseas NESC (1991: 142) found that only 3 per cent felt they could not live in Ireland even with a good job. The NESC report on emigration was based on a sample of 2000 individuals who had left school in 1981/2 and were interviewed on three separate occasions – May 1983, November 1984, and post-November 1987. These interviews were related to the issues of employment and emigration. In 1987 33 per cent of the sample were overseas and 8 per cent definitely intended emigrating (NESC, 1991: 125).

So why do people with jobs leave Ireland? The NESC report suggested that the most important factors concerned 'trading up' in terms of employment. This involved moving to positions of higher status and avoiding the over-certification process that exists in Ireland which forces people to take positions that they feel over-qualified for and so on. In short the most important reasons for migration involve the search for upward mobility. This search was most important amongst the middle class, many of whom are attracted by the pull factors of the core, that is the relative abundance of quite elevated posts. These positions are limited in Ireland and as such Ireland is viewed as having a small opportunity structure. Emigration is part of a career strategy for these people.

> For many of the better educated middle class, on the other hand, emigration appears to be seen more as a normal option in career planning. Here the larger and better opportunity structure of the combined Ireland–UK–EC and even US, labour market appears to be seen as almost equally accessible as that of Ireland's own, and emigration is not much more problematic than internal movement in Ireland. (NESC, 1991: 160)

This is in marked contrast to the emigration of the working class. This latter group are more likely to be pushed out of Ireland by unemployment and are more inclined to leave Ireland without having secured employment overseas and so on.

IRELAND'S PROFESSIONAL EMIGRATION AND THE
INTERNATIONAL DIVISION OF LABOUR

These emigration patterns make a lot more sense if Ireland's role within the
International Division of Labour is examined. As stated, Irish industry
lacks significant headquarters facilities, there is a high percentage of
branch plant facilities set up by foreign multinationals, and the indigenous
sector is weak. This has led to a situation wherein Irish professionals feel
unhappy with the quality of work and the opportunities for them in Ireland.
These features appear to be most pronounced in industries dominated by
multinational firms. Alongside the globalisation of capital, production, and
product markets there has emerged an international labour market.

Wickham (1987, 1989) has shown how Irish engineers are part of an
international labour structure and that for many of these engineers the
fulfilment of their career aspirations entails movement overseas. In his
survey sample he suggested that 25 per cent of graduate engineers had
made some practical plans to emigrate (Wickham, 1987: 11). This, added
to the fact that in 1986 when the research was carried out, over 33 per
cent of Irish engineering graduates went abroad, demonstrates the significance of migration. The reasons for Irish emigration have been portrayed
as largely financial, in the case of those who leave stable jobs, by the
media (*Irish Independent*, 27 July 1989) and, indeed, this view is
implicitly suggested by Culliton *et al.* (1992). Although salary, tax, and
so on are important they are not determining factors (NESC, 1991). One
feature that appears consistently in the research on professional emigration is the view that emigration allows one to gain exposure to work
skills, experience, etc. which in turn supposedly enables one to progress
up a career ladder. This feature must be part of any serious analysis of
professional migration. Amongst engineers this career factor was present
(see Figure 5.2).

If one groups together the categories: 'more interesting work', 'experience', and 'promotion' for the sample of engineers they account for 40.1
per cent of the reasons for migrating. I am not dismissing the importance of
the taxation system or financial incentives I am merely suggesting that
reform in these areas alone is not the total solution. All three variables that
have been grouped together are in some way connected to a career move.
'More interesting work' for these people is synonymous with more technically challenging work which will allow them to keep abreast of the
changes in a rapidly developing field. This ensures that their experience
and qualifications are kept up to date and therefore these people are more
marketable.

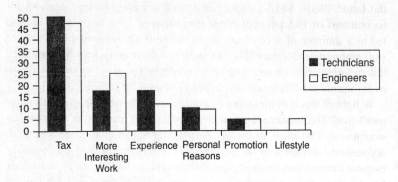

Source: Wickham, 1987: 11.

Figure 5.2   The reasons for considering emigration amongst Irish electronics
staff (%)

Wickham (1989) has suggested that this level of emigration amongst
engineers will continue, if conditions abroad are favourable, because the
Irish industrial base is not 'high tech'. Despite this industrial base, these
graduates receive a 'high tech' education giving rise to a mismatch
between the education system and the local industrial reality. This mismatch guarantees an element of dissatisfaction amongst engineers when
they enter the labour market. This dissatisfaction is reflected in discussions
through comments about the quality of the work, the lack of R&D facilities, the lack of promotional opportunities and so forth. This incongruity is
solved via emigration, which in turn provides core countries with a cost
free skilled labour supply. In the more advanced economies these engineers
feel they will receive the quality experience they seek. Whether or not they
get this exposure has yet to be documented, however, there is little
doubt that this work is to be found in these destination states given the
international division of labour. Sterne (1987) has argued that similar
processes operate in the Irish computer industry.

Are these trends reflected within Irish accountancy? The answer appears
to be 'yes'. As highlighted emigration amongst Irish accountants rose
sharply over the 1980s and it was consistently high amongst the Business
and Commerce graduates who enter accountancy in large numbers (HEA,
1991). This increased emigration came at a time of unprecedented growth
for the profession, in particular the Big Six, both nationally and internationally (see Chapters 1 and 2). Over the course of the 1980s the ICAI's
membership expanded by some 69 per cent (Hanlon, 1991). Despite this
growth there was still an overall shortage in the supply of accountants in

the latter 1980s. FSIA (1988) anticipated a growth in the demand for accountants of 13.5 per cent per annum between 1986 and 1990. This had led to a shortage of accountants in 1988 and to the increased poaching of staff amongst practices (FSIA, 1988). Hence the accountant who emigrated did so voluntarily, in line with most graduate and professional migration over the course of the previous decade (Tansey, 1990; NESC, 1991).

In light of this it is important to ask the question why did these accountants leave? The answer again is partly explained by financial or income considerations. The most important reasons for emigrating given by those accountants abroad who were surveyed (from here on referred to as the migrant sample) and for those accountants surveyed and based in Ireland are listed in Figure 5.3.[4] There are differences between these two groups and there are differences between these two and those in Figure 5.2. The most noticeable difference between engineers and accountants is the factor 'more interesting work'. Technically demanding work is not a feature which greatly concerns accountants, they feel that the work, particularly auditing, has little intrinsic reward of itself (see Chapters 3 and 4). The variable 'better experience' encapsulates, to a limited extent, 'more interesting work' but it is larger in scope than the narrower definition used for engineers. From my semi-structured interviews with accountants 'better experience' appears to concern issues such as exposure to new specialisms and indeed to other non-technical, social and commercial skills (see Chapter 4).

There are also variations between the accountants overseas and those in Ireland. Personal reasons play a greater role in the emigrating decisions of those accountants based in Ireland. This is not as surprising as it may first

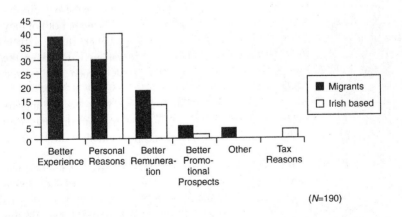

(*N*=190)

Figure 5.3   Most important factors when deciding to emigrate, per cent

appear given that the Irish based accountants are older on average, for example 40 per cent of those overseas are 30 years of age or less in comparison with only 20 per cent of those in Ireland. The older Irish based accountants would therefore have more family considerations to take into account when contemplating emigration. This is significant for Ireland because although there is evidence to argue that there was in the nineteenth century a trend for family groups to emigrate (Mageean, 1985) the overwhelming process since then has been for these emigrants to be young single people (Jackson, 1963; NESC, 1991).

A feature that the two accountancy groups share is the relatively poor showing of financial factors in the emigration decision making process. This is quite different to the engineers for whom the tax system is a major impetus in their consideration of emigration (see Figure 5.2). One would have thought that accountants, given the popular perception about them, rather than engineers would have been more interested in financial considerations. This poor showing of financial matters exists despite the fact that the salary gap between newly qualified accountants in Ireland and the UK is relatively large, some 33 per cent (Davis *et al.*, 1993).

As with other professional migrants much of this process can be explained by the impact, or at least the perceived impact, that migration has upon career prospects.

ACCOUNTANCY AND THE INTERNATIONAL LABOUR MARKET

An international labour market for professional workers has arisen within global capitalism in the past twenty years (Salt, 1986; Massey, 1988b). Accountancy has also created such a market. This international market is primarily confined to the largest multinational firms (Beaverstock, 1989, 1990; Hanlon, 1991). These markets are part of a global strategy by the Big Six to shift employees from areas of over-supply (or at least areas with less of a shortage) to areas of greater demand. Hence the movement of people is encouraged when it is of corporate benefit. Beaverstock (1990), when talking about UK accountants, highlighted a number of reasons explaining why practices use migration:

(1)　Staff tipped for promotion to partnership level are sent abroad for career development and training. In particular, it is the aspect of international business experience that is stressed.
(2)　Employees are encouraged to go abroad to directly meet staff shortages in overseas' offices.

(3)   Staff who generally have a 'wanderlust' are facilitated by moving them to an office abroad in order to keep them within the international organisation.

Beaverstock has also suggested a number of reasons as to why people avail of these opportunities to go abroad. These reasons are:

(1)   Gain international experience as part of a career strategy. Some UK accountants who are denied an international move will join another Big Six firm in order to do so. The benefit of international experience is made plain to these accountants by the fact that to become a Big Six partner in the UK one needs international exposure.
(2)   Personal development is another reason as to why individuals migrate abroad. Although this factor is always closely related to career development.
(3)   Financial gain. It benefited UK accountants to go to certain destinations.

This internationalism is of growing importance in the past decade. Between 1983 and 1989 the overseas offices of the Big Six increased by 36 per cent (Beaverstock, 1990: 156). The increasingly international nature of the producer services is not surprising given the changes within the global economy outlined in Chapter 1.

The notion that the large international practices dominate this labour market is reinforced by the statistics for accountants in the migrant sample, 66.7 per cent were trained in a Big Six firm and 34.4 per cent were currently employed by the Big Six. The corresponding figures for those who stayed in Ireland are 59.8 per cent and 20.6 per cent respectively. Likewise of those accountants based in Ireland who had taken some positive step to emigrating the most popular enquiry was to ask about an intra-firm transfer. Roughly 25 per cent had taken this route, in comparison with this only 12 per cent had opted for the second most popular choice, to apply directly to an employer overseas.

Like their UK counterparts the Irish practices are now beginning to look for international experience when they are considering potential partners. For example Peter O'Neill, a Big Six Director, commented:

On the whole emigration benefits a person's career, yes ... most people leaving would go to us abroad ... that sort of thing is very beneficial to the person's future. I think that it means an opportunity at an early stage to apply your skills in a different arena to develop personal qualities of self-reliance, independence, maturity, to learn how to cope with different situations, with different people, and in many cases to benefit professionally from, for example in the States the typical job is much larger and in many cases more complex, you also have a different work ethic in the States, good or bad.

He went on to state:

Yes, yes very strongly of that view [that potential partners would increasingly need international exposure]. I actually wish we had more partners who had taken a planned career stage abroad.

Accountants are very much aware of the growing importance of global experience. When asked did temporary emigration enhance one's career back in an Irish practice the results were as in Figure 5.4. Similar views were held by both those abroad and those in Ireland hence they have been grouped together in Figure 5.4. However, when both groups were asked about what type of industrial organisation views temporary emigration as a big plus differences emerged despite the fact that both groups broadly felt it was advantageous (see Figure 5.5). As can be seen both groups rejected the category for small firms completely. This makes sense as these organisations would conduct less international business and as a consequence they would have less need for international experience.

Why do these groups differ as regards industry but not practice? Both groups have roughly the same percentage of people in industry. Those based in Ireland had 47 per cent in practice and 53 per cent in industry. The corresponding figures for those abroad were 48 per cent and 52 per cent respectively. This may be slightly unusual given the younger age of those

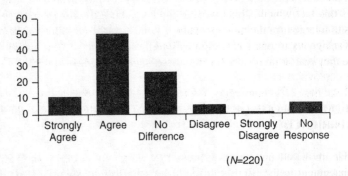

(*N*=220)

Figure 5.4   Temporary emigration enhances one's career in practice upon returning to Ireland (%)

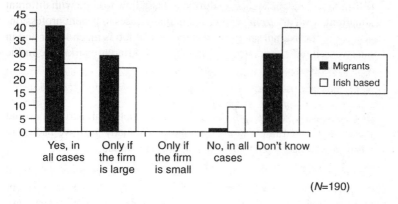

Figure 5.5   Temporary emigration enhances one's career in industry upon return-ing to Ireland (%)

abroad, as one would have expected fewer people to have made the move out of practice. However, what is noticeable is that the accountants abroad are much more exposed to large and/or international firms and hence to international labour markets and the value of international experience. 34.4 per cent and 37.6 per cent of those overseas are in the Big Six or a large industrial organisation, a mere 12 per cent are in a small firm or a practice. The Irish based sample are a lot less concentrated in large organisations, in either industry or practice, than their overseas counterparts. Only 20.6 per cent and 35.1 per cent are in either a Big Six practice or a large industrial firm. 30 per cent are in a small firm or practice. Added to this difference is the fact that those people overseas were more likely to be trained in a Big Six practice, 66.7 per cent as opposed to 59.8 per cent. I would suggest that it is this fact which explains the difference. The greater the exposure one has to a large firm the more predisposed one is to the idea that migration is advantageous to one's career. What are these advantages one might ask? Are they real or imaginary? It is to these issues that I now turn.

THE MYTHOLOGY OF INTERNATIONAL TECHNICAL EXPERIENCE[5]

What are the advantages to be gained by working outside Ireland? Senior management in the Big Six talked about things such as working in a new culture, independence, self-reliance, maturity, new ideas and so forth, for example Conor Hackett, a Big Six partner, stated:

It is an advantage for people to have worked abroad in terms of gaining international experience. For example, if people go to the US they've experience of dealing with US clients, US accounting standards – while they're broadly similar they're not precisely the same, the terminology they use, they have dealt with individuals and know their names so that when they get back here they'd find themselves working for US clients so that's an advantage. It also gives people broader experience, knowledge of other cultures, etc.

The above, plus the qualities listed by Peter O'Neill (see p. 167), are not technical. They are commercial and social skills (see Chapter 4). The technical skills that are highlighted will not be of use to an accountant in Ireland, for example American Accounting Standards where they are different to Irish Accounting Standards cannot be implemented in Ireland. Emigration is concerned with character building, the development of self-reliance, maturity, ability to make contacts overseas and so forth. This is quite different to the reasons for which engineers emigrate. There are definite technical reasons for emigration amongst engineers due to the international division of labour. Within accountancy, as will be highlighted later on, the international division of labour is less pronounced and it operates in a different way.

Accountancy seniors feel that emigration will give them levels of responsibility and experience that they find difficult to get in Ireland.

if salaries continue at their present levels and trends continue leaning as they seem to do because there is such a shortage of labour, people will just be attracted by lifestyle and the relative responsibility which they are given quite easily. (Peter Daniels, Big Six, Senior)

They go abroad for the experience of a different level of work. You come here to Ireland your big firm will be only a £100 million turnover, you go abroad and your big company say in England is a £100 million profit. It is the level, larger scale, prestige on your CV at the end of the day. The fact that in time people will say, you know what I mean, the prophet is never respected in his home land type thing. You're better to go away and come back no matter where you are career wise. (Cathal Murray, Big Six Assistant Manager)

if you come back from abroad, from London, looking for a job here, say, say you want a manager's job and you said oh I've worked on this and I've worked on that yeah it goes down well. The bigger the better you know. It is the level of responsibility rather than say size, you know I was a supervisor on this job with so many staff. It's the number of staff on the audit as well as the turnover, it's kind of the two things. They'd say how many people did you supervise and you'd say two or whatever, seven people on a large job. That goes down well. (Jean Devoy, Big Six Supervisor)

These are not the only reasons given for emigrating. Many accountants gave personal reasons – desire to travel, family reasons and so on; however, when they were talking about career orientated factors the above quotes were typical. Hence although the senior management within the practices stressed commercial or social features to emigration, for example getting to know people, developing self-reliance, etc. The potential emigrants, that is the seniors, talked about areas such as control of an audit, performing larger technical jobs, exposure to greater responsibility and so on. Often the seniors referred to these issues in technical terminology although they were really talking of managerial or commercial issues – control of an audit and hence budgets, managing larger numbers of people than one would get the opportunity to do in Ireland, being responsible for greater financial assets and so forth – in short the ability to bring in profit. When the accountants who were actually overseas were asked what they saw as the greatest work advantages to be gained by migrating they ranked the following list accordingly (see Figure 5.6).

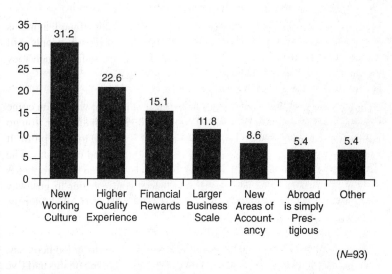

(*N*=93)

Figure 5.6   Work advantages to be gained overseas, migrant sample (%)

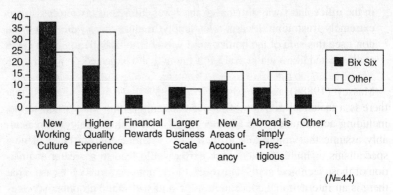

Figure 5.7   Greatest work advantages to be gained from emigrating, by size of practice, migrant sample (%)

There appears to be roughly a 40–60 split between technical and non-technical factors in favour of the latter (I have grouped together 'higher quality experience', 'larger business scale' and 'new areas of accountancy' as technical factors in the sense that they expose one to new accounting techniques). Hence those who have actually gone abroad appear to feel that there are definite technical advantages to emigrating. Yet if one simply examines those in a Big Six practice the importance of the technical advantages is slightly diluted (see Figure 5.7).

As is shown in Figure 5.7 the accountants in Big Six practices overwhelming opt for the non-technical advantages to be got from migrating. Some 60 per cent of these accountants choose a non-technical advantage. In comparison with this medium practice and small practice based accountants are somewhat more inclined to pick technical reasons for emigrating (the figures for the 'other' category should be treated with great caution due to the small numbers involved, a mere 12). Despite these perceived advantages the reality it appears can be different. For example Frank Rogers (US Big Six Manager) commented on his experience overseas that

> I went up to Montreal to help them get their US tax practice started. When I got up there they had a partner and a Canadian senior manager. Through their own palace intrigue the partner was booted soon after I arrived so it was just me and the senior manager and she was a lovely person but not very good at managing people and she was very difficult to work with. She was very focused on her own potential promotion to partnership and so she, to the extent that she possibly could, kept all the good work to herself and gave me all the shit. We were the only two senior American tax people

in the office and I was a manager and I was filling out tax returns, it was extremely frustrating. I learnt a lot simply because there were issues you don't see this side of the border and I was able to soak them up but I was really treated like a junior you know, more than I expected.

Massey (1988b) and Leyshon *et al.* (1989) have both suggested that there is a technical division of labour emerging within the service sector, including accountancy (see Chapter 1). Accepting this, one could reasonably assume that emigrating to the places where a concentration of new specialisms or highly skilled work exists would lead to a greater acquisition of these technical skills. However, this is not necessarily the case. That there is an international concentration of skill within the producer services sector is beyond doubt (Gillespie and Green, 1987; Sassen, 1988; Leyshon *et al.* 1989; Friedmann and Wolff, 1982, Hanlon, 1991). These skilled areas of the producer services are concentrated in regions that are economically dynamic and have large scale corporate headquarters complexes. Accountancy, as part of the business service sector, has concentrated its most prestigious, highly skilled and lucrative functions within the major cities (see Chapter 2). The reason for this is quite straightforward: it is in these cities that multinationals locate their regional or global headquarters and it is these offices that provide the market for services such as international tax, management consultancy and so on. Gillespie and Green (1987) have highlighted how the suppliers and receivers of producer services locate within close proximity to one another.

This concentration of producer services within what have been termed 'global or world cities' (Sassen, 1988) with their widespread control and planning functions for international corporations has been recognised by Irish accountants. An international hierarchy has emerged within accountancy which ranks geo–economic regions in terms of status and in terms of benefiting career development. Accountants who are contemplating emigration divide the globe into three markets: a money market, a pleasure market, and a career development–experience market. This division is agreed upon by both the senior management and the foot soldiers.

There are three different answers when one is thinking of going abroad. If you want for example to go off and build up a nest egg quickly without thinking about improving your professional skills you might go to somewhere that is perceived to be a hardship posting, somewhere like the Middle East. If you want to go somewhere where you get sun and sand and an easy sort of life you go to somewhere like the Bahamas or Bermuda where the work isn't too taxing but is highly specialised in banking and insurance. If you want to go somewhere you are going to be stretched professionally with very demanding work you might go to somewhere like New York or Hong Kong or London. (Kenneth Byrne, Big Six Partner)

Yeah we would certainly see that [an international hierarchy]. The West Indies, the Bahamas all those places are very nice I think. You've got the sun and the sea and I don't know what. The work you get can be pretty routine. It's either doing very large financial service companies that aren't really located there or else doing things like returns. But for experience the places we would feel are good would be London, New York, maybe Canada, elsewhere in the States. That is probably it, we've a lot of people who've gone to Australia in the last while but I don't think the experience is necessarily great. For the rest of Europe, mainland Europe, we would always encourage people to go to Germany both for the fact that they'll learn German and the auditing is different. (Stephen Flanagan, Big Six Partner)

These sentiments were echoed by the seniors:

No there are various degrees, if you go to Bahrain or somewhere like that no it's not going to be very good ... you'd make a lot of money but it wouldn't be a career move ... the States are good, London is not bad for a stint, some European countries, not like smaller ones like Luxembourg. (Nicola Byrne, Big Six Senior)

I think interviewers might have the attitude that you're basically going to say Bermuda because its tax free, fantastic social life but what about the work element? They might view you as a bit of a waster which mightn't necessarily be true but it has that connotation ... but places like Hong Kong, intense, hard working, financial centre, along with New York and London, they might view you as more ambitious than if you come back with a sun tan. (Mark Dawson, Big Six Senior)

The survey samples broadly endorsed these opinions. Those based in Ireland ranked a number of destinations in the order shown in Figure 5.8.

When those abroad were asked to pick a first preference destination to work in for CV purposes they presented the results shown in Figure 5.9.

Hence there is broad agreement on where it is advisable, from a career perspective, to work and where not. The reasons for this are quite logical. The key functions of control and coordination within the global economy

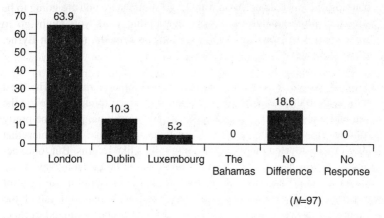

Figure 5.8   Ranking of foreign workplaces by prestige for CV purposes by Irish based accountants (%)

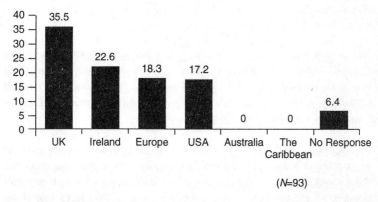

Figure 5.9   Ranking of destinations in terms of most valuable experience by migrant sample (%)

are found in a limited number of areas. As accountancy is largely concerned with these functions it is 'natural' that the 'best' experience is to be found there.

It is widely held by those abroad that as regards the various specialisms within accountancy – auditing, general practice, information technology, management consultancy and tax – that London was the premier destination in a list made up of London, Dublin, The Netherlands and The Cayman Islands. The only specialism where London lost out to another region was in the area of general practice. General practice work is quite similar to the work carried out by a small practice and as such it relies a great deal on things such as networking with small business people, knowledge of the local tax environment and so on; this other region logically enough was Ireland. International exposure is of no benefit in this area because of the nature of the work and the clients.

Theoretically the preference that accountants have for the large centres of corporate power makes sense and should lead to career enhancing experience. However, the reality is not quite so straightforward. If one wants to reap the full benefits of international exposure within practice it appears to be the case that one should only stay overseas for eighteen months to two years before returning to Ireland.[6] The exchange programmes run by the Big Six last roughly this long. An accountant who has stayed any longer runs the risk of losing touch with the Irish environment, the contacts he or she has made and so forth, and these things are of vital importance for promotion to partnership (see Chapter 4).

If one only has a year or two to gain international experience how much can one learn of a technically advantageous nature? I would suggest that the actual amount of technically useful material one can pick up is quite limited. The fact that a person is new in an office will mean that his or her superiors will be reluctant to give that person large scale responsibility until their capabilities have been thoroughly established. This would appear a reasonable suggestion in the light of the extensive evaluation procedures endured by accountants within the Big Six (see Chapter 4). Hence the migrant has to spend time proving him or herself.

It is the most difficult issue we face and unfortunately it has all the hallmarks of the X process. First you make the glossy book, tell everyone how wonderful it's going to be then send them out there and we don't want to hear from them again and so the only way to find out how it's going to be is to talk to other people who've done it. And you know when I came here it was a huge cultural shock because the profession here is much more detail orientated, much more risk adverse, we won't work on that that's too risky, procedures are different, the internal control procedures are different, culturally the firm is very different from London, the expectation level is different, and you had come from another office to the X office which is somewhat parochial in itself and they didn't quite know what to make of you. So they weren't going to give me anything good because you hadn't been here that long anyway and coming from London your perception is they don't have anything good anyway and so you're now kicking your heels saying Jesus what've I done. But slowly you do the classic X thing, you shut your mouth, knock on doors, and demonstrate you can do it and I think you're right a year and a half is just not enough. (John Barnes, British US Based Big Six Senior Manager)

Another factor is quite simply why should a practice give responsibility and training to an employee who will not be there for any great length of time? Surely it is in the host practice's interests to groom its own people for this work as they will be a better long term investment? This would be especially true for the core economies as they are receivers rather than exporters of personnel. This fact was commented upon by some of the accountants interviewed.

It [receiving increased responsibility whilst abroad] depends upon how long you're staying there, if you are not staying very long people don't want to throw a lot of responsibility at you ... if you are there a long time I don't think it is a great problem, I think then it is the capabilities of the individual. (Liam Hamilton, Big Six Senior)

One returned migrant noted this shortage of extra or increased experience.

Working in the Los Angeles office was like working in Dublin. We used the same files, the same programmes and the same terminology – we even used the same paper. The only difference was that the guys working beside me had American accents. (Keith Talent, ex-Big Six Senior)

Supposing one breaks through the 'trust' and 'duration of stay' barriers one may, theoretically, be able to pick up valuable experience that is of relevance to an Irish environment in the year or so that is left. However, even at this point there are problems.

One of these problems arises if one stays in auditing. It is reasonable to assume that many of the younger migrants are in auditing as they move from auditing departments in Ireland and are thus inexperienced in the newer, more skilled areas of accountancy. If one is in an auditing department overseas then one is more likely to be engaged in larger audits. However, technically in the Anglo–American world auditing is broadly similar except for different accounting standards which are peculiar to individual countries and hence inapplicable to Ireland. The only difference is one of scale rather than technical knowledge. If one is in Continental Europe the traditions are so dissimilar technically to the Irish tradition that the knowledge is again quite useless in an Irish context.

Finally, one may legitimately ask why Irish accountants need to go in such large numbers to a major city in the core, if they move out of auditing then learn a detailed area of a new specialism, such as international tax or management consultancy, for the small Irish market with its significant lack of corporate muscle? These people go to world cities like London or New York because these cities are *different* to Ireland in the sense that they have a high concentration of economic power. For example

I don't know if too many people abroad would say God we've got to get to Ireland to work. Ireland itself is just a spot really. There's a very small stock exchange here, the whole economics is just so small a lot of people wouldn't have even heard of Ireland ... its very, very small and as such its not a major player in banking or stock exchange or international business. (Mark Dawson, Big Six Senior)

I mean you don't hear too many people talking about Ireland all that much. I mean its not a financial capital. I mean its, being honest, people talk about New York, London ... in Australia Sydney a bit, Hong Kong, Japan, I mean they're all financial centres but they don't with Ireland ... it has two or three very big companies that have an impact overseas but it's not a lot. (Greg O'Driscoll, Big Six Manager)

The fact that Ireland is not a 'major player' nor a large international financial centre would lead one to suggest that the skills required in Ireland would not entail all the skills that have been concentrated in these major conurbations (see Chapter 1 and Chapter 2). If these skills are required it would seem more likely that a Dublin based Big Six office would buy them from its London based partner on the relatively rare occasions that they are needed rather than encourage large scale migration in the hope that some of these people would return with the desired know how. Neither are the Irish Big Six seeking these skills to trade internationally as this is forbidden within their partnership agreements. Even outside the international practices accountancy services could not be traded internationally with ease unlike manufactures (Davis *et al.*, 1993).

COMMERCIAL AND SOCIAL ASPECTS TO EMIGRATION AND THE EMERGENCE OF AN INTERNATIONAL ELITE LABOUR MARKET

If the above arguments are correct then accountancy would appear to be quite different to engineering and computers in terms of the advantages to be gained by going overseas. After all it is conceivable that an engineer may learn new techniques or skills in California that he or she may put to use in Ireland. I am not suggesting that Irish accountancy has nothing to learn from abroad. What I am saying, however, is that technically what is to be learned does not explain why emigration rose dramatically in the 1980s nor does it explain the qualities or advantages it gives migrants upon their return despite the technical factors listed by the migrant sample. Those who are abroad obviously feel that emigration gives them something as an overwhelming 97.8 per cent stated they would recommend temporary migration to other Irish accountants.

The advantages of emigration are social and/or commercial. Technically something may be learned but it is the commercial and social skills one encounters that are career enhancing. The senior management talk of non-technical skills (see Peter O'Neill and Conor Hackett quotes on p. 167, 170). So do the seniors although some of this is couched in technical terms (see Mark Dawson quote on p. 174).

> I think you've hit off other people [if you've been abroad], you've got on, you're able to understand international business, you've got an international perspective rather than a very localised one. I think there are a lot of things … you've also got initiative … you're in the States you're going to work hard, you're going to come under budget pressures, partner pressures are a lot higher there, etc. (Peter Walsh, Big Six Senior)

> If we've got an issue where a US company is trying to relocate in Reading say and the manager says 'Jesus I know such and such over there' and calls them up and sets the contact with them that's invaluable and whether because this guy's a phenomenal golfer and played golf with everybody in the firm and met some good technical people or whether the guy's a technical guy and met them that way it doesn't matter. He's given us the contact, the open door. (Tom Wallace, US Big Six Manager)

> Yeah I'd say so [that working abroad is viewed differently to working in Ireland]. It's just the fact that you had the guts to go abroad and go into a totally different environment, country and everything and work there successfully for a year or two and then come back again. (Barbara Wilkinson, Big Six Senior)

If it is for social and commercial factors such as 'working in an international business environment', 'having the guts to go abroad' 'making contacts with individuals abroad', 'dealing with budget pressures and partner

pressures', 'developing self-reliance' and so forth why is there an international hierarchy of status? Why is Trinidad and Tobago not as prestigious
as New York? Surely one shows more self-reliance and maturity, etc. if one
goes to Outer Mongolia to work than if one goes to London and works there
whilst living with Irish friends? How can this conflict be explained?

Harvey (1989) has suggested that post-modernist culture is ephemeral,
lacks depth, and is judged on appearance value. However, this culture is
not shaped in a vacuum; it is shaped by the market. For example, the move
from Fordism to Flexible Accumulation entailed intensifying the labour
process and speeding up turnover time. This in turn entailed the speeding
up of consumption time. To do this fashion was mobilised in the mass
market – clothes, marketing, advertising and so on stressing the ephemeral-
ity of products and the importance of image. These features gave rise to a
rootlessness and a throwaway aspect to culture and lifestyle in the 1980s
and a subsequent, and seemingly paradoxical, return to family values, etc.
as a means of establishing some form of stability (Harvey, 1989: esp.
Chapter 17). I would suggest that emigration within accountancy is a little
similar in the sense that it is concerned with image, signs, communication
and so forth and that these appearances have direct corporate benefits as
with Harvey's ephemeral culture in Flexible Accumulation. Irish migrants
are encouraged to go abroad by the Big Six to enhance their careers. This
enhancement comes via the acquisition of social and commercial skills
rather than technical ones. In light of what was presented in Chapter 4 this
is perhaps unsurprising. However, although one would assume many of
these skills could be developed anywhere, as they are of a highly personal
nature – independence, maturity, self-reliance and so on, there emerged an
international pecking order. This hierarchy places the global cities at the
top. Again this is not surprising given that it is cities like these that have
witnessed the greatest growth in producer services and hence the greatest
shortage in accountants and other professionals (see Chapter 1). Thus the
requirements of the international labour markets in the Big Six helped to
shape the emerging migrant culture within the Irish Big Six.

> I think also there is a self-fulfilling prophecy about the place. They see
> one go and they feel they have to follow ... they're a bit like a bunch of
> sheep. (Greg O'Driscoll, Big Six Manager)

There is one proviso to moving to these cities, or indeed moving overseas
generally, and that is time. To be of maximum benefit upon returning the
stay has to be quite short – a year to two years. I am not suggesting that this
is a simple cause–effect relationship but, like Harvey, I am suggesting that

the requirements of the Big Six international labour market affected the intensification of a migrant culture.

The core economies offer advantages to the Big Six migrant. They are viewed as being capitalist, hard working, intense, profit orientated, commercially aware, and so forth. Simply put they are seen as tightly controlled and budget orientated with modern management skills, which improve one's ability to make profit. With the emergence of the commercialised professional these management skills are of increasing importance in accountancy and as a result migration to the core symbolises adherence to these standards and a willingness to learn and implement them. It gives one business virtues. This exposure allows one to suggest that one has the same values, beliefs, experiences and so on as those at the economic heartland.

This development can possibly be explained in terms of commercialisation. As business globalised those who are managing it have sought to develop a commitment to commercialism from their professional employees. However, this commercialism, both at a corporate and a national level, is limited spatially. One cannot be commercial in any group or place, one can only be commercial if one feels or wants to feel solidarity with the core as it is these regions that have developed the new commercial ethos and specialisms within certain professions (see Chapter 4 for an examination of this within accountancy and Galanter and Palay, 1991 for law). Gellner (1964) has suggested that when Nationalism is first starting in a country language, symbolism, communication in all its forms becomes very important. It is through communication that people assert their common identity with one another and their difference to other groups. The same is true within accountancy. Migration to the core is highly symbolic. It symbolises a commitment to business, a commitment to industriousness, and a commitment to the new profitability. Upon returning it highlights to employers that, other things being equal, you have made this commitment and the other potential candidate for the post has not. In short emigration to these commercial centres symbolises that one is prepared to make the ultimate sacrifice in order to become 'trustworthy'.

Going to the periphery does not convey the same meaning. There are a variety of reasons for this. Places like the Bahamas do not have large scale corporate headquarters hence they do not have the same environmental factors such as control, planning, and coordination that exist in the core. There is also a belief that the cultural value system in the periphery is different to that of the core. It is viewed as being less intense and less competitive. Much of this is perception. One accountant argued that he had received very good experience in Bermuda although he had a difficult time trying to convince prospective employers of this. The acceptance that it is the actual experience a person receives rather than the geographical location they were based in which is important appears to be found more in industry than in practice (although this assumption is based on a handful of interviews).

> I don't know [if the international hierarchy abroad is valid], if you're looking at somebody I think you look at the experience they have and the job you're trying to put them into, so if they've the experience for the job regardless of why that's okay. (James Hughes, ex-Big Six-Financial Controller)

The reason for the Big Six reluctance to employ people from the periphery in comparison with the core is because they have not developed or exhibited the same belief in the sought after social and commercial skills. Industry is more likely to require new technical skills thus they will examine the technical background of the migrant. In comparison with this the Big Six will not require this technical experience both because the periphery is highly specialised in a limited market and if these services are required they can be imported from the global partnership. This is not to suggest that industry is employing vast quantities of migrants who have been to the periphery. I would assume, although I do not have the data to prove it, that industry's views upon the periphery are not radically different to those of practice.

WHO GOES AND WHO STAYS

How, if at all, are those who migrate different to those who stay? One would expect those who migrate to be younger, better educated, trained in the Big Six, and to be more likely to work in a large organisation either in practice or industry.

Those accountants who are abroad tend to be younger, 40 per cent are under 30 in comparison with 20 per cent of those based in Ireland. There is a slightly disproportionate percentage of females amongst the migrants – 11.8 per cent versus 10.3 per cent but this gap is so small as to be insignificant. Likewise there appears to be very little difference in terms of educational background (see Figure 5.10).

There are also similarities in terms of class backgrounds (see Figure 5.11). Broadly speaking the class backgrounds are similar, although those who have migrated appear to be less likely to be in a professional/managerial category. This is in line with the NESC argument that it is those people who seek upward mobility that leave. There are greater differences in terms of

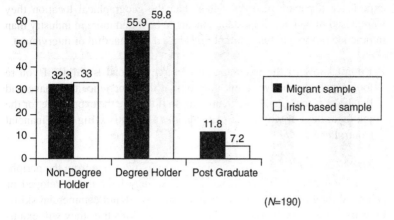

Figure 5.10   Education level of both migrants and Irish based accountants (%)

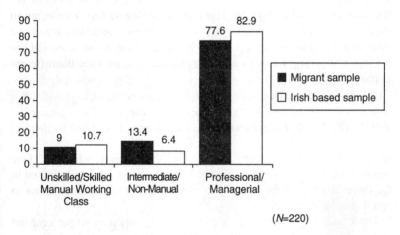

Figure 5.11   Fathers' class background for Irish based and migrant samples (%)

fathers' educational background (see Figure 5.12). Migrants' fathers are generally better educated. This may in some sense encourage migration in their children. The fathers despite being educated chose to stay in Ireland but they may have passed on some migratory propensity to their children.

Whilst acknowledging these broad similarities there is one important difference. This difference concerns the work histories of the two samples.

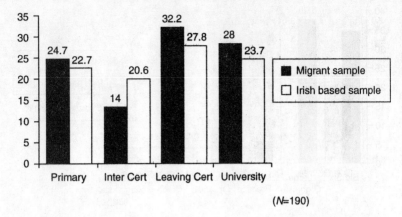

Figure 5.12   Fathers' educational background for both the migrant sample and the Irish based sample (%)

The emigrants have had greater exposure to international or large organisations thus reinforcing my hypothesis that these firms, through the creation of international labour markets, have encouraged emigration (see Figures 5.13 and 5.14). The divergence between the two groups is significant, especially in Figure 5.14. The migrants are more concentrated in large firms. This is to be expected given the links between international exposure, large firm experience, and career development. The Irish based accountants are less likely to work in such international organisations. The fact that almost

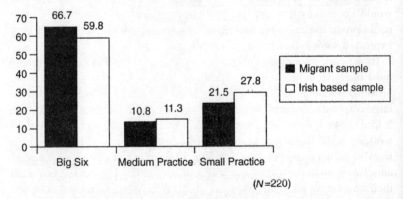

Figure 5.13   Size of practice trained with for both the migrant sample and the Irish based sample (%)

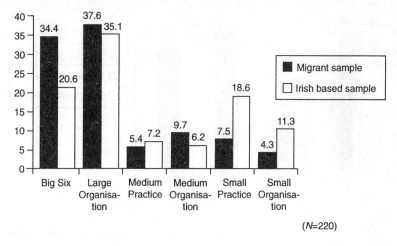

Figure 5.14   Size of organisation currently employed in (%)

one in three Irish based accountants work in small practices or organisations would lead one to suggest that migration and international exposure
would be of little use to them on returning as these firms would largely be
serving a local market. In contrast only 11.8 per cent of the migrant sample
work in a small practice or industrial firm. Again this is logical as working
in a small practice requires local contacts for promotion, something which
migrants would not have. Working in a small organisation overseas would
not give one the international expertise that many migrants seek and even if
a small firm did give one this opportunity the likelihood is that the firm
would be unknown to prospective employers in Ireland hence the gain
could prove useless. This latter point is important as some 76.3 per cent
expressed some form of intention to return.

If one concentrates on those accountants under 35, that is the migrants
most likely to have emigrated during the 1980s, this divergence in work
histories is maintained. The migrant groups are still more likely to work in
large corporate concerns. A number of points need to be noted about Figure
5.15. Despite the increased percentage of Irish based accountants under 35
working in the Big Six or a large organisation (62.2 per cent of this sample
work in such a firm in comparison with 52.4 per cent for all those accountants based in Ireland) they are still less concentrated in these firms than
their migrant counterparts. Migrants under 35 have likewise increased their
concentration in large concerns – 79.2 per cent of this subgroup work in
such places as opposed to 72.0 per cent for the total migrant sample. A

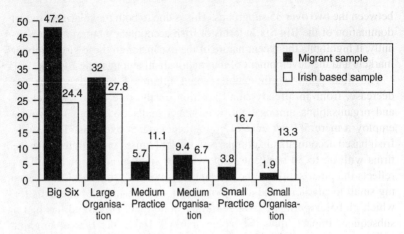

Figure 5.15   Size of organisation currently employed in for those under 35 (%)

massive four out of five young migrants now work in a large or international firm. Within this overall picture the role of the Big Six has increased. Roughly one in two migrants under 35 work for a Big Six practice.

Although the Big Six have increased the number of young accountants that they employ both at home and abroad, as one would expect given their dominance of the profession (see Figure 5.16), it appears reasonable to say that they have siphoned off Irish accountants to their international labour market. As can be seen from Figure 5.16 there is very little difference

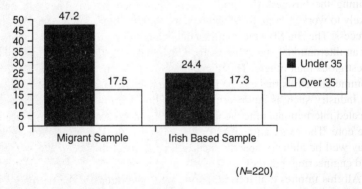

(N=220)

Figure 5.16   Percentage of Irish accountants, in Ireland and overseas, employed by the Big Six firms

between the two over 35 subgroups. This is due to both the relatively recent domination of the Big Six in terms of Irish accountancy but, more importantly, it highlights the recent nature of the expansion in these global labour markets and the development of internationalism amongst the Big Six.

The final point worth making about Figures 5.14 and 5.15 is the decrease, from an already small position, in the role of small practices and organisations amongst those migrants under 35. These firms now employ a mere 5.7 per cent of young accountants overseas. The young Irish based accountants in comparison are still quite concentrated in these firms with up to 30 per cent employed in a small practice or firm. This reflects the polarisation of the accountancy market into a local firm serving small local clients and an international firm serving global clients for which global experience is increasingly important. This trend has had a subsequent impact upon the labour market. Today the typical migrant accountant leaves a Big Six firm to join a Big Six firm, or as a second choice, an international organisation overseas. In terms of education and class the migrant and the Irish based accountant are quite similar. The area of the most substantial difference appears to be the increased likelihood of the migrant staying within a large organisation with some form of international connection.

CONCLUSION

All of the above would lead one to suggest that emigration is linked to international firms and career development. Those who go overseas are the upwardly mobile middle class who view global experience as the means of joining the business decision makers upon their return. They are more likely to work in large firms and believe that this migration is necessary for success. The Big Six have facilitated this migration process via the creation of an international status hierarchy which makes certain destinations more prestigious than others. This prestige is given due to supposed social and commercial skills that can be picked up rather than technical skills, unlike an industry such as engineering. Multinational firms thus appear to have created international elite labour markets that encourage people to move to the core. The exact attractions in this move for the individuals concerned may well be industry specific, hence the differences between accountancy and engineering, but they all seem to relate to the issue of social mobility.

All this implies that Ireland, and indeed other areas of the periphery, is still unable totally to control its own destiny. Changes in the tax structure and so on will not eradicate professional migration as the international economy has established other attractions for migrants. This leads one to suggest that there are similarities between Ireland's emigration today and that of previous eras although the exact mechanisms are different (Hanlon, 1992). Ireland's peripherality is still present, it has merely undergone a transmutation.

6 Accountants and the Class Structure: To Serve or be Served? That is the Question

INTRODUCTION: WHY EXAMINE ACCOUNTANCY AND CLASS?

The class position of experts and professionals is worth examining for a variety of reasons. Firstly, they form part of that broad category the 'middle class' and hence, at a popular level at least, they are taken as living proof of Marxism's irrelevance. At another level it has been suggested that this middle or service class has taken over the dynamic function that Marxism historically gave to the proletariat. Thirdly, even outside of the Marxist tradition the role of the middle class has been problematic. It has been argued that professionals have been, and continue to be, a benign influence upon society protecting the public interest, often to the detriment of their own self-interest, out of an altruistic service code (Freidson, 1973). I would hope that Chapter 4 has dispelled the notion of a benign professional operating in the public interest, at least within accountancy. In a somewhat similar vein Child (1982) has proposed that there may well emerge a conflict between the manager and the professional within large bureaucracies as both of these groups see control of the labour process as their own prerogative. In contrast to this Crompton (1990) dismisses such an idea and sees the the manager and the professional very much in the same light: both are expert labour.

The Marxist tradition has had great difficulty in explaining the rise of the service class, locating them within the class structure, and explaining their role.[1] These difficulties also apply to accountants. This is not surprising given that many chartered accountants go on to hold posts such as that of financial director; such a position can pay up to £76 000 per annum plus supply a car worth £20 000 in the City of London (Dixon, 1992), likewise in Ireland the average chartered accountant who is qualified sixteen to twenty years earns roughly IR£40 000 (LSCA, 1990). Given that accountancy and the other areas where large numbers of accountants work, for example financial services (LSCA, 1990), have grown rapidly throughout the 1980s, an adequate explanation of their role within the class structure would be beneficial. Many of the previous attempts to explain the future of both these people and the role they play have to be discounted in the case of accountants, particularly deskilling and proletarianisation (see Chapter 3 for an analysis of the deskilling arguments).

Accepting that the proletarianisation arguments concerning the professions are inadequate this chapter will try to locate accountants within the class structure through a Marxist analysis of capitalism's development over the past century. The primary reason for a Marxist analysis is control. I believe that the key issue in any theory of class is how it understands and prioritises control. Of all the major sociological traditions Functionalism, Weberianism, Social Interactionism and so on I would suggest that Marxism provides the most comprehensive explanation and understanding of control within the workplace, although it is by no means faultless. I am placing accountants within the service or new middle class because they exert control over their own labour process, over the labour processes of others and/or over surplus value when they are at the height of their careers. Before delving into this further an overview of both the main Marxist and Weberian theses on the service class will be presented.

A WEBERIAN ANALYSIS OF THE SERVICE CLASS

At a common sense level a Weberian explanation of the class structure within late capitalism appears to be the most appropriate methodology for studying class. Such an analysis concentrates primarily on the market position of the individual, that is the 'quality' and price of the labour power that an individual has to sell. This shapes the work situation of a person; the more highly prized a form of labour power is the better the pay, conditions, and security one will experience at work. People of broadly similar working conditions, status, and value on the labour market form classes (Marshall *et al.*, 1988; Goldthorpe, 1980). Developing parallel with this market is the growth of bureaucracy within capitalism. This bureaucracy requires different levels of expertise and hence different labour skills. The growth of bureaucratic structures leads to the need for highly differentiated labour skills and labour qualities that are satisfied through the market (Smith, 1987). It is largely the interaction between the labour market and this bureaucracy that separates individuals into classes.

There are a number of criticisms to be made of the Weberian thesis. It has been accused of being functionalist. It suggests the labour market became differentiated to the degree it has simply to satisfy the needs of an expanding bureaucratic network, but it does not adequately explain why this bureaucracy was formed. The relationship between the labour market and capital is not this straightforward, as will be demonstrated later on in the chapter. The concentration on the labour market, as opposed to the production process and the relations within this process, is incorrect; as will be highlighted it is these latter relationships which shape the labour market and this market then goes on to shape the class structure.

A second criticism of the Weberian approach is that by concentrating on the labour market it is impossible to limit the number of classes, theoretically the number of classes could be infinite. Weber suggested four classes – a capitalist class, a propertyless white collar intelligentsia, a petty bourgeoisie, and a manual working class (Mackenzie, 1982). Goldthorpe (1980), possibly the most influential Weberian class analyst living in Britain today, has suggested six classes – two service classes, two intermediate classes, and two working classes. On the other hand Runciman (1990) argues for the existence of seven classes in modern Britain – an upper class, three middle classes, two working classes, and an underclass. The reason for these differences is due to the fact that to form a class a group of individuals must have similar lifestyles[2] and so on. But what any particular theorist considers similar and where one draws the class line is a matter of commonsense and personal preference.

This is not to suggest that the Weberians are completely without merit. Goldthorpe (1980, 1982) has described some very significant changes in the British class structure throughout the post-war era. He has rightly pointed out how the expansion of the service class has been the most noticeable and significant feature of these alterations. He attributes much of this to the structural changes within the UK economy in the post-war boom which led to the creation of 'more room at the top'. As a result of this the service class in 1980 made up roughly 20–25 per cent of the working population. He suggests that in absolute terms there has been a significant degree of mobility in Britain, although relatively the inequalities within the class structure have remained. He highlights quite nicely how the service classes are especially good at maintaining their position and how the working classes are relatively ineffective at achieving mobility (Goldthorpe, 1980). As the expansion at the top levels out Goldthorpe argues that a degree of class polarisation will set in.

> Even in the presumably very favourable context of a period of sustained economic growth and of major change in the form of the occupational structure, the general underlying processes of inter-generational class mobility – or immobility – have apparently been little altered, and indeed have, if anything, tended in certain respects to generate still greater inequalities in class chances. (Goldthorpe, 1980: 85)

Goldthorpe has also made other useful insights, he concentrates on the issue of class mobility as do Stewart *et al.* (1980) in their penetrating examination of clerical work. In contrast the issue of career mobility is often ignored by Marxists (see Carchedi, 1975; Poulantzas, 1979).

However, even from within the Weberian camp Goldthorpe's work has been criticised. For example he has been taken to task for neglecting the role of women within the class structure.[3] But it is not on this issue that I wish to criticise Goldthorpe.[4] Goldthorpe (1982) has suggested that the service class are characterised by four features; they have a code of service, relative security of employment, prospects of material and status advancement, and they are trusted. It is this last point that I wish to focus upon as I believe that the other three features are contingent on this trust. The service class are trusted for two reasons in Goldthorpe's view, because authority must be delegated, and because specialist expertise must be used in an increasingly complex world, this use entails a degree of trust in the expert.

This argument assumes a number of things. The first is that authority is delegated to those with expertise, be it bureaucratic – managerial or professional – technical. Implicit within this argument is a belief in a technical meritocracy, albeit, to use a contradictory term, an unfair meritocracy wherein one's social background gives one an unfair advantage in acquiring these technical skills. But it is the fact that people are trusted because technically they can do the job which is the underlying point. However, as has been highlighted by people like Offe (1976) and Lovering (1990) for workers in general, and by Chapters 4 and 5 for accountants in particular, gaining trustworthy status is a matter that hinges on social and/or commercial criteria as much as, if not more than, technical issues.[5] Goldthorpe himself alludes to this. He acknowledges that the growth of the service class was not inevitable rather it came about because of a whole series of social, political, and organisational choices. Yet he neglects to examine these choices. An analysis of these decisions would highlight how it emerged that a large section of the working population came to be trusted. Goldthorpe never asks why it was that certain workers were trusted and others were not. He appears simply to assume that those who are trusted have to be trusted because they have certain expertise. This is true for all service class workers in his eyes as he himself dismisses the distinction between those with managerial expertise and those with professional expertise as being rather spurious. I would suggest that this weakness is a direct result of his Weberian approach. Because of its concentration on the market it can only suggest that one particular skill is in more or less demand than another. Thus at senior management level in the UK accountants are in demand more so than in Germany; in Germany engineers provide much of the staff for top level management (Glover and Kelly, 1987; Lawrence, 1980). However, this descriptive analysis is not enough to provide an adequate explanation of why this is the case. To explain why such a situation arises entails concentrating on the labour process and the relations of production. This requires a Marxist approach.

A MARXIST ANALYSIS OF THE NEW MIDDLE CLASS

That Marxism has had difficulties in explaining the rise of the service class need almost be left unstated. Smith (1987) and Armstrong *et al.* (1986) have examined a plethora of Marxian writings upon the subject and have found each theorist wanting in some regard. The major criticisms of the Marxist tradition stem from the fact that Marx argued that there were only two great social classes – the bourgeoisie and the proletariat (Marx and Engels 1967; Marx 1976b). As suggested the key to any Marxian class analysis is the examination of the social relations of production. These relations are dominated by the search for profitability. Marx believed that this search led capitalists to deskill and degrade labour at every opportunity. Hence labour is homogenised and distinctions between labour are made upon criteria such as gender, age, race and so forth (Marx, 1976b: 545). Within this system professionals were to become part of the proletariat (many of these points were reiterated by Braverman (1974) and other labour process theorists, see Chapter 3). At another level competition between capitalists would destroy the petty bourgeoisie and they too would be forced into the proletariat (Marx and Engels, 1967: 88).

These two predictions have been proved false. Both the salaried middle class and the self-employed petty bourgeoisie are still with us. The former have grown throughout the advanced world over the course of this century and the latter have recently reversed the decline they had experienced, since at least the end of World War II, in some Western economies (Chapter 1). As a result of these features an adequate theory of the service class is obviously required.[6]

As mentioned there have been numerous theorists on the new middle class; however, three of these theorists appear to have more credibility than the others. These are Poulantzas, Wright, and Carchedi. Each of these writers has tried to explain the growth of the service class, its role, and its location within the overall class structure. I will first examine the work of Poulantzas.

Poulantzas' analysis of class is based on three foundation stones. These are:

(1)   Marx's labour theory of value.
(2)   Emphasis on the place of an individual in the social division of labour rather than the conditions of work experienced by that individual.
(3)   Class structure precedes class struggle. Thus the adoption of collect- ive working class modes of struggle by members of the new middle class does not make these people working class.

Poulantzas also suggested that in certain instances the ideological and political levels within class formation put a group of workers in the service class when they are economically part of the working class. Therefore, although the economic level is the most important plane for forming the two primary classes this is not an universal rule, political and ideological factors can not be dismissed. Political relations are basically relations of control and authority typically found in work. Ideological relations on the other hand refer to the distinction between manual and mental labour; this distinction effectively enables the exclusion of manual workers from knowledge by the new middle class or the new petty bourgeoisie to use Poulantzas' terminology (Mackenzie, 1982).

Poulantzas argues that the new middle class coordinate the labour pro- cess and that they control this process for capital. This latter feature he sug- gests was primarily a political function which furthers the reproduction of capitalist class domination of the production process. However, unlike other Marxist writers he feels that the new middle class are not in a contra- dictory class location because their exploitative role prevails over any other functions they may have. Likewise all performers of mental labour have an ideological role which dominates their participation in the produc- tion process. This role entails denying knowledge to the working class and legitimating the devaluing of manual labour. The bridge between mental and manual labour can never be crossed, hence there is an insurmountable class barrier between the two workforces.

Poultantzas also argues that the new middle class are not a class in the sense that the working and capitalist classes are. The new middle class is quite fractioned. It is torn between the ideologies and values of the two dominant classes. Different fractions will identify with different classes. A whole series of factors in the class struggle could push groups in certain ways.

There are a number of very serious difficulties with Poulantzas' work. Mackenzie (1982) has highlighted three in particular:

(1)   It is ahistorical.

(2)   There is no discussion or account of resistance or conflict and it gives no role to the individual.

(3)   Because Poulantzas believes that productive labour is only to be found in the manual production of things (Poulantzas, 1979: 221) his idea of the working class, the dynamic class within society, offends common sense. According to his definition the working class in the USA would comprise roughly 20 per cent of the working population. Marx would have rejected this idea of productive labour. For Marx it was not the product that defined whether or not a worker was productive but the social and economic organisation involved in the work.

Having highlighted these very serious failings in Poulantzas' work it is important to note that there is one major advantage to be found in it. He highlights the centrality of control within the class structure and is quite right to suggest that it is this which separates the service class from the working class rather than some vague notion of skill and marketability. As suggested earlier, for the author this is the key issue to be examined in any analysis of the class structure, especially one which seeks to separate the working and service classes and to explain the position of the latter.

Wright's work also seeks to look at class in terms of roles played in the production process. In his book *Classes* (1985) he suggests that as regards exploitation where one stands in the production process determines one's class position. The concept of exploitation is based around three issues: ownership of capital, control of organisational assets, and skill or credentials. The degree to which one has or has not got these three advantages conditions the extent to which exploitation takes place. Hence somebody with control of some organisational assets, for example a middle manager, can both exploit those below him or her and be exploited by those above him or her. This allows for contradictory class locations. In Wright's opinion the new middle class have a dual role as both exploiters and exploited. The way in which the degree of exploitation is measured is primarily through evaluating the extent of autonomy a person experiences in their work.

Wright seeks to place individuals and the roles they exercise within the class structure, and in so doing he has to be commended. Unfortunately the end result of this process is problematic. He derives twelve classes from this operation, seven of which he suggests are in contradictory locations. Within this there are examples that, as with Poulantzas, offend common sense – a pilot has less autonomy than a school cleaner (see Wright, 1985; Marshall *et al.*, 1988). There are also other difficulties in his work. Mackenzie (1982) has highlighted that Wright's work is ahistorical and static.[7] Smith (1987) and Marshall *et al.* (1988) have suggested that his emphasis on the use of credentials and the labour market is Weberian. I would suggest that these two criticisms are intertwined. Because his approach is ahistorical we are given a static snapshot of the labour market and the skills that are highly sought on that market. If an historical account of this labour market were given we would see why these skills were sought after and the solutions they offered capital at various points of crises. These solutions allow capital to rectify, at least temporarily, one of its perennial dilemmas – controlling labour in the production process.

As with Poulantzas, Wright provides us with a number of insights. He emphasises the role of the production process, he seeks to account, in some form at least, for the individual and he expresses the idea that people can operate in contradictory class locations and as such the boundaries between the classes in the late twentieth century are quite blurred. He also suggests in his work that the role of trade unions, political parties and so on have a part to play in shaping the ideological and political aspects to the class struggle and the class structure. This latter point is nicely highlighted by the contrasting of the USA and Sweden.

I have left Carchedi's work until last in this section partly because most Marxist examinations of accountancy, which we will discuss in the next section, use Carchedi's insights a great deal but also because I feel it is the most beneficial analysis.

Carchedi (1975) concerned himself with the economic identification of the new middle class although he accepted that the political and ideological identifications of this group were also important. He defined the new middle class in terms of certain functions that were performed within capitalism. There were two sets of these functions, the function of the collective worker, and the global functions of capital. The former basically entail coordinating and unifying the labour process and as such this labour is productive.

To perform the function of the collective worker means to take part in the complex scientifically organised labour process as part of the collective labour-power, to produce collectively use values in order to produce surplus value. (Carchedi, 1975: 25, emphasis in the original)

This idea stems directly from Marx. Marx stressed the fact that when workers are brought together in a coordinated fashion their productive power is increased. However, with the increased coordinating and unifying functions of the collective worker and the existence of the desire for the greatest possible self-valorisation of capital within capitalism, there is an increase in worker resistance against the domination of capital. This leads to a greater need for control over labour power on the part of the capitalist. Hence under capitalism with the development of coordination and unity comes the emergence, or at least the intensification, of superintendence.[8]

> The work of directing, superintending and adjusting becomes one of the functions of capital, from the moment that the labour under capital's control becomes cooperative. As a specific function of capital, the directing function acquires its own special interests. (Marx, 1976b: 449)

It is these latter functions that Carchedi calls the global functions of capital.

> Therefore, *to perform the function of capital basically means to carry out the work of control and surveillance*. (Carchedi, 1975: 24, emphasis in the original)

As Marx himself highlighted, with the growth of the large scale enterprise both the collective labour functions and the global functions of capital would be passed on to employees. Carchedi argues that certain groups, whom he calls the new middle class, can perform both these sets of functions. Those performing the global functions of capital may be broken down into three clusters. First is, top management who have real economic ownership – capitalists. Second are those who perform global functions of capital and not the functions of the collective worker, although they do not have real economic ownership. Third are those who perform both the global functions of capital and the functions of the collective worker. This latter group are the new middle class.

The mix between the functions performed varies from occupation to occupation but clearly the new middle class are in a contradictory class location. Carchedi suggests that the greater the proportion of global functions of capital performed the less chance there is that this group of workers will be proletarianised and the closer its links or identification with capital will be. As suggested proletarianisation entails the loss of these global functions. Merely coordinating and unifying the labour process ensures that a particular job or occupation will be proletarianised and that these people will at some point join the ranks of the working class. Avoiding proletarianisation entails gaining an expertise or a skill, namely that of controlling or manipulating surplus value, which is then valuable on the labour market. This proletarianisation process will take place on a large scale within the new middle class due to the logic of profitability within capitalism. This logic will demand the devaluing of skilled or expensive labour. As with Wright the new middle class are both exploiters and exploited, or oppressors and oppressed if they are involved in the non-productive areas of the economy, and it is this which is at the heart of their contradictory location.

As with Poulantzas and Wright, there are weaknesses within Carchedi's work. It has been suggested that his work is ahistorical and does not take account of resistance and class struggle (Smith, 1987). Perhaps more importantly, Nichols (1986) has posed some serious questions such as can the collective labour functions and the global functions of capital be separated in the way that Carchedi suggests? How do we establish where one function ends and the other begins? Are supervision and coordination not two sides of the same coin? If they are then is not exploitation a necessary and productive part of the surplus value producing process? These are very pertinent questions and they remain unanswered in Carchedi's work and indeed in much of the academic work to be scrutinised in the next section.

Despite these shortcomings Carchedi's theory is helpful. Like Poulantzas and Wright he grasps the central issue concerning class: the degree to which one is controlled or one controls. He seeks, albeit incompletely, to highlight why those in the new middle class are different from the working class and states that the key thing which separates the two is performance of the global functions of capital.

A MARXIST INQUIRY INTO ACCOUNTANTS AND THE CLASS STRUCTURE

As stated, the Marxists that have researched the accountancy profession, and there has not been an overwhelming abundance of them, have generally made use of Carchedi's class analysis. The two theorists that have been most influential in this area have been Terence Johnson and Peter Armstrong.

Johnson (1980) rejects the idea that knowledge is a given object; he argues rather that it is a product of social power. Hence professional knowledge, like all other knowledge, is not neutral nor is it developed in a vacuum, instead it is manufactured within a power structure. Accountants have developed knowledge that allows them provide Carchedi's two functions. The class position of accountants is determined by the fact that they are appropriators of surplus value for capital, hence they perform at least some of Carchedi's global functions. Thus, for Johnson, accountancy is unambiguously tied to the requirements of the bourgeoisie.

The general characteristics of accountancy, as it has developed since the late nineteenth century in Britain, have been such that the occupation has always been subject to large measures of corporate control. The modern accountancy profession was largely brought into being by the demands of corporate business first, as a form of internal company control and then as a form of accounting to the risk bearer by means of public audit. (Johnson, 1972: 66)

The fact that there are both the functions of the collective worker and the global functions of capital means that two distinct strands of professional knowledge have emerged (Johnson, 1977). These strands can broadly be defined in terms of technical know how and indetermination. Technical expertise is concerned with the coordination and unity of the labour process. Like all technical knowledge it is vulnerable to appropriation by others and deskilling. Technical knowledge can be deskilled because on its own it can be codified and mapped out in a logical, although often complicated, way. Once this has occurred the skill can be broken down into more and more less complicated constituents. As such it is increasingly simplified. It is for this reason that those elements of the new middle class who simply perform the tasks of technical coordination are proletarianised. To exercise the global functions of capital one needs to develop a certain degree of indeterminacy around the particular skills a profession may have (for a greater discussion of the concept of indeterminacy, see Jamous and Peloille, 1970). Indeterminacy revolves around the idea that aspects concerning the professional organisation of knowledge should be mystified and protected. Thus professions argue that their work is not purely technical, there are also a whole range of other factors that are equally important to the work. These other factors can only be understood after a long apprenticeship or socialisation process. Accountancy exhibits this indeterminacy. In Chapter 3 it was shown why accountancy, or particularly auditing, will not be deskilled; some of the reasons proffered were the level of intuition involved, the need to talk to people, the feeling one gets for a set of accounts – a feeling which comes only from experience and so on.

Johnson (1977) goes on to argue that there is a constant tension between the capitalist and the new middle class because the capitalist constantly seeks to lower the level of indeterminacy involved in the work by subordinating work activities to rational managerial definitions. The managerial prerogative is to stress technicality and hence to push this class closer and closer to the proletariat.

Within such an environment a fissure has opened up within accountancy. The profession in Johnson's opinion is being polarised and has moved away from the old notion of colleagueship to a more blatantly hierarchical structure (Johnson, 1986). One section of the profession is increasingly being proletarianised via the loss of its global functions of capital. This segment of the profession is now primarily made up of information gatherers who simply perform collective labour functions. At the other end of the spectrum there are the controllers. These people carry out vital functions of control for capital by installing and supervising financial and other control mechanisms. These two groups are related in that both the technical and indeterminacy knowledge of the latter facilitates the proletarianisation of the former.

> Thus while their function in servicing capital creates the conditions of indetermination in relation to their own [the 'elite' accountants] organisation of knowledge as work the very same function has the effect of stressing the technicality of the work activities of their colleagues – subordinates, creating the conditions for work devaluation. (Johnson, 1977: 108)

In Chapter 3 I have taken Johnson to task on a number of issues so at this point I will refer the reader to p. 82. However, Chapter 3 did not address class and it is concerning this that I wish to make one last criticism. Like many Marxists Johnson has no account of mobility in his work. This is largely because the structure is given almost complete dominance over the actor. However, the role of the individual is important especially in an occupation where people are promoted. As described already in this work (see Chapters 1 and 4) chartered accountants experience high degrees of occupational mobility. One consequence of this is that even though a 25 year old chartered accountant may be in a technical and thus potentially proletarianised position, for example that of a senior wherein the superiors are quite aware of the indeterminacy skills and, therefore, a senior's mystifying abilities are useless, it is unlikely that he or she will question his or her allegiance to capital or view him or herself as proletarian in light of the fact that the individual is almost certainly guaranteed some form of promotion and mobility.

Once again having criticised Johnson I would like to suggest that there are perceptive insights in his work. By acknowledging that what is determined knowledge or skill depends upon the power relations within a society, Johnson accepts that expertise on the labour market does not depend upon the 'quality' of the skill in some objective sense but rather upon the particular capacity of particular classes to define what is or is not expertise. This capacity is unequal and as a result the capitalist class define skill in their interest, which primarily lies in controlling labour power in order to produce the maximum surplus value. This is a point that is ignored by a Weberian approach. The Weberians appear uninterested in the fact that the labour market is subordinate to the productive process in this way.

The second advantage of Johnson's thesis is that he brings Carchedi's endeavours a step further. Johnson provides a framework, through his use of the technical–indeterminacy distinction, of analysing how expertise is deskilled and proletarianised. He rejects the functionalist notion that one's place in the hierarchy depends upon one's technical abilities and rightly points out that to maintain a favourable position within the class structure non-technical capacities are required.

Finally, Johnson does try to give an historical description of the development of accountancy and its links with capitalism, although I would suggest that his account is insufficient. Possibly more than anyone else the person who has tried to examine the historical role of accountants and their emergence as global functionaries of capital is Armstrong.

Armstrong's argument centres around two interrelated points. These points are that control of the labour process is central to capitalism (although it is not the only problem, see Armstrong, 1986), and that certain groups emerged to provide solutions to this problem of labour control. This latter feature leads to inter-professional rivalry as different professions seek to ingratiate themselves to capital. The consequences of these two interrelated problems are never predetermined. Armstrong argues that for a profession to maintain its global functions of capital it must continue to provide solutions to one or other of capital's difficulties. Armstrong refers to such a plan of campaign as a 'collective mobility strategy' (Armstrong, 1985). For such a strategy to be successfully embarked upon a profession must find a problem area within capitalism, criticise the existing solutions and the professions that advocate them and then provide a better, that is more profitable, solution on the basis of their professional techniques. He suggests that accountants have been particularly successful at pursuing such strategies in the Anglo–American world. Accountants have been able successfully to maintain their hold on key functions for capital through stressing the indeterminacy of their skills.

Armstrong (1987) highlights how accountants came to dominate UK management and how they first entered the important position of global functionary. He suggests that they provided solutions to the problems of extracting surplus value, realising surplus value, and allocating surplus value. What follows is largely a brief summary of Armstrong's 1987 paper.

Although accountants had been involved in some costing and budgetary control within firms in the late nineteenth century their presence was not widespread. In fact cost accounting during this period was primarily undertaken by engineers and hence it was they and not accountants who extracted surplus value through controlling costs. Until World War I the future of cost accounting was open in terms of who would come to dominate it and it could very easily have been developed by engineers given that the prestigious accountancy firms were not involved in its early development.

If accountants did not provide this global function of capital exactly which one did they provide? The answer is that accountancy's main global function at this time lay in the realm of allocation: accountants allocated surplus value largely through their involvement with bankruptcies. Again this decision making function need not have been restricted to accountants; in fact it had been provided by lawyers who for some reason allowed accountancy, which had grown up as a subordinate branch within law (see Chapter 2), to commandeer this function independently.

The second way within which members of the profession became global functionaries was through the audit. The fact that they were the only legal auditors placed accountants in a powerful position between both the managers and the owners of public companies.[9] Accountants thus had a second crucial say in the allocation of surplus. This position also allowed them to define a crisis in terms of the balance sheet and the interpretation of the balance sheet in turn was shaped by the accountancy profession. The audit also provided them with a spring-board from which greater corporate control could be garnered, namely the monitoring of individual branches, departments and so forth.

It was mainly through the audit and the role it gave accountants that the profession moved into the area of extracting surplus value. This was done during World War I where for a whole series of reasons accountants moved into the region of costing within firms (for a further discussion of this see Chapter 2; Armstrong, 1987; and Jones, 1981). This move allowed accountants to control labour through the use of budgets. As a result accountants were now able to extract, realise and allocate surplus value.

The inter-war period and beyond led to a whole range of changes in corporate control and in corporate structure which further facilitated accountants in extending their global functions through costings, control of investment, and control of labour. Thus the fact that accountants had a power base in the allocation of surplus value allowed them to gain control of other functions and as a result of this they gained their pre-eminent position within British management. They did not achieve this simply because of the techniques they possessed. It was achieved via a collective mobility strategy through which they outmanoeuvred other professions such as engineering and law. They have continued to do the same today with personnel managers (Armstrong, 1986) and IT specialists (Murray and Knights, 1990).

The fact that there is nothing predetermined about these processes allows for inter-professional competition. Armstrong (1985) has used the concept of indeterminacy to explain why some professions succeed and others do not. For example, a profession must put forward a solution to a particular dilemma within capitalism which is more profitable than rival suggestions. However, to reap the benefits of this the profession must mystify its remedy somewhat so that this answer cannot be improved upon by other professions, nor can the profession be downgraded by capital.

As with Johnson, Armstrong (1991) accepts that capital seeks to drive down the costs of delegated authority and the costs of those who carry out these global functions. However, this is problematic as these people have relatively large degrees of power due to the positions they already hold and the trust that has been placed in them. This trust comes from a greater distrust of the rest of the workforce and it is maintained through the greater salary and the better working conditions given to trusted as opposed to distrusted labour. Within this there is a contradiction – trust is purchased. Under capitalism trust has been commodified. It is not given to those with certain objective technical expertise as the Weberians would suggest, rather it is bought from those groups that will provide profitable solutions to the control problems, amongst other things, within capitalism. Which groups these are is not simply down to technical skill, it is also related to other indeterminate factors. These factors allow for a degree of mystification, thus bumping up the price of this labour and they also entail a perceived unambiguous commitment to capital. As a result of these processes management is problematic because not only is the issue of which group manages constantly up for grabs but furthermore capital seeks to cheapen this trusted labour as much as possible. Added to all this is the fact that within the idea of trusted labour there is the incongruous fact that this trust is bought.

The above section highlights the central points of Armstrong's thesis. He demonstrates how accountancy defeated its rivals within the Anglo–American world and now provides the largest slice of managerial labour within UK and US capitalism; he also suggests reasons as to why this did not happen in other states (Armstrong, 1987). As a consequence of this accountants took over key global functions of capital. He argues that today accounting influences and controls labour in three key ways:

(1) Allocation of budgets for departments and judgment of the performance of the labour within these departments.

(2)   Rationalisation of decisions of allocation, which leads to the concentration of labour and capital in those areas that yield greatest surplus value. This indirectly puts disciplinary pressure on those areas that yield less surplus.

(3)   The fact that accounting is now the meta-language that workers have to try and engage if they wish to challenge capital in a 'realistic' way.

A number of criticisms of Armstrong's work have been made. It has been argued that his writing is functionalist in parts, for example the idea that accountants need to be involved in the direct control of labour has been described as simplistic and functionalist. Murray and Knights (1990) argue that the reality is more complicated than this. They suggest that other specialisms, for instance engineering in the coalmining industry, may directly control labour whilst a different specialism, e.g. accounting may be dominant in resource allocation. These authors also state that a specialism need not necessarily increase surplus value for capital in order to achieve collective mobility. While both of these criticisms may be valid I would view them as being somewhat spurious. To take the first criticism, Armstrong's work need not necessarily be tied to the idea that accountancy directly supervises labour; surely actions such as resource allocation or the search for greater yields of surplus value exert control over the engineering supervisors and as such over labour in coalmining more generally? Secondly, a specialism may not necessarily increase surplus value for capital, although I would argue that it generally does, but by not doing so the specialism would leave itself more vulnerable to displacement by a more successful collective mobility strategy carried out by a more profit orientated occupational group. Armstrong's work is very beneficial. It builds upon the work of Carchedi and, to some extent, Johnson and provides us with quite a detailed description of the rise of the accountant in British management.

MOBILITY, CONTROL AND CLASS

At this point I want to return to the issue of contradictory class location and the separation of control and coordination within the production process. The class position of accounting trainees and seniors can I believe be explained by using a modified form of Carchedi's work as developed by Roslender (1990). Roslender accepts the criticisms concerning the impractical separation of the control and surveillance functions from the functions of coordination and unity of the labour process. He states that this separation can only be carried out at an analytic level. He also argues that

Carchedi is unclear as to how he regards the 'other' function of the collective labourer, namely technical or intellectual work. To solve these problems he modifies Carchedi's work so that first, the functions of capital embraces the work of both control and of coordination and secondly, the functions of the collective labourer are identified with technical or intellectual labour only. If one accepts this then all management, at least theoretically, has some productive function to it, that is all those who are involved in control are to some extent involved in productive coordination. We then return to Carchedi's difficulty. These managers are in a contradictory class location, partly exploited and partly exploiter. It is the mix of these two roles that is important in deciding where an individual's class allegiance lies. These people are neither working class nor capitalist, they lie somewhere in between. Where they lie in relation to the two 'great' classes is the question.

Some light can be thrown on this question by examining the class location of the chartered accountant. In practice a senior's control over his or her work process is not far removed from the control exercised by a skilled manual worker (see Chapter 3). Hence if one merely examined this aspect of accountancy a senior would be a member of the working class. However, he or she is not a member of the proletariat for two very important reasons – mobility and control of or influence over surplus value.

Mobility

Because of the Marxist preoccupation with structure the role of mobility tends to be somewhat disregarded. The class identification of a person is obviously influenced by where they realistically feel they will be in, say, ten or twenty years time. As has been mentioned already in this chapter an accountant has a genuine prospect of career advancement and of making it to the top of the occupational hierarchy either with legal and real ownership of capital – partner – or with effective control of organisational assets – financial director, company secretary, financial controller and so on. Because of this accountants will accept tightly controlled or possibly more tightly controlled conditions than those experienced by the working class (see Chapters 3 and 4). They know that someday they will be the controllers rather than the controlled and therefore align themselves clearly to capital. Hence in terms of class identification and class alliance mobility must be taken into consideration. This situation would most likely be different for accounting technicians. Jack (1992) has suggested that the large firms will make increasing use of these technicians and that they will be used to carry out the routine tasks currently performed by accountants. One would also expect that over time these technicians would develop a working class identity as it is most likely that they would not be 'trustworthy', unlike accountants, and hence they would be refused mobility. Mobility – or more correctly the lack of mobility – would shape these workers at an ideological and political level in a way that was different to today's accountant.

Control of or Influence over Surplus Value

This second feature is related to the first, and indeed largely determined by it. With mobility will come an influence over surplus value and, by implication, labour. As already described accountants have a great deal of influence on the extraction, realisation, and allocation of surplus value. The same may be said of other private service workers, for example investment analysts, bankers and even advertisers or marketing people. It is this characteristic of their work which gives them control not only over their own labour but over that of others. This control extends to other professionals in some instances – the advancement of financial or cost controls within public service areas such as health and education. It is upon the basis of this commitment to capital and upon their willingness to be commercial and profitable that these employees become trusted and can then expand their global functions through building a career. These features further tie them to capital. Although they perform some productive functions through their work as collective labourers as one progresses up the ladder this labour will increasingly diminish although, unlike Carchedi, I would suggest that it is never completely obliterated – surely even a board of directors mapping out corporate strategy over the next five years has some coordinating function?

Other new middle class members such as doctors, lecturers, army officers and so on derive their control of surplus value in a fundamentally different way. The private sector, new middle class professional gets this influence by expansion of his or her organisation through capitalist competition. In contrast with this the public service, new middle class professional receives his or her influence through the political arena and the decision to expand the state sector. I would suggest that this fact may lead to different class identifications or alliances on the part of the 'commercialised' and the more public orientated sections of the new middle class, the point being that the commercialised wing is firmly attached to capital.

The above two features are therefore important if one wants to suggest how this middle class will act. It is not enough to know where at some fixed point a person fits into the structure. One must also know the realistic mobility a worker will experience and the means by which he or she will control and gain control over surplus value and the labour processes of others in order to understand their class identification.

THE NEW MIDDLE CLASS AND CASINO CAPITALISM[10]

When discussing the service class, to use their terminology, Lash and Urry (1987: 194) made a number of very pertinent points:

(1) Knowledge has been appropriated away from the working class and incorporated into the professions, institutions of science and so on, effectively into the service class and this latter class increasingly serves capital on its *own* terms.

(2) The causal powers of the working class have been/are being eroded as it is subject to control and reproduction by the service class.

(3) The power of the service class appears as legitimate power based upon technical rationality.

(4) A career is now the preferred form of work in society and access to one is based upon education. In turn such credentials and attainment structures shape the stratification of the society.

(5) The service class' interests are not the same as those of capital. In fact much of today's politics is shaped by divisions within the service class or between sections of that class and capital.

(6) A major division in all the advanced economies is the one between the public and private sectors of the service class. The relative power of the former has had a major influence upon the character and strength of the socialist movement.

(7) Much labourist struggle is directed against the service class rather than a depersonalised capitalist class.

(8) Potential oppositional groups to capital are nevertheless very large.

(9) The state is under pressure from the demands made on it by many service class interest groups and at the same time it is viewed as something to be struggled against as it is deemed too strong.

(10) The service class has been partly responsible for creating new social movements such as the Green Movement.

There are a number of important features to Lash and Urry's challenging thesis. The most important one is the suggestion that the working class has ceded its dynamic role to the service or new middle class and that capitalism's movement from an organised to a disorganised structure is largely down to this latter class. It is a thesis that I disagree with although certain aspects of it are correct; for example it is true to say that the service class is divided, that its interests are not identical to the interests of capital, and that potentially the opposition to capital is very large. However, I would suggest that capital is currently setting about resolving these contradictions through its recent and continuing restructuring.

Lash and Urry argue that the creation of the service class was not inevitable, rather it came about due to a series of choices. These choices centred around the adoption, first in the USA but later on in Europe, of Scientific Management Principles. This choice led to the expansion of professional or expert labour both within the private sector through the enlarging of management control and within the public sector through the expansion of state services such as education and health. All of this was accelerated with the corporatist deals done during the 1930s and beyond. The authors suggest that these changes altered the balance of power within the advanced economies, largely weakening labour and transforming capital.

The transition to Fordism led to a number of changes within the West following World War II and continuing right up until today. This transformation led to the collapse of working class politics and indeed to the disintegration of class politics in general, the control of the state over capital was severely weakened, internationalisation increased at a rapid rate, the managerial and/or professional strata within society expanded and this group increasingly put forward its own agenda, the service sector grew and the importance of the city declined, there was cultural fragmentation and so forth. Eventually all these processes led to a move away from a Fordist structure. All of this was not inevitable but Fordism effectively sowed the seeds of its own demise. There are serious weaknesses in this whole position which were addressed earlier in Chapter 1.

A second explanation for this alteration is available. It is one that stresses the structured nature of the metamorphosis from Fordism to what has been labelled Flexible Accumulation (Harvey, 1989). This thesis largely addresses the altering regime of accumulation over the past twenty years. Hence out of the ashes of Fordism came Flexible Accumulation (Harvey, 1989; Gordon *et al.*, 1982; Harrison and Bluestone 1988). Using the approach laid down by these Marxist writers a number of criticisms of the Disorganised Capitalism thesis can be addressed.

As stated in Chapter 1, the Fordist regime of accumulation was based upon a compromise between capital and labour. This compromise centred around the segmentation of the labour market into the primary labour market, the primary subordinate labour market, and the secondary labour market. This latter market was largely excluded from the benefits of this compromise and was characterised by part-time, dead-end employment typically carried out by women and/or minorities. In terms of capital there were also two type of firms: core firms operating in the core areas of the economy, characterised by long-term stable growth and dominant market shares, and peripheral firms operating in the less profitable and less stable areas of the economy – typically these firms employed a lot of secondary market labour (Gordon *et al.*, 1982). Let me once again remind the reader that Fordism had a degree of flexibility.

These labour markets did not represent various levels of skill or quality, rather they were control mechanisms and as such were part and parcel of what Edwards (1979) has called bureaucratic control. The idea that labour markets are control mechanisms is not new nor unique to Gordon *et al.*. Offe (1976, 1985) to name but one has forcefully argued that the labour market is dominated by ascriptive features (for a further discussion of these points and accountancy see Chapter 4). This is a crucial point and one which Lash and Urry ignore. They suggest that entry to the service class is based upon educational credentials but they do not discuss the purpose of these qualifications. Credentialism is largely a means of closing access to labour markets. Offe (1985) has highlighted how the labour market is restricted from acting as a free market and hence it acts as a means of supervision. There are three ways in which this is done. First is the fiction that labour is a true commodity; labour is a unique commodity, unlike other commodities it is not brought into the world in the quantity nor quality desired by the market nor can it be withdrawn from the market with the ease that other goods can. Second, restrictions exist on the market, for example employers' associations, trades unions, entry to skill acquisition or education is closed to many, etc.; all these things limit the freedom of the market. Third, what Offe calls 'contemporary functional disturbances', e.g. the spatial strategies of capital, oversupply of labour in the West, political shift to the right and so on. These three features mean that the labour market can never be entirely free. If one accepts the proposition that access to the labour market is impeded and that the labour market is segmented in the way that Gordon *et al.* suggest then entry to the primary labour market, that is the service class market, is closed. This market has largely been closed by the strategies of capital and as such one must seriously question the belief that the group of workers that capital created via this market will bite the hand that feeds them.

At this point it is insightful to return to our accountants. Hopper and Armstrong (1991) have shown how accountants have come to dominate large areas of management in the USA not because of economic nor technical imperatives but because they could control labour. They controlled labour through internal costing. It was accounting's ability to control labour that facilitated the transition from the 'foreman's empire' structure of the late nineteenth century which had at that point run into difficulties in achieving high levels of profitability. The move towards the homogenisation of labour that followed this in the early twentieth century led to the expansion of managerial, technical, and clerical employees. This solution to capital's crisis of profitability created problems of its own. These were temporarily overcome by using accounting information to protect shareholders' dividends via throwing the costs of such a policy onto a disorganised labour movement. Such policies often led to excess capacity in times of slump or a shortage during boom times. This had consequences for labour in terms of speed ups of production, seasonal layoffs and so forth in order to ensure that targets were met throughout the 1920s. Likewise throughout the welfarist compromise which followed this period the accounting techniques of monopoly pricing were developed. Monopoly pricing techniques protected the partial accord between capital and the organised labour movement by pushing the harsher traits of such a system onto the firms and labour in the peripheral segment of the economy. Hopper and Armstrong go on to highlight how the current agency theory being developed within accountancy is tied to the changes taking place in capitalism today.[11] This agency theory is a new form of labour control, it stresses ideas such as flexibility and a widespread return to the notion that labour is a variable cost. The return to the notion of labour as a variable cost is in contrast to the situation that prevailed under Fordism. It applies the idea of cost to *any* relationship wherein authority is delegated.

By adapting their techniques to provide new solutions to the labour control problem, albeit that these solutions are temporary, accountants successfully fought off any young pretenders to their crown as the major source of senior management personnel. It is because of its success at dealing with challenges to capital that accountancy has achieved the position it has in Anglo–American capitalism; no doubt a similar analysis would reveal the same for engineering in Germany and Sweden. These service class members have always sided with capital in this way because one only gets into the occupation and then progresses up the ladder if one is prepared to pursue capital's interests rigorously (see Chapters 4 and 5).

This is not to say that the interests of the service and the capitalist classes are identical. Lash and Urry are correct in stressing the differences between the two (as are Nichols, 1969; Salaman, 1982 and a whole host of others); however, although there are differences the service class will not pose a major challenge to capital on its own nor will it shape society in its own interest. The reason for this is that the service class does not serve capital on its own terms as Lash and Urry have suggested. The service class, at least its private sector wing, engages in inter-class competition to decide who will serve capital rather than who will serve the service class. This may partially explain why between 1984 and 1986 600 000 middle to upper managerial employees, service class members, lost their jobs in the USA (Harrison and Bluestone, 1988: 38). These workers were obviously an unnecessary drain upon the surplus value being created and their removal would have been initiated by other service class members devising plans to increase profitability for capital.

What is taking place within capitalism today is not disorganised. What it is is an intensification of, amongst other things, old policies, for example an intensification of labour market segmentation. As a result of this the service class has possibly been split in two and the class structure as a whole has been polarised (see Conclusion). Within all this change accountants have further aligned themselves to capital. This intensified segmentation of the labour market is a means by which capital seeks to further subjugate labour and regain some of the ground it conceded in the postwar period. Access to any particular segment is controlled largely through normative features such as race, gender and, class rather than through meritocratic factors such as education or skill, although these may ostensibly be the entry criteria.

As suggested in Chapter 4 the move to graduate recruitment by the Big Six[12] has largely been a control mechanism whereby those entering the profession are middle class or have been made middle class by their participation in the university system. That the Irish university sector is largely closed to the working class has been well established (Breen *et al.*, 1990). Yet as Chapters 3 and 4 demonstrated the intellectual content of the accountancy training period hardly justifies the need for a degree. Despite this 75 per cent of those surveyed who had a degree stated that it was very important or important to their receiving their first job. As highlighted by one of John O'Grady's quotes in Chapter 4 (p. 116) the important benefits that a degree gives one are largely social – an argument reinforced by the fact that 30 per cent of the graduates surveyed had degrees in areas unrelated to accountancy such as engineering, arts, social science (this trend is continuing today see McManus, 1992).

The unwarranted nature of this qualification comes to light when one examines the current use these accountants make of their university education. 66 per cent ($N = 97$) stated that they made *no* current use of their third level education and only 30 per cent stated that their university education was an important or a very important factor in getting them their current post, quite a decline in terms of the importance attached to it when entry to the profession was at stake. Thus one could legitimately argue that the holding of a degree is completely irrelevant to the work of an accountant and, from a purely meritocratic–technical point of view, gaining one is a waste of three or four years. Its advantage is simply that it makes one acceptable to the employers.

One could explain the recent introduction of these graduate recruitment policies by the Big Six in terms of this intensified labour market segmentation. Education is not being used in a meritocratic sense but rather as a means of, potentially at least, ensuring loyalty to capital. Gaining a degree is merely the first step on the ladder, to proceed to the next rung greater demonstrations of loyalty are required. If this argument is correct, and I would argue strongly that it is, then one must seriously question the thesis that the new middle class are real contenders for the role as the dynamic force within capitalism. On its own this class has not seriously challenged capital nor sought to enforce its own agenda; even one of Lash and Urry's examples of a challenge to capital, that is the opposition by the management of the time to the introduction of Taylorism, is better explained using Armstrong's inter-professional competition thesis rather than suggesting it was an example of capital's partial resistance to the service class' introduction of Scientific Management (see Lash and Urry, 1987: 171).

It has been the working class that have challenged capital throughout capitalism (Gordon *et al.*, 1982). The Fordist regime of accumulation led to the expansion of the state, the growth of a professional service class, increased working class power and so on. However, these processes eventually led to a crisis in profitability to which capital has responded (see Chapter 1).

Many of the results of this response have been documented in Chapter 1 but one important feature was neglected and this is the fissure within the service class. Broadly speaking this divide entails the emergence of two groups; on the one hand there is the public sector service class, e.g. doctors, academics, civil servants, etc. and on the other there is the 'commercialised', private sector service class – accountants, lawyers, engineers. These two groups are subject to different control mechanisms, different career paths, different spatial mobility patterns and so forth (Chapter 4). Crucially they also have different interests in terms of state expansion, state spending, etc. The public or bureaucratic professionals would, one presumes, want to maintain or expand current levels of state expenditure whilst the commercialised service class would seek to limit such policies as far as possible. If this analysis is accurate then the interests of the two groups are fundamentally opposed: the public sector group will try to uphold some form of Fordist compromise whilst the commercialised group will aspire to shattering such a compromise. As mentioned it is by state expansion and

political choice rather than capitalist competition that the public sector service class expand their control over surplus value and society. I would
argue that their desire for a form of Fordist, or possibly more accurately,
bureaucratic society centres around their own self-interest and an expansion of their own influence rather than some altruistic sense of justice.
Accountants are quite definitely in the commercialised segment and their
interests are inextricably linked to the interests of capital – they are functionaries of capital. Lash and Urry are right to state that the service class is
split but it is this very split that stops the service class from being the
dynamic force within society. It is also significant that during the post-war
boom it was the public sector wing of the service class that experienced the
greatest degree of growth; however, with the restructuring that capital initiated in the past twenty years it is the commercialised service class, that is
that section of the class that is most closely allied to capital, which has witnessed the largest growth. Restructuring has severely weakened the working class (Harrison and Bluestone, 1988; Sassen, 1991) but I would suggest
it has also weakened that section of the service class most likely to threaten
capital at the expense of its more pliable colleague. This is a factor somewhat ignored by the Disorganised Capitalism theorists. Obviously this is an
approximation and in reality the distinction is not this straightforward.

CONCLUSION

I have argued in this chapter for a Marxist analysis of accountancy's role
within the class structure. The chapter has sought to demonstrate how
accountants have acted both historically and contemporaneously in favour
of capital. They do this primarily in three ways:

(1)   They set budgets against which to evaluate workers.
(2)   They move capital and thus labour into the areas of greatest
      profitability.
(3)   Accountancy provides the meta-narrative within which labour has to
      challenge capital.

Despite their controlling role these workers are productive both within
practice and industry because control and coordination cannot in reality be
separated and as such control has some productive function. This latter
point presents a problem because one must seriously ask, when does coordination give way to control? Both foremen and managers control and
coordinate, so are they the same? The answer to this is obviously 'no', but

one must look to mobility and the realistic level of control yielded by a person at the high point of their career. This requires a detailed knowledge of the occupation being discussed in order to incorporate the concept of mobility. This is not to say that the class structure is unimportant, it merely says that on its own it only gives us a snapshot of a society and cannot explain fully the ideas of class alliance and class identification.

As has been postulated the service class is not the changing force within society nor is it homogeneous. Under Flexible Accumulation this class has been reshaped so that at least one section of it suits the needs of capital and this 'commercialised segment' is subject to internecine warfare in order to further reinforce the privileged position of its various occupations. Because of the role within capitalism played by this commercialised fraction its future is closely bound to that of capital. As a consequence it is inherently conservative (see Goldthorpe, 1982 for reasons as to why this will be so, although he incorrectly talks about the *whole* class). The second service class fraction, that made up of the public service, has different interests and these are more closely tied to the expansion of the state. One could argue that the survival of this segment is indirectly tied via the state to a functioning capitalist economy. This may or may not be the case; however, the point is that the interests of this fraction are not as directly tied to the interests of capital as its commercial counterpart. As such these workers may, potentially at least, form an alliance with the working class to challenge the increased power and freedom of capital.[13]

On the basis of the foregoing the Disorganised Capitalism argument has to be rejected. What we are witnessing today is a greater intensification of capital's attempt to control labour and the accumulation process. This has been or is currently being done through further market segmentation. Within capitalism it is still the working class that provides the challenge to capital, albeit that it is a lot weaker today than in previous eras, and the working class may increasingly need alliances with elements of the service class.

Conclusion: Flexible Accumulation and the Commercialised Service Class

This book set out to do one thing. That was to highlight how the organisation, control, and ideological outlook of certain service class employees, particularly accountants, has altered in the new regime of accumulation which has emerged. All of this entailed a redefining of what it means to do professional work. In order to convincingly argue in favour of this redefinition four points had to be made. (1) It sought to destroy the myth that professionals are not controlled nor socialised in very specific and rigorous ways. (2) It wanted to examine the notion of objectivity within the area of professional work. (3) It sought to explain why Irish accountants emigrate and the role of the large accountancy multinationals within this process. (4) It tried to analyse the way in which professional work has been redefined within the new regime of accumulation.

The overall conclusion of this work must be that the one group of key controllers within capitalism examined – accountants – are themselves more tightly controlled than other, less 'responsible', personnel. This control process entails a whole variety of socialisation procedures which are designed to sift out the trustworthy from the untrustworthy. The notion of 'trustworthiness' revolves around commercial criteria. Accountants have historically acted in the interests of capital rather than labour and this is possibly more true today than at any other time. Hence it cannot be claimed that the profession, or the knowledge it makes use of, is neutral. Both have been developed within a socially constructed system, therefore, neither is objective.

Today accountants themselves will explain why they need to be commercial. This is different to the past possibly because during the 1980s it was acceptable to talk about commercialism and to denigrate public service. If accountants are to be commercial then they are required to behave in a certain manner. As Chapter 4 outlined this entails giving the customer, that is capital, what he or she wants. This is ensured through a whole variety of control mechanisms and incentives. An accountant's training is not really about developing technical expertise, although this obviously is a factor, it has much more to do with becoming acceptable, trustworthy, commercially aware or whatever other term one cares to use.

215

In short it concerns the development of business virtue. If all of the above is correct then the profession cannot be deemed neutral nor public orientated nor a public watchdog and the theories of people like Bell (1974) or Freidson (1973) have to be rejected.

Chapter 5 brought this examination of control a step further by arguing that for Irish accountants the development of business virtue is completed by a 'spell abroad'. However, this spell cannot be spent anywhere – a trip to the Bahamas is all very well and good if one wants to be exotic and interesting in the pub; however, of what use is that to a hard pressed accountancy firm? Such a firm requires someone who has been to a place like London, New York, or Tokyo despite the fact that these places offer scant international experience. I would suggest that the belief that one gets a real insight into how business in the real commercial world operates by going to certain locations is a fine piece of mystification. The reality is that these accountants when they go abroad receive similar experience to the people that remain in Ireland. All of this, however, is not to say that the two groups are perceived as being the same. The former accountants are viewed as being made of the right stuff; they have had the guts to take the risk (and what a risk it is) of going to say somewhere like London. All of these traits really revolve around the fact that the accountant who goes abroad is prepared to submit to the consummate purgation. Because these global cities have been touted as the centres of the commercial world and full of great experience gathering opportunities and, as such, are perceived to be better than Dublin the 'seriously career minded' are prepared to make the journey. Whether or not one believes the mythology is unimportant one has conformed to it and made the commitment; one has put the icing on the cake. This is not to suggest that people who go abroad do not benefit from their experience, rather what is being argued is that technically having been overseas has little to offer and whether one has been to London, Calcutta or Kingston is of little technical importance.

Because of these socialisation procedures and the fact that the successful can be trusted labour process theories such as deskilling, professionalisation, flexible specialisation and so on are of little value when one seeks to understand accountancy (see Chapter 3). It may appear somewhat incongruous but as a labour process accountancy involves being trusted to make decisions; however, having stated that one is also supervised and rigorously controlled to ensure, initially at least, that this trust has not been misplaced. As Chapter 3 demonstrated to understand professional work two points must be borne in mind. As labour processes they are very often immune from deskilling because they demand unique responses in many cases, a fact which Johnson and others fail to account for. This, however, does not mean that the control of this work is left in the hands of the professional who carries it out nor does it mean that this professional is then free to act for the common good. It is to prevent such occurrences that the second aspect to professional work has emerged. As Chapter 4 highlighted accountants, and I would argue other professionals, are controlled through the use of a wide variety of carrots and sticks. These carrots and sticks are defined, and indeed redefined, to accommodate the requirements of the regime of accumulation of any particular epoch (see Chapter 6). Chapters 4, 5, and 6 argued that under the Flexible Accumulation regime the incentives and sanctions centre around the issue of, what I have called, commercialism.

So what does this analysis tell us about capitalism in the late twentieth century? It has been argued in this study that we have moved away from a Fordist to a Flexible regime of accumulation. The primary reason for this has been the declining rate of profitability that emerged as an effect of the capital–labour compromise under Fordism. Increasing the rate of profitability entailed the intensified segmentation of the labour market, a process which is based on ascriptive rather than technical factors. This intensification has given rise to an increasingly spatially dispersed, complex, yet economically concentrated system. This system is manipulated by trusted segments of the labour force. Accountants are one such segment and as such they have benefited from the shift in regimes.

However, neither this shift nor the role of accountants within it was predetermined. It is possible that capital could have responded differently to the crisis of profitability. On top of this, accountancy has altered its nature somewhat to take advantage of the move to Flexible Accumulation; one example of this is the rise of agency theory (see Chapter 1). Another, and more important, example is the changing ideology within accountancy. At the heart of this is the move towards commercialisation but it is also represented by other changes, for example innovation in services offered by the practices, the use of advertising, global expansion, creation of new products and so on. In essence it means giving the client what he or she requires in as many different areas as possible. Accountancy is now a fully fledged, profit orientated business. I would suggest it probably always has been, but today it has come out of the closet.

Accountancy is not the only profession to move down this road. Law is also fast heading this way. I would argue that there is now a clear fissure within the service class which is based around the issue of commercialisation. One segment is commercial whilst the other is, broadly speaking, bureaucratic and/or public service orientated. Naturally this crude segmentation is an approximation to the reality. This fragmentation of the service class is closely related to the Flexible Accumulation regime's intensified

segmentation of the labour market. With the renewed emphasis on profitability only those areas of the labour market which are directly profitable
have grown substantially. This meant destroying the strength of labour in
various market sectors and allowing the commercial service class segments
to grow; provided they could be trusted. Non-commercial service class
areas such as public sector employees did not expand as fast because they
were unprofitable and had a different ethos or ideology; these features pre-
vented them from being manipulated into becoming profitable as easily as
the commercialised sector. In short the non-commercial service class is
something of a dinosaur from the Fordist past that cannot be trusted to be
commercial.[1]

All of this implies that the disorganised and post-industrial schools are
wide of the mark. The professional or service class are not the dynamic
sector within society. Profitability still exists in Flexible Capitalism, a fact
which Lash and Urry accept. However, what is incorrect about their analysis is that they suggest that the service class has an agenda of its own, that
this agenda takes primacy over profitability and hence they argue that the
service class is dominant. Yet, somewhat incongruously, they also argue
that the service class is functional to the process of capital accumulation. I
have argued that what has actually occurred is evidence of the fact that the
issue of capital accumulation is dominant and that it is this which has
shaped the service class; so much so that it is the service class'
commercialised segment which has grown most rapidly in the recent past.
In contrast to this under Fordism the public sector–bureaucratic service
class experienced rapid growth which has now all but withered away.
Another feature of the inaccuracy of Lash and Urry's thesis is that when
they talk of the service class they talk of it largely in Fordist terms, i.e.
managers in large bureaucracies, educators, engineers, social workers, etc.
rather than in terms of the new growth areas such as accountants, lawyers,
bankers and so on. Thus although they explicitly state that the service class
is not homogeneous they never examine the differences; this is a pity as it
would have proved insightful.

On the other hand this work has sought to examine one element within
this divided service class and it has been argued that the issue of profitability and commercialisation has fashioned this element. This leads me to suggest that although Lash and Urry's Disorganised Capitalism thesis
describes Flexible Capitalism very well, it does not explain it. What does
explain Flexible Accumulation? As with all other regimes it can be
explained by the search for profitability. This search led to the weakening
of the working class, the division, or at least the intensified division, of the
service class, and the return of profitability levels reminiscent of the 1960s.

This regime unlike its predecessor is uncompromising and as a result it has polarised the class structure of certain advanced societies in a way not witnessed since World War II. The commercialised service class are one of the key beneficiaries within this new regime (see Chapter 1). To use a paradoxical phrase yet again, this regime is flexible in its search for profitability but rigid because this search is all it contemplates. Certain professions, particularly I would suggest accountancy, are aware of this and have sought to take advantage of it. Accountancy has exhibited greater flexibility in the past fifteen years than many other professions by adapting and changing in all sorts of ways. However, the profession has also been rigid: it changes only if the price is right. This pursuit and flexibility on behalf of the commercialised professions distinguishes them from other professions concerned with both profit and other things, for example education, the civil service, science and so forth. Capital and profit have shaped the service class, not vice versa. Because of the continued importance of profit within Flexible Accumulation the position of the post-industrialists is untenable.

Capital has thus hit back and regained some of the losses it suffered under the Fordist regime. It is in light of this process that the emergence of the commercialised professions and the splitting of the service class should be seen.[2] The two sections of the service class derive their growth and ideologies in different ways. The bureaucratic service class depends primarily either on the expansion of the state or on an expansion of the internal labour market (ILM) in a way somewhat akin to Edwards' bureaucratic organisation. As a result of this one would expect these people to favour some form of Fordist compromise and to value other things as well as profit. Lash and Urry to some extent have recognised this by acknowledging the fact that in those states where Fordism, in the broadest political and economic sense, was strongest, say Sweden and Germany, the process of disorganising is weakest. On the other hand, the commercialised service class depend upon the issue of profitability at every level within the organisation for their elevation. Thus only by being commercial can one prosper, both organisationally and individually. As a consequence of this these people are more individualistic and inclined to believe in the equity of the marketplace. Generally speaking these are the adherents to Thatcher's enterprise culture. Growth depends solely on profitability and on giving the client whatever he or she wants and can pay for. These issues are part of the more general polarisation of the class structure in the advanced world. As the film character Bob Roberts in the film of the same name, a right wing US Senator, rather simplistically says, 'The times they are a changing back'.

Appendix 1: Scripts for Semi-Structured Interviews with Accountants

INTERVIEWS WITH YOUNG ACCOUNTANTS WITHIN PRACTICE AND INDUSTRY

Education

Are you a graduate/non-graduate? Ever considered going to college? Is there any noticeable difference in the way graduates and non-graduates are treated? Are they taught the exact same things within the same depts? Are they trained together? With the increase in MBA students in accountancy over the years is there a difference in how MBAs are trained and everybody else? When finished on average what type of work do MBA students perform? Why? Are there any differences in the speed with which promotion is gained among non-grads, grads, and MBAs?

Training

Are there any differences in the training systems of small, medium, and large firms? Are there significant differences in the quality of training between medium and BigEight firms? What are the advantages and disadvantages of a Big Eight training? What are the advantages and disadvantages of training in a medium practice? Does a person become specialised in one dept, e.g. auditing as opposed to gaining an overall ability? How is one judged within practice and can a trainee be let go if they are deemed unsuitable?

Polarisation

Is it fair to say that the bulk of graduates and, thus better quality staff, go to the Big Eight firms? Is it possible for medium sized firms to take large clients from the Big Eight? Why/Why not? What client advantages can a Big Eight firm offer? What advantages can a small or medium practice offer their clients? Do these three groups of practices – small, medium, and Big Eight – compete in the same markets?

With recent mergers and potential mergers if the Big Eight become the Big Five can the medium practices ever close the gap? If not can they maintain their present size? Why/Why not? What effect will these mergers have on the profession here? Because there are fewer large firms competing for graduates will the cost of labour be affected? Will these fewer firms require less staff? In terms of competition are these mergers good for the profession as a whole or clients? For you personally and other accountants will it in any way affect your future career prospects?

Career Paths

Practice
There appears to be three career paths for accountants – practice, industry, and emigration – which one do you think you will choose? Why? There appears to be

a general feeling that it takes too much time and effort to become a partner in a Big Eight firm, is this the case? Why/Why not? Are there any great differences in being a partner in a Big Eight as opposed to a non-Big Eight practice? With the Big Eight becoming the Big Five won't promotion to partnership become even more difficult? Will this lead to tension within the firm or at least to mobility out of the Big Eight by quality staff? Are there differences in the mobility rates of practice/industry.

Industry
What are the differences between work in industry and practice? Which is the more challenging and varied? In industry do you receive more or less autonomy? Is rapid promotion easier in industry? Is it easier for Big Eight staff to enter industry? Does your training in practice equip you for industry? Do you feel the Big Eight and non-Big Eight staff will perform differently in industry? Which do you think will be better? Very briefly, why would you or why would you not go into industry?

Emigration
Why, with a shortage of accountants in Ireland, do 20 per cent emigrate every year? Although the money is an important factor in emigration the other main reason appears to be the prestige to be gained from working abroad is this true? Why can this status not be gained here? Do you think having this work on your CV would be an important factor in terms of promotion if an accountant returned to Ireland? Is it easier for Big Eight staff to find work overseas? Are the Big Eight better equipped for the work overseas? Is the work overseas very different technically from here?

In terms of status work is all work performed abroad viewed as high status or is it only work performed in particular countries or cities? For instance is work done in the Bahamas as prestigious as work done in London? Why would you or would you not emigrate? Will Irish accountants continue to emigrate? Will this be affected by recent mergers?

Setting Up Your Own Practice

Will you set up your own practice? Is it harder for Big Eight staff to set up their own practice seeing as they deal mainly with large firms and it is unlikely that they would develop the personal contacts to take these away from the Big Eight? How difficult is it now to establish a successful practice? Is it easier or harder than before? Will the number of practices in the foreseeable future increase or decrease?

Work Processes

How do you spend your average day? What technical skills do you need to be an accountant? What are the skill differences in auditing, IT, management consultancy, etc.? How did your time in college prepare you for practice? Are the courses good at teaching the technical skills of the job? How computer literate do you feel you are? Where did you learn to use computers? Do you think computers will ever be an important part of your job?

SCRIPT FOR THE INTERVIEWING OF BIG SIX PARTNERS

Biographical

Have you ever worked in industry? Which do you feel would provide the most interesting and challenging employment – practice or industry? Why? Will you stay in practice?

Did you attend university? What degree did you do? Did what you learn in your degree have any relevance to the work of an accountant? Do you think being a graduate is a major benefit to an accountant?

What qualities do you feel were of decisive importance in your promotion to partner? Do you think all partners should exhibit these traits?

If your son or daughter was an accountant where would you advise him or her to work, both in terms of the specialisms within the profession and in terms of place, i.e. London, Dublin, New York, etc.? Why would you give such advice? Would you encourage them to leave practice?

Strategy and Structure Within the Big Six

In the next ten years will the Big Six be

(1)   Multi-discipline,
(2)   Limited companies,
(3)   Have increased hierarchical levels within them, i.e. more ranks between say manager and partner? ·

Do you feel the recent merger boom within accountancy was a good or a bad thing from the viewpoint of a non-accountant? Will these mergers increase or are they going to tail off? Why did these mergers take place, how important were reasons such as geographical coverage increased economic power, '1992', a general sense of 'merger-mania'? Within what was previously the Big Eight who initiated them? How important a factor is the level of concentration within other sectors of the economy as regards forcing practices towards concentration?

With the increased international nature of business do the Big Six encourage their best people to spend some time abroad? Is a period abroad seen as an advantage by firms in other areas of the economy? Do many foreign accountants come to Ireland? Why/Why not? Where are the best places to go as regards gaining experience? In your experience what type of accountant goes abroad? Did you yourself spend some time away?

Staffing Issues

In my survey 70 per cent of degree holders felt that their degree was important to their getting employment with the Big Six, yet they found that it was of little use to them in accountancy, so why have the Big Six moved towards recruiting graduates? What are the important differences that exist between graduates and non-graduates? Which group are better?

With the increased importance of experience related areas within accountancy such as management consultancy, information technology, etc. what plans do you have to hold on to more staff or are your present retention rates high enough?

Does it make an important difference to your career been trained in a Big Six firm? Are these differences justified?

It has been suggested to me that a Big Six training is quite narrow and special-ised, concentrating upon auditing, as such it is deemed to be mundane. Would you accept this criticism? Is it true to say that the best place to get an accountancy train-ing is in a medium practice? Will a computer programmer ever replace an account-ant on a computer audit?

Control

How is promotion decided upon? Are budgets the overriding criterion upon which the decision is made?

Do you keep detailed files upon all staff? What would be disastrous for an employee in terms of their future with the firm? How is such an employee eased out of the practice? Why do firms use individual salary scales and assessments?

How are managers distinguished from one another when deciding who is and who is not partnership material? Generally speaking what traits are looked for in a partner? Do all partners have an equal say in the decision? Does the decision have to be unanimous or is it a simple majority decision? Do people have to buy into the partnership? Roughly what type of figure is required? Will the partnership provide loan facilities?

Is there any way a partner can be 'sacked'? What would provide the circum-stances for doing this? How is the decision reached?

What is a partner's job? Is it fair to say that the manager runs the practice day to day and the partner formulates policy? Is the partner's job mainly to seek new clients? Is it getting harder to become a partner?

How is the Irish section of a Big Six practice influenced by the larger firm? Can the international firm impose things upon the Irish branch that the Irish partners do not want? Does the policy of the international firm have to be ratified by the Irish branch through voting? Is the Irish firm autonomous to a large degree?

Is accountancy moving towards a business internationally and away from a 'pro-fession'? If so what dangers and benefits are there in this for Irish accountancy?

Why are accountancy services not traded internationally in the same way as, say, cars are? What accountancy services are traded internationally? Does Irish account-ancy sell these abroad and can it compete with a place like London? Are there any services that a Dublin Big Six practice needs to buy from an international affiliate more than two or three times a year? Where are these services bought? If one was emigrating would it make most sense to go to such a place?

Appendix 2: Questionnaire for Irish Based Accountants

Dept of Sociology,
Arts Building,
Trinity College,
Dublin 2

Dear

This is a questionnaire about accountants. It has the support of the Institute of Chartered Accountants in Ireland (ICAI) and it is from the ICAI that I received your name. This survey questionnaire is part of a research project that I am working on as part of my Ph.D studies at Trinity College; as such I would be very grateful for its completion and return for purely selfish reasons.

However, there are also less personal motives involved. Accountants are a largely ignored group and at times a very misunderstood profession. It would be beneficial to have some knowledge of the profession due to its important place within industry and also within the increasing vital financial services sector. I hope that my research will throw some light on a number of issues including how the profession has become international, how this has influenced Irish accountants, why accountants emigrate and what the role of accountants is and will be in the future within Irish industry.

The questionnaire covers areas such as educational background, training, emigration, career aspirations, etc. and it will try to trace levels of satisfaction or dissatisfaction within the profession. I would greatly appreciate a prompt return of the questionnaire via the free post mechanism as I wish to give a preliminary summary to the ICAI.

There will be instructions throughout the text, in most instances, please tick the appropriate box. Needless to say all information will be treated as confidential and the questionnaires will only be viewed by myself, the information will only take the form of aggregate numbers. All confidentiality will, therefore, be respected.

Throughout the questionnaire some phrases are used that may need some clarification. These two phrases are 'industry', by which is meant all jobs that are non-practice, and the 'Big Eight', by which is meant the largest international accountancy firms. These eight international firms have actually decreased in number to six and this number may decrease again but for the sake of simplicity I will stick to what is most familiar. A medium practice is one where the practice has five or more partners and a small practice is one where there are less than five partners. I would like to thank you for your time and cooperation and I would like to inform you that some of the results of the survey should be published in the ICAI's newsletter.

Yours sincerely,
Gerard Hanlon

This section of the questionnaire asks for some straight-forward biographical detail. In most instances please answer the question by ticking the appropriate box.

Biographical Data
(1.1)   Name _____
                      (Please Write In)

(1.2)   Age   ☐☐

(1.3)   Gender
Male   1 ☐
Female   2 ☐

(1.4)   Educational Level
Non-Degree Level   1 ☐
Degree Holder   2 ☐
Post-Graduate Degree Holder   3 ☐

(1.5)   **This question is divided into two groups, practice and industry. What is meant by industry in this questionnaire is really non-practice, thus it includes areas such as the financial services sector. Please tick the appropriate box.**
What size organization are you currently working in and within which area?

Practice:
Big Eight   1 ☐
Medium (5 or more partners)   2 ☐
Small (under 5 partners)   3 ☐

Industry:
Large Organisation (100+ employees)   4 ☐
Medium Organisation (30–100 employees)   5 ☐
Small Organisations (under 30 employees)   6 ☐

(1.6)   What is your present position at work, e.g. financial controller, partner, etc.
_____
                      (Please Write In)

Training
This section will cover areas of your training as an accountant and it is designed to highlight similarities and dissimilarities between practices of various types. There are also some questions relating to the way third level education helps in the training process of accountants.

  In many instances the questions are divided up into practices based on size. These sizes are derived in the same way as those in the section above. For those of you who have trained with a practice that subsequently merged with a 'Big

Eight' firm would you please, for the purposes of this questionnaire, use the category reserved for 'Big Eight' employees.

(2.1)   Were/Are you trained in a

'Big Eight' practice   1 ☐

Medium practice   2 ☐

Small practice?   3 ☐

(2.2)   Would you describe your training as being or having been

Too General   1 ☐

General   2 ☐

Specialised   3 ☐

Too Specialised   4 ☐

Don't Know?   5 ☐

(2.3)   Which practices do you feel give the best training? **Please tick *one* box**

'Big Eight' practice   1 ☐

Medium practice   2 ☐

Small practice   3 ☐

No Difference   4 ☐

(2.4)   **If answered yes to the above question please answer this next question, if not then please go on to question (2.6). This next series of questions are on how your university education helped you at accountancy.**
How important was your university education in helping you to gain your first post in accountancy?

Very Important   1 ☐

Important   2 ☐

Of Some Importance   3 ☐

Not Important   4 ☐

Irrelevant   5 ☐

(2.5)   Are you able to use most of what university taught you in your current position?

Yes   1 ☐

No   2 ☐

(2.6)   In which subject area was your degree?

Business Studies/Commerce   1 ☐

Science   2 ☐

Social Sciences, e.g. economics, politics   3 ☐

Arts   4 ☐

Medicine/Dentistry   5 ☐

Engineering   6 ☐

(2.7)   This question is for people who have a university education *and* are working in a different organisation to the one they trained with. All other respondents please go on to the next question.

In your opinion was your university education an important factor in your successful application for the position you now occupy?

Very Important   1 ☐

Important   2 ☐

Of Some Importance   3 ☐

Not Important   4 ☐

Irrelevant   5 ☐

Emigration

The next section is concerned with emigration. It applies to all respondents as I am trying to discover what you perceive to be the advantages or disadvantages of emigrating and your reasons for these beliefs.

(3.1)   Will you take up a job abroad in the next two years?

Yes   1 ☐

Seriously Considering It   2 ☐

A Possibility   3 ☐

No   4 ☐

(3.2)   What steps have you taken as regards emigration? Please tick all the appropriate boxes.

Enquired at foreign embassies   1 ☐

Contacted foreign employers   2 ☐

Applied for work abroad   3 ☐

Contacted friends abroad about employment
there   4 ☐

Made enquiries about an intra-firm transfer   5 ☐

Other   6 ☐

None   7 ☐

(3.3)   The following is a five point scale ranging from yes to no, it concerns a list of destinations where people may head to if they are emigrating for work related reasons, please tick the appropriate box for *each* destination.

Theoretically, if you were ever to emigrate where would you consider going?

	Yes	Likely	Possibly	Unlikely	No
London	☐	☐	☐	☐	☐
Rest of UK	☐	☐	☐	☐	☐

Brussels/Paris/Frankfurt	☐	☐	☐	☐	☐
Other EC	☐	☐	☐	☐	☐
New York/LA/Chicago	☐	☐	☐	☐	☐
Other USA	☐	☐	☐	☐	☐
Canada	☐	☐	☐	☐	☐
Melbourne/Sydney	☐	☐	☐	☐	☐
Other Australia	☐	☐	☐	☐	☐
Caribbean	☐	☐	☐	☐	☐
Middle East	☐	☐	☐	☐	☐
Hong Kong/Tokyo	☐	☐	☐	☐	☐

(3.4) If you were to emigrate for what reasons do you feel you would do so? **(Please rank in order of importance from 1 to 5 where 1 is the most important).**

Personal	1	☐
Better Pay	2	☐
Favourable	3	☐
Better Promotion Prospects	4	☐
Good, long term career move	5	☐

(3.5) As regards your career in Ireland is a period abroad seen by employers as

Very Good	1	☐
Good	2	☐
No Effect	3	☐
Bad	4	☐
Very Bad	5	☐
Don't Know	6	☐

(3.6) Which organisations are most favourable in their attitude towards returned emigrants? **Please tick one *only*.**

The 'Big Eight'	1	☐
Large Private Companies	2	☐
Medium Practices	3	☐
Medium Companies	4	☐
Small Practices	5	☐
Small Companies	6	☐
State/semi-state bodies	7	☐
No Difference	8	☐
Don't Know	9	☐

(3.7) The following are a list of specialisms within accountancy and a list of places where each is practised, please tick which place would generally give an accountant the most beneficial experience in the various specialisms. Please tick one box per line.

	London	Dublin	Cayman Islands	Holland	No Difference
Auditing	☐	☐	☐	☐	☐
General Practice	☐	☐	☐	☐	☐
Information Technology	☐	☐	☐	☐	☐
Management Consultancy	☐	☐	☐	☐	☐
National and International Tax	☐	☐	☐	☐	☐

(3.8) In general which of the following is the most prestigious place to have worked when presenting a CV?

London   1 ☐
Dublin   2 ☐
Cayman Islands 3 ☐
Luxembourg   4 ☐
No Difference 5 ☐

(3.9) For people who have recently qualified, and wish to emigrate to a job that is of comparable standing to the one they have, which sized practice gives the best experience to facilitate this move?

'Big Eight'   1 ☐
Medium Practice 2 ☐
Small Practice 3 ☐

Industry
This section is again aimed at all respondents. It is concerned with working as an accountant in industry, however, as stated previously, by industry what is really meant is non-practice, thus it also includes areas such as the financial services sector.
(4.1)   **This question is for those who are currently in practice, all others please go on to the next question.**
Will you leave practice?

Definitely Yes   1 ☐
A Strong Possibility 2 ☐
Maybe/Maybe Not   3 ☐
A Slight Possibility 4 ☐
Definitely No   5 ☐

(4.2) **This question is for all respondents.**
The following is a list of items upon which a general work environment may be judged. I would like you to compare industry to practice on this scale, please do so by ticking *one* box *per* line.

Industry is	much better than practice	better	same	worse	much worse than practice
Salary	☐	☐	☐	☐	☐
Perks	☐	☐	☐	☐	☐
Promotion Chances	☐	☐	☐	☐	☐
Interesting Work	☐	☐	☐	☐	☐
Work Colleagues	☐	☐	☐	☐	☐

(4.3) Which provides the most interesting and challenging work?

Practice 1☐
Industry 2☐
No Difference 3☐
Neither 4☐
Don't Know 5☐

(4.4) Does it help to have emigrated for a while if one wants to join industry?

Yes in all cases 1☐
No in all cases 2☐
Only if the firm you want to join is large 3☐
Only if the firm you want to join is small 4☐
Don't Know 5☐

(4.5) Does having third level education give you an advantage when wanting to join industry?

Yes 1☐
No 2☐
Don't Know 3☐

(4.6) **If you have answered No to the question above please go on to the next question (4.7), otherwise please answer this question. Please tick one box only.**
In what way does a third level education benefit you?

Makes you technically a better accountant 1☐
Gives you better management capabilities 2☐
Gives you a more social contacts in industry 3☐
Gives you a more rounded education which is a big benefit in industry 4☐
Other (please specify) 5☐

(4.7)   All respondents please answer this question.
Which group finds it easier to join industry?

'Big Eight'	1 ☐
Medium	2 ☐
Small	3 ☐
No Difference	4 ☐
Don't Know	5 ☐

(4.8)   Which group is actually better equipped to join industry?

'Big Eight'	1 ☐
Medium	2 ☐
Small	3 ☐
No Difference	4 ☐
Don't Know	5 ☐

Practice
This section refers to work in practice and it would be appreciated if all respondents would answer the relevant questions.
(5.1)   Is it too hard to become a partner in an existing practice?

Yes	1 ☐
No	2 ☐
No harder than previously	3 ☐

(5.2)   Which practices are harder to become a partner in?

'Big Eight'	1 ☐
Medium	2 ☐
Small	3 ☐
No Difference	4 ☐
Don' Know	5 ☐

(5.3)   Temporary emigration significantly helps one to gain promotion in practice.
Please tick the appropriate box to indicate your view on this statement.

Strongly Agree	1 ☐
Agree	2 ☐
No Difference	3 ☐
Disagree	4 ☐
Strongly Disagree	5 ☐

(5.4)   Third level education is an important factor in deciding who gets promotion within practices. Please tick the appropriate response.

Strongly Disagree	1	☐
Disagree	2	☐
No Difference	3	☐
Agree	4	☐
Strongly Agree	5	☐
Don't Know	6	☐

Own Practice
This section deals with the pros and cons of setting up one's own practice.
(6.1)   Will you set up your own practice?

Yes	1	☐
No	2	☐

(6.2)   Is it better to set up a general practice or a specialised practice (say for example as simply an auditor or a management consultant)?

General	1	☐
Specialised	2	☐
No Difference	3	☐

Miscellaneous
This final section covers a variety of areas. Once again this section is to be filled out by everyone and I would like to take this opportunity to thank you for your help, it is much appreciated.
(7.1)   The following is a list of items that make a job attractive. How would you rank these in terms of importance when looking for a future job (number within the boxes from 1 through to 7 where 1 is the most important)?

Technically Demanding Work	1	☐
Secure Employment	2	☐
Good Promotion Prospects	3	☐
Good Salary	4	☐
Good Fellow Workers	5	☐
High Responsibility	6	☐
Job Satisfaction	7	☐

(7.2)   **This question and the next are concerned with your general background.**
At what stage did your father complete his education?

Primary	1	☐
Inter Cert.	2	☐

Leaving Cert.   3 ☐
University   4 ☐

(7.3)   What was your father's occupation?

(Please Write In)

Once again I would like to thank you for your cooperation and I want to reassure you that all of this data will be treated confidentially,

Gerard Hanlon

Appendix 3: Questionnaire for Migrant Sample

Dept of Sociology,
Arts Building,
Trinity College,
Dublin 2

Dear

This is a questionnaire about accountants. It has the support of the Institute of Chartered Accountants in Ireland (ICAI) and it is from the ICAI that I received your name. This survey questionnaire is part of a research project that I am working on as part of my Ph.D studies at Trinity College; as such I would be very grateful for its completion and return for purely selfish reasons.

However, there are also less personal motives involved. Accountants are a largely ignored group and at times a very misunderstood profession. It would be beneficial to have some knowledge of the profession due to its important place within industry and also within the increasing vital financial services sector. I hope that my research will throw some light on a number of issues including how the profession has become international, how this has influenced Irish accountants, why accountants emigrate and what the role of accountants is and will be in the future within Irish industry.

The questionnaire covers areas such as educational background, training, emigration, career aspirations, etc. and it will try to trace levels of satisfaction or dissatisfaction within the profession. I would greatly appreciate a prompt return of the questionnaire via the free post mechanism as I wish to give a preliminary summary to the ICAI.

There will be instructions throughout the text, in most instances, please tick the appropriate box. Needless to say all information will be treated as confidential and the questionnaires will only be viewed by myself, the information will only take the form of aggregate numbers. All confidentiality will, therefore, be respected.

Throughout the questionnaire some phrases are used that may need some clarification. These two phrases are 'industry', by which is meant all jobs that are non-practice, and the 'Big Eight', by which is meant the largest international accountancy firms. These eight international firms have actually decreased in number to six and this number may decrease again but for the sake of simplicity I will stick to what is most familiar. A medium practice is one where the practice has five or more partners and a small practice is one where there are less than five partners. I would like to thank you for your time and cooperation and I would like to inform you that some of the results of the survey should be published in the ICAI's newsletter.

Yours sincerely,
Gerard Hanlon

This section of the questionnaire asks for some straight-forward biographical detail. In most instances please answer the question by ticking the appropriate box.

Biographical Data
(1.1)   Name _____
                              (Please Write In)

(1.2)   Age   ☐☐

(1.3)   Gender
Male   1 ☐
Female   2 ☐

(1.4)   Educational Level
Non-Degree Level   1 ☐
Degree Holder   2 ☐
Post-Graduate Degree Holder   3 ☐

(1.5)   **This question is divided into two groups, practice and industry. What is meant by industry in this questionnaire is really non-practice, thus it includes areas such as the financial services sector. Please tick the appropriate box.**
What size organization are you currently working in and within which area?

Practice:
Big Eight   1 ☐
Medium (5 or more partners)   2 ☐
Small (under 5 partners)   3 ☐
Industry:
Large Organisation (100+ employees)   4 ☐
Medium Organisation (30–100 employees)   5 ☐
Small Organisations (under 30 employees)   6 ☐

(1.6)   What is your present position at work, e.g. financial controller, partner, etc.
_____
                              (Please Write In)

Training
This section will cover areas of your training as an accountant and it is designed to highlight similarities and dissimilarities between practices of various types. There are also some questions relating to the way third level education helps in the training process of accountants.

In many instances the questions are divided up into practices based on size. These sizes are derived in the same way as those in the section above. For those of you who have trained with a practice that subsequently merged with a 'Big

Eight' firm would you please, for the purposes of this questionnaire, use the category reserved for 'Big Eight' employees.

(2.1)   Were/Are you trained in a

'Big Eight' practice	1 ☐
Medium practice	2 ☐
Small practice?	3 ☐

(2.2)   Would you describe your training as being or having been

Too General	1 ☐
General	2 ☐
Specialised	3 ☐
Too Specialised	4 ☐
Don't Know?	5 ☐

(2.3)   Which practices do you feel give the best training? **Please tick *one* box**

'Big Eight' practice	1 ☐
Medium practice	2 ☐
Small practice	3 ☐
No Difference	4 ☐

(2.4)   **If answered yes to the above question please answer this next question, if not then please go on to question (2.6). This next series of questions are on how your university education helped you at accountancy.**

How important was your university education in helping you to gain your first post in accountancy?

Very Important	1 ☐
Important	2 ☐
Of Some Importance	3 ☐
Not Important	4 ☐
Irrelevant	5 ☐

(2.5)   Are you able to use most of what university taught you in your current position?

Yes	1 ☐
No	2 ☐

(2.6)   In which subject area was your degree?

Business Studies/Commerce	1 ☐
Science	2 ☐
Social Sciences, e.g. economics, politics	3 ☐
Arts	4 ☐

Medicine/Dentistry   5 ☐
Engineering   6 ☐

(2.7) **This question is for people who have a university education *and* are working in a different organisation to the one they trained with. All other respondents please go on to the next question.**
In your opinion was your university education an important factor in your successful application for the position you now occupy?

Very Important   1 ☐
Important   2 ☐
Of Some Importance   3 ☐
Not Important   4 ☐
Irrelevant   5 ☐

Emigration
The next section is concerned with emigration. It applies to all respondents as I am trying to discover what you perceive to be the advantages or disadvantages of emigrating and your reasons for these beliefs.
(3.1) Why did you emigrate? **If more than one reason please number in order of importance.**

Better Renumeration   1 ☐
Better Experience   2 ☐
Better Promotion Chances   3 ☐
Personal Reasons   4 ☐
None of the Above   5 ☐

(3.2) Will you return to Ireland?
Yes   1 ☐
Possibly   2 ☐
No   3 ☐

(3.3) 'Working abroad allows people greater career mobility in terms of promotion if one decides to return to Ireland.' Please indicate how you feel about this statement.

Strongly Agree   1 ☐
Agree   2 ☐
No Difference   3 ☐
Disagree   4 ☐
Strongly Disagree   5 ☐

(3.4) Which organisations in Ireland are most favourable in their attitude towards returned emigrants? **Please tick *one* box.**

The 'Big Eight'	1 ☐
Large Companies	2 ☐
Medium Practices	3 ☐
Medium Companies	4 ☐
Small Practices	5 ☐
Small Companies	6 ☐

(3.5) Which of following areas is the best as regards gaining valuable experience for future use here in Ireland with a large organisation? **Please rank in order of importance where 1 the most important.**

UK	1 ☐
USA	2 ☐
Ireland	3 ☐
Continental Europe	4 ☐
Caribbean	5 ☐
Australia	6 ☐

(3.6) The following are a list of specialisms within accountancy and a list of places where each is practised, please tick which place would generally give an accountant the most beneficial experience in the various specialisms. Please tick one box per line.

	London	Dublin	Cayman Islands	Holland	No Difference
Auditing	☐	☐	☐	☐	☐
General Practice	☐	☐	☐	☐	☐
Information Technology	☐	☐	☐	☐	☐
Management Consultancy	☐	☐	☐	☐	☐
National and International Tax	☐	☐	☐	☐	☐

(3.7) What are the greatest work advantages that a young accountant could gain from emigrating as opposed to an accountant who stayed in Ireland? **Please tick *one* box.**

Financial Rewards	1 ☐
Learn a Foreign Language	2 ☐
They would have worked in a different culture	3 ☐
They would have seen a larger business scale	4 ☐

They would have worked in areas
not available in Ireland 5☐

They would have gained higher quality
experience abroad 6☐

Just working abroad is prestigious 7☐

There are no advantages that
could not be gained in Ireland 8☐

(3.8) If you were to return to Ireland do you feel your time abroad would increase your likelihood of promotion?

Yes 1☐

No 2☐

Don't know 3☐

(3.9) Would you recommend emigration, temporary or otherwise, to a young Irish accountant?

Yes 1☐

No 2☐

(3.10) **This question applies only to those who feel that they *will not or may not* return to Ireland. All others please go to the next section.**

Why will you not return to Ireland? **If more than one answer please rank all appropriate answers where 1 is the most important.**

Lack of employment opportunities
in my field in Ireland 1☐

Financial incentives too great abroad 2☐

Current or potential position very
good in present place 3☐

Working in Ireland would not be as challenging 4☐

Personal Reasons 5☐

None of the above 6☐

Industry
This section is again aimed at all respondents. It is concerned with working as an accountant in industry, however, as stated previously, by industry what is really meant is non-practice, thus it also includes areas such as the financial services sector.

(4.1) **This question is for those who are currently in practice, all others please go on to the next question.**
Will you leave practice?

Definitely Yes 1☐

A Strong Possibility 2☐

Maybe/Maybe Not 3☐

A Slight Possibility	4 ☐
Definitely No	5 ☐

(4.2) This question is for all respondents.
The following is a list of items upon which a general work environment may be judged. I would like you to compare industry to practice on this scale, please do so by ticking *one* box *per* line.

Industry is	much better than practice	better	same	worse	much worse than practice
Salary	☐	☐	☐	☐	☐
Perks	☐	☐	☐	☐	☐
Promotion Chances	☐	☐	☐	☐	☐
Interesting Work	☐	☐	☐	☐	☐
Work Colleagues	☐	☐	☐	☐	☐

(4.3) Which provides the most interesting and challenging work?

Practice	1 ☐
Industry	2 ☐
No Difference	3 ☐
Neither	4 ☐
Don't Know	5 ☐

(4.4) Does it help to have emigrated for a while if one wants to join industry?

Yes in all cases	1 ☐
No in all cases	2 ☐
Only if the firm you want to join is large	3 ☐
Only if the firm you want to join is small	4 ☐
Don't Know	5 ☐

(4.5) Does having third level education give you an advantage when wanting to join industry?

Yes	1 ☐
No	2 ☐
Don't Know	3 ☐

(4.6) If you have answered *No* to the question above please go on to the next question (4.7), otherwise please answer this question. Please tick *one* box only.
In what way does a third level education benefit you?

Makes you technically a better accountant	1 ☐
Gives you better management capabilities	2 ☐
Gives you a more social contacts in industry	3 ☐

Gives you a more rounded education
which is a big benefit in industry   4 ☐
Other (please specify)   5 ☐

(4.7)   All respondents please answer this question.
Which group finds it easier to join industry?

'Big Eight'   1 ☐
Medium   2 ☐
Small   3 ☐
No Difference   4 ☐
Don't Know   5 ☐

(4.8)   Which group is actually better equipped to join industry?

'Big Eight'   1 ☐
Medium   2 ☐
Small   3 ☐
No Difference   4 ☐
Don't Know   5 ☐

Practice
This section refers to work in practice and it would be appreciated if all respondents would answer the relevant questions.
(5.1)   Is it too hard to become a partner in an existing practice?

Yes   1 ☐
No   2 ☐
No harder than previously   3 ☐

(5.2)   Which practices are harder to become a partner in?

'Big Eight'   1 ☐
Medium   2 ☐
Small   3 ☐
No Difference   4 ☐
Don' Know   5 ☐

(5.3)   Temporary emigration significantly helps one to gain promotion in practice.
Please tick the appropriate box to indicate your view on this statement.

Strongly Agree   1 ☐
Agree   2 ☐
No Difference   3 ☐
Disagree   4 ☐
Strongly Disagree   5 ☐

(5.4) Third level education is an important factor in deciding who gets promotion within practices. Please tick the appropriate response.

Strongly Disagree	1	☐
Disagree	2	☐
No Difference	3	☐
Agree	4	☐
Strongly Agree	5	☐
Don't Know	6	☐

Own Practice
This section deals with the pros and cons of setting up one's own practice.
(6.1) Will you set up your own practice?

Yes	1	☐
No	2	☐

(6.2) Is it better to set up a general practice or a specialised practice (say for example as simply an auditor or a management consultant)?

General	1	☐
Specialised	2	☐
No Difference	3	☐

Miscellaneous
This final section covers a variety of areas. Once again this section is to be filled out by everyone and I would like to take this opportunity to thank you for your help, it is much appreciated.
(7.1) The following is a list of items that make a job attractive. How would you rank these in terms of importance when looking for a future job (number within the boxes from 1 through to 7 where 1 is the most important)?

Technically Demanding Work	1	☐
Secure Employment	2	☐
Good Promotion Prospects	3	☐
Good Salary	4	☐
Good Fellow Workers	5	☐
High Responsibility	6	☐
Job Satisfaction	7	☐

(7.2) **This question and the next are concerned with your general background.**
At what stage did your father complete his education?

Primary	1	☐
Inter Cert.	2	☐
Leaving Cert.	3	☐
University	4	☐

(7.3)   What was your father's occupation?

_____

(Please Write In)

Once again I would like to thank you for your cooperation and I want to reassure you that all of this data will be treated confidentially,

Gerard Hanlon

Notes and References

1 The Post-industrial Mirage

1. A global city is a city such as London, i.e. it has large scale corporate, political, financial and cultural resources.
2. The audit entails the examination of a company's accounts by an 'independent' accountant or firm of accountants in order to ensure that these accounts give a 'true and fair' picture of the firm's finances to shareholders, the state and other interested parties (see Chapter 3 for a more detailed look at the audit).
3. For a further discussion of the form of work organisation flexible specialisation entails see Chapter 3 or Piore and Sabel (1984).
4. Although again this figure is quite low by international standards, the rate for the EC is 28 per cent (Commission of the European Communities, 1989: Table 60).
5. Sales workers have been included despite the fact that 20 per cent of this group are auctioneers, insurance sales personnel, etc. and security workers have been included despite incorporating the police because the vast bulk of the increase in this latter category is accounted for by private personnel.
6. The relevance of Bell's ideas on the quality of work in 'post-industrial' occupations is examined in Chapter 3.
7. Northern Ireland was considered as part of Ireland as the chartered accountancy body the Institute of Chartered Accountants in Ireland (ICAI) is an all-Ireland body.

2 The Formation of a Polarised Profession

1. This move to London was mirrored in the USA by the dominance of New York and to a lesser extent Chicago (Richards, 1981; Stevens, 1984).
2. In contrast the German system was based on maintaining secrecy and on hiding reserves (a feature outlawed in the UK in the 1920s) whilst in Sweden the Company Act 1944 put the emphasis on protecting the company from its shareholders and in certain instances reducing their dividends in order to ensure adequate growth and stability; this was in direct opposition to the Anglo–American experience (see Gallhofer and Haslam, 1991; Jönsson, 1991).
3. Chapter 6 examines the role that accountants and accountancy firms play in the extraction, realisation and allocation of surplus value.
4. This feature is of great importance today in all large organisations. It is also one that has been implicated as possibly the major advantage accountants, in the Anglo–American world, have over other professions within management. This is because it gives them greater ability to control the labour process, one of the fundamental necessities behind management (see Hopper and Armstrong, 1991).

5.   Likewise, in Sweden engineers organised cost accounting within organisations. When cost accounting was evolving in Sweden during the 1920s and 1930s there was a power struggle on the committee established to oversee its development. This struggle centred upon whether or not costing should be standardised or left to specific and contextual evaluation procedures. The advocates of this latter position wanted to adapt the costing mechanisms used in their US subsidiary and as such they explicitly did not want cost accounting to become dominated by engineers. The former position was adopted by committee members who were also engineers with a heavy manufacturing firm ASEA. They advocated the adoption of standard costs across the board based upon the actual product rather than the context as they argued it was more applicable to the Swedish economy. In the end it was the engineers who won the day and they dominated cost accounting, and internal management, for the next 50 years (Jönsson, 1991: 532–6).

6.   This was also a reflection of the fact that in the preceding two decades accountants had established a virtual monopoly on the audit anyway.

3   Accountancy as an Elite Labour Process within Flexible Accumulation

1.   Unless the audit is outside Dublin or another regional centre, in which case they will keep in contact by phone every day or second day depending on the manager.

2.   This is only done on the more complex computer systems as all young Big Six accountants are now relatively conversant with information technology.

3.   If that judgment is incorrect the partners' personal assets are liable!

4.   Of which accountants themselves form a very major part.

5.   As we shall see in Chapter 4 the idea of being 'professional' has undergone a change within accountancy.

6.   See McGovern (1992) for a description of a similar system with Irish engineering and pharmaceutical firms.

7.   The same danger exists for small firms sub-contracting to the Big Six (see John Peters quote on p. 96).

8.   This latter figure may decline somewhat in the future as the Big Six consolidate their position through organic growth rather than the incorporation of smaller practices and thus small firm accountants.

4   Flexible Accumulation and the Emergence of the 'Commercialised Professional'

1.   Added to the above conflict is the fact that at present 50 per cent of Irish accountants work within industry and are hence directly concerned with profitability and commercialism as opposed to the 'public interest'.

2.   This point is a little weak as one can think of many groups that spend time studying by themselves but do not become preoccupied with their own self-interest, for example Buddhists.

3. Admittedly, promotion to a partnership level has become increasingly difficult but nevertheless it is an attraction.
4. One may buy a greater amount if one has the resources and the partnership permits you to but this appears to be unusual.
5. See Stewart *et al.* (1980) for an account of the high rate of mobility into the traditional service class within organisations.
6. This may also go on in specialised areas within accountancy but it is not the case in auditing.
7. The use of these informal networks appears to be paralleled in the chemical and electronic industries (McGovern, 1992).
8. On the basis of McGovern's work engineers and chemists would appear to lie somewhere in between.
9. Given the fact that many accountants go on to hold elite business positions, for example 15.2 per cent of the sample stated that they themselves were company directors, it is reasonable to assume that many of the sample whose fathers were also accountants were marked down as directors, etc. so that the total whose fathers were accountants could actually be increased.

5 Accountancy and the International Division of Labour

1. Although Corcoran *et al.* (1992) have suggested that Ireland's employment structure is now quite similar to that of Britain and the USA.
2. Lynn (1968) also suggests that young professional migration was occurring in the relatively successful 1960s.
3. Again, one must remember, these figures are inaccurate as they only account for those who leave a year after graduation.
4. Let me remind the reader at this point that there were two independent samples, one of accountants based overseas and another of accountants based in Ireland. Although much the same questions were asked there were some differences on the topic of emigration (see Appendixes 2 and 3).
5. By 'technical' what is meant is the physical skills required for adequate functional performance; for example in auditing these would be the ticking and totting, the defining of the audit scope, the implementation of accounting standards, the application of tests to ensure the client's accounting controls were secure and so on (see Chapter 3). At a managerial level the technical skills and the commercial skills overlap. Managers have to be technically good and as such are able to ascertain from documentation received and so forth whether or not the audit scope is correct, etc. However, they also need commercial skills. They must be able to control the audit team and limit time wasting on such non-commercial things as a thorough search for the 'true and fair' account of the client's finances. Other skills required revolve around issues such as profits being made and fees got in on time and so on. These are commercial skills as opposed to the technical ones outlined above (although obviously the two overlap to some extent). These divisions are based on those outlined in Chapter 4.
6. Incidentally some 36.6 per cent of those abroad stated they definitely wanted to return home and a further 39.8 per cent felt that returning home was a

possibility. Of course not all of these will return: the recent NESC report
estimated that only 25 per cent of their 1983 sample returned.

6 Accountants and the Class Structure

1. I shall use the terms 'service class' and 'new middle class' interchangeably throughout this chapter.
2. Incidentally this definition of class is wider than those Weberian definitions that stress common income and working conditions.
3. Outside of saying that the feminisation of certain occupations led to the upgrading of men, Goldthorpe has little to contribute on the rise of the female workforce (see Marshall *et al.*, 1988).
4. Although I feel Goldthorpe is incorrect to ignore the role of women within the labour market and within the class structure to the extent that he has.
5. See also Chapter 2 for a brief discussion of the fact that accountancy skills are dominated by other groups in Sweden and Germany for a whole series of non-technical factors.
6. Having stated all of this, Marx's work is somewhat contradictory as he also envisaged a situation wherein the service class could grow in both his early and late work (see Smith, 1987; Bell, 1974).
7. Although Mackenzie was writing before Wright completed his book *Classes*, I would suggest that the criticism is still valid.
8. I will argue later on that this distinction between coordination and supervision cannot be separated at a practical level.
9. Although the importance of the legal guarantee is open to question (Armstrong, 1987).
10. 'Casino capitalism' refers to the emergence in the 1980s of an economy characterised by financial speculation on a grand scale, fictitious capital formation, personal aggrandisement, large scale indebtedness, yuppie culture, close attention to symbolic capital, etc. (Harvey, 1989: 329–35).
11. For a brief description of agency theory, see Chapter 1.
12. 74 per cent of new entrants into the profession were graduates in 1987 (Walsh, 1988).
13. This is more likely to have an impact in the case of Europe than in the case of the USA for a whole series of historical reasons (see Lash and Urry, 1987).

Conclusion

1. This is not to say that like the dinosaur this segment will simply disappear: it may change or be forced to change. The reforms in the Health and Education systems within the UK, and to some extent Ireland, should be viewed in this context.
2. The split in the service class does not mean that the non-commercialised wing will simply become working class, nor indeed that they will ally themselves to the working class.

Bibliography

ABERCROMBIE, NICHOLAS (1991) 'The Privilege of the Producer', in Russell Keat and Nicholas Abercrombie (eds), *Enterprise Culture*, Routledge, London, pp. 171–85.

ADAMS, DON (ed.) (1971) *Education in National Development*, Routledge and Kegan Paul, London.

ALLEN, JOHN (1988) 'Towards a Post-Industrial Economy?', in Doreen Massey and John Allen (eds), *Restructuring Britain: The Economy in Question*, Sage Publications, London, pp. 99–135.

AMIN, SAMIR (1980) *Class and Nation: Historically and in the Current Crisis*, Heinemann, London.

ARMSTRONG, PETER (1985) 'Changing Management Control Strategies: The Role of Competition between Accountancy and Other Occupational Professions', *Accounting, Organizations and Society*, pp. 129–48.

ARMSTRONG, PETER (1986) 'Management Control Strategies and Inter-Professional Competition', in D. Knights and H. Willmott (eds), *Managing the Labour Process*, Gower, Aldershot, pp. 19–43.

ARMSTRONG, PETER (1987) 'The Rise of Accounting Controls in British Capitalist Enterprises', *Accounting, Organizations and Society*, 12, pp. 415–36.

ARMSTRONG, PETER (1991) 'Contradiction and Social Dynamics in the Capitalist Agency Relationship', *Accounting, Organizations and Society*, 16, pp. 1–25.

ARMSTRONG, PETER, CARTER, BOB, SMITH, CHRIS and NICHOLAS, THEO (1986) *White Collar Workers. Trade Unions and Class*, Croom Helm Beckenham.

ARMSTRONG, PHILIP, GLYN, ANDREW and HARRISON, JOHN (1984) *Capitalism Since World War Two – The Making and Breakup of the Great Boom*, Fontana, London.

ATKINSON, JOHN (1984) 'Management Strategies for Flexible Organisations', *Personnel Management*, 16 (August) pp. 28–31.

BARRAS, RICHARD (1984) *Growth and Technical Change in the UK Service Sector*, The Technical Change Centre, London.

BEAVERSTOCK, J.V. (1989) *High Skilled Professional and Managerial Labour Migration: The Case of Large Chartered Accountancy Firms*, Working Papers on Producer Services, 9, University of Bristol and Services Industries Research Centre, Portsmouth Polytechnic.

BEAVERSTOCK, J.V. (1990) 'New International Labour Markets: The Case of Professional and Managerial Labour Migration within Large Chartered Accountancy Firms', *Area*, 22.2, pp. 151–8.

BELL, DANIEL (1974) *The Coming of Post-Industrial Society*, Heinemann, London.

BELL, DANIEL (1976) *The Cultural Contradictions of Capitalism*, Heinemann, London.

BLESSING, PATRICK (1985) 'Irish Emigration to the United States 1800–1920: An Overview', in P.J. Drudy (ed.), *The Irish in America: Emigration, Assimilation and Impact, Irish Studies*, vol. 4, Cambridge University Press, Cambridge, pp. 11–38.

249

BOHDANOWICZ, JANET (1984) *Who Audits the UK, Financial Times* Business Information, London.

BRAVERMAN, HARRY (1974) *Labour and Monopoly Capital*, Monthly Review Press, New York.

BREEN, RICHARD, HANNAN, DAMIAN, ROTTMAN, DAVID and WHELAN, CHRISTOPHER (1990) *Understanding Contemporary Ireland*, Gill and Macmillan, Dublin.

BRISTON, RICHARD (1989) 'Wider Still and Wider', *Accountants Magazine*, (August), 16 pp.

BRITTAN, SAMUEL (1989) 'The Thatcher Government Economy Policy', in D. Kavanagh and A. Seldon (eds), *The Thatcher Effect*, Oxford University Press, Oxford, pp. 1–37.

BROWN, C.J.F. and SHERIFF, T.D. (1986) 'Deindustrialisation: A Background Paper' in Frank Blackaby (ed.), *Deindustrialisation*, 2nd edn, Gower, Aldershot, pp. 233–63.

BURAWOY, MICHAEL (1979) *Manufacturing Consent – Changes in the Labour Process Under Monopoly Capitalism*, University of Chicago Press, Chicago.

BURAWOY, MICHAEL (1988) 'Thirty Years of Making Out', in R.E. Pahl (ed.), *On Work: Historical, Comparative and Theoretical Approaches*, Basil Blackwell, Oxford, pp. 190–209.

CAIN, MAUREEN (1983) 'The General Practice Lawyer and The Client – Towards a Radical Conception', in Robert Dingwall and Phillip Lewis (eds), *The Sociology of the Professions*; Macmillan, London, pp. 106–30.

CAIRNCROSS, ALEC (1986) 'What is De-industrialisation?', in Frank Blackaby (ed.), *De-industrialisation*, 2nd edn, Gower Aldershot, pp. 5–17.

CALLAGHAN, JOHN (1993) 'Fraud: Don't Blame the Auditors', *The Irish Times*, 11 March 1993.

CARCHEDI, G. (1975) 'On the Economic Identification of the New Middle Class', *Economy and Society*, 4(1), pp. 1–86.

CASTLES, STEPHEN and KOSACK, GODULA (1985) *Immigrant Workers and Class Structure in Western Europe*, 2nd edn, Oxford University Press, Oxford.

CAUSER, G. and JONES, C. (1990) 'Technical Workers, Work Organisation and Career Structures in the Electronics Industry', paper presented at the 'Organisation and Control of the Labour Process Conference', Aston University (28–30 March).

CHAMBERS, MICHAEL (1986) *Managing Your Career in Law*, Chambers and Partners, London.

CHILD, JOHN (1982) 'Professions in the Corporate World: Values, Interests and Controls', in D. Dunkerley and G. Salaman (eds), *International Yearbook of Organisation Studies, 1981*, pp. 212–41.

CHILD, JOHN (1988) 'Managerial Strategies, New Technology and the Labour Process', in R.E. Pahl (ed.), *On Work: Historical, Comparative and Theoretical Approaches*, Basil Blackwell, Oxford, pp. 229–57.

COGHLAN, DENIS (1992) 'Government Under Pressure Over Jobs', *Irish Times*, 21 August 1992.

COHEN, ROBIN (1987) *The New Helots – Migrants in the International Division of Labour*, Avebury, Aldershot.

COLLINSON, DAVID, KNIGHTS, DAVID and COLLINSON, MARGARET (1990) *Managing to Discriminate*, Routledge, London.

COMMISSION OF THE EUROPEAN COMMUNITIES (1989) *Employment in Europe*, European Commission, Brussels.

COOKE, PHILIP (1988) 'Spatial Development Processes: Organised or Disorganised?', in Doreen Massey and John Allen (eds), *Uneven Redevelopment: Cities and Regions in Transition*, Hodder and Stoughton, London, pp. 232–49.

COOLEY, MIKE (1981) 'The Taylorisation of Intellectual Work', in Les Levidow and Bob Young (eds), *Science, Technology and the Labour Process*, vol. 1, CSE Books, London, pp. 46–65.

CORCORAN, T., SEXTON, J.J. and O'DONOGHUE, D. (1992) *A Review of Trends in the Occupational Pattern of Employment in Ireland 1971–90*, FAS/ERSI Manpower Forecasting Studies Report 2, FAS/ESRI, Dublin.

COUNSELL, GAIL (1988) 'Multidiscipline and the Megabuck', *Accountancy* (March), pp. 67–71.

CROMPTON, ROSEMARY (1990) 'Professions in the Current Context', *Work, Employment and Society*, Special Issue (May), pp. 147–66.

CROMPTON, R. and SANDERSON, K. (1990) *Gendered Jobs and Social Change*, Unwin Hyman, London.

CROTTY, RAYMOND (1986) *Ireland in Crisis – A Case of Capitalist Colonial Underdevelopment*, Brandon Books, Cork.

CULLEN, L.M. (1972) *An Economic History of Ireland Since 1660*, Batsford, London.

CULLITON, JIM, BARRET, SEAN, BROUGHAN, MARY, CAHILL, BERNIE, CASSELLS, PETER, HANRAHAN, DENIS, HASKINS, CHRIS, QUINN, LOCHLANN and KELLY, JOHN (1992) *A Time For Change: Industrial Policy for the 1990s*, Stationery Office, Government Publications, Dublin.

DANIELS, P.W., LEYSHON, A. and THRIFT, N.J. (1986) *U.K. Producer Services: The International Dimension, Working Papers on Producer Services*, 1, University of Bristol and The Services Industry Research Centre, Portsmouth Polytechnic.

DAVIS, EVAN, HANLON, GERARD and KAY, JOHN (1993) 'What Internationalisation in Services Means: The Case of Accountancy in the UK and Ireland', in Howard Cox, Jeremy Clegg and Grazia Ietto-Gillies (eds), *The Growth of Global Business: New Strategies*, Routledge, London.

DE JONQUIERES, GUY (1986) 'Europe's Quest for Foreign Investment: A War of Diminishing Returns', *Financial Times*, 10 November 1986.

DIRSMITH, MARK, W. and COVALESKI, MARK, A. (1985) 'Informal Communications, Nonformal Communications and Mentoring in Public Accounting Firms', *Accounting, Organizations and Society*, 10, pp. 149–69.

DIXON, MICHAEL (1992) 'Time For Advertisers to Find a New Joke', *Financial Times*, 12 February 1992.

DORE, RONALD (1976) *The Diploma Disease: Education, Qualification and Development*, George Allen and Unwin, London.

DRUDY, P.J. (1985) 'Irish Population Change and Emigration Since Independence', in P.J. Drudy (ed.), *The Irish in America: Emigration, Assimilation and Impact, Irish Studies*, vol. 4, Cambridge University Press, Cambridge, pp. 63–86.

DRUDY, P.J. (1986) 'Migration Between Ireland and Britain Since Independence', in P.J. Drudy (ed.), *Ireland and Britain Since 1922, Irish Studies*, vol. 5, Cambridge University Press, Cambridge, pp. 107–24.

EDWARDS, RICHARD (1979) *Contested Terrain*, Heinemann, London.

EHRENREICH, BARBARA (1984) 'Women and Multinationals', in P. Ayrton, T. Engelhardt and V. Ware (eds), *World View (1985)*, Pluto Press, New York.

EISENHARDT, KATHLEEN, M. (1989) 'Agency Theory: An Assessment and Review', *Academy of Management Review*, 14(1), pp. 57–74.

FARMAR, TONY (1988) *A History of Craig Gardner and Co – The First Hundred Years*, Gill and Macmillan, Dublin.

FINANCIAL SERVICES INDUSTRY ASSOCIATION (FSIA) (1988) *The Financial Services Industry: Manpower and Training Needs – Report of the Focus Group*, FSIA, Dublin.

FITZGERALD, KYRAN (1987) 'The Top Accountancy Firms', *Finance* (December), pp. 8–14.

FITZPATRICK, JIM and KELLY, JOHN (eds) (1985) *Perspectives on Irish Industry*, Irish Management Institute, Dublin.

FREIDSON, ELLIOT (1973) 'Professionalisation and the Organisation of Middle Class Labour in Postindustrial Society', in Paul Halmos (ed.), *Professionalisation and Social Change*, University of Keele, Sociological Review Monograph, No. 20, pp. 47–59.

FRIEDMANN, JOHN and WOLFF, GOERTZ (1982) 'World City Formation: An Agenda for Research and Action', *International Journal of Urban and Regional Research*, 6(3), pp. 309–44.

GALANTER, MARC (1983) 'Mega Law and Mega-Lawyering in the Contemporary United States', in Robert Dingwall and Philip Lewis (eds), *The Sociology of The Professions*, Macmillan, London, pp. 152–76.

GALANTER, MARC and PALAY, THOMAS (1991) *Tournament of Lawyers: The Transformation of the Big Law Firms*, University of Chicago Press, Chicago.

GALLHOFER, S. and HASLAM, J. (1991) 'The Aura of Accounting in the Context of a Crisis: Germany and the First World War', *Accounting, Organizations and Society*, 16 5/6, pp. 487–520.

GALLIE, DUNCAN (1991) 'Patterns of Skill Change: Upgrading, Deskilling or the Polarisation of Skills', *Work, Employment and Society*, 5(3), pp. 319–53.

GELLNER, ERNST (1964) *Thought and Change*, Weidenfeld and Nicolson, London.

GERSHUNY, JONATHAN and MILES, IAN (1983) *The New Service Economy*, Frances Pinter, London.

GIBSON, NOELEEN (1987) 'The Export Market in Irish Accountants', *Finance* (December), pp. 8–14.

GILLESPIE, A.E. and GREEN, A.E. (1987) 'The Changing Geography of Producer Service Employment in Britain', *Regional Studies*, 21(5), pp. 397–411.

GLOVER, IAN, A. and KELLY, MICHAEL, P. (1987) *Engineers in Britain: A Sociological Study of the Engineering Dimension*, Allen & Unwin, London.

GOLDTHORPE, JOHN, H. (1980) *Social Mobility and Class Structure in Modern Britain*, Clarendon Press, Oxford.

GOLDTHORPE, JOHN (1982) 'On the Service Class, Its Formation and Future', in Anthony Giddens and Gavin Mackenzie (eds), *Social Class and the Division of Labour*, Cambridge University Press, Cambridge, pp. 162–85.

GORDON, DAVID, EDWARDS, R. and REICH, M. (1982) *Segmented Work, Divided Workers*, Cambridge University Press, New York.

GREENWOOD, R., BROWN, J. and HININGS, C.R. (1991) 'Merging Professional Service Firms', paper presented at the 'Third Interdisciplinary Perspectives on Accounting Conference', Manchester University (July).

HAKIM, CATHERINE (1989) 'New Recruits to Self-Employment in the 1980s', *The Employment Gazette*, 97(6), pp. 286–97.

HAKIM, CATHERINE (1990) 'Core and Periphery in Employers' Workforce Strategies: Evidence from the 1987 ELUS Study', *Work, Employment and Society*, 4(2), pp. 157–89.

HALES, MIKE (1980) *Living Thinkwork – Where Do Labour Processes Come From?*, CSE Books, London.

HANLON, GERARD (1991) 'The Emigration of Irish Accountants – Economic Restructuring and Producer Services in the Periphery', *Irish Journal of Sociology*, 1, pp. 52–65.

HANLON, GERARD (1992) 'Graduate Emigration: A Continuation or a Break With the Past?', in Patrick O'Sullivan (ed.), *The Irish World Wide, vol. 1*, Leicester University Press, Leicester, pp. 183–95.

HANNAH, LESLIE (1976) 'Strategy and Structure in the Manufacturing Sector', in Leslie Hannah (ed.), *Management Strategy and Business Development*, Macmillan, London, pp. 184–202.

HANNAN, DAMIAN (1970) *Rural Exodus*, Geoffrey Chapman, London.

HARPER, RICHARD (1989) 'An Ethnography of Accountants', unpublished Ph.D Dissertation, Faculty of Economic and Social Studies, Manchester University.

HARRIS, LAWRENCE (1988) 'The UK Economy at the Crossroads', in Doreen Massey and John Allen (eds), *The Economy in Question*, Sage Publications, London, pp. 7–44.

HARRISON, BENNETT and BLUESTONE, BARRY (1988) *The Great U-Turn: Corporate Restructuring and the Polarising of America*, Basic Books, New York.

HARVEY, DAVID (1989) *The Condition of Postmodernity*, Basil Blackwell, Oxford.

HASTINGS, A. and HININGS, C.R. (1970) 'Role Relations and Value Adaptation: A Study of the Professional Accountant in Industry', *Sociology*, 4, pp. 353–66.

HIGHER EDUCATION AUTHORITY (HEA) (1989) *First Destination of Award Recipients in Higher Education (1988)*, HEA, Dublin.

HIGHER EDUCATION AUTHORITY (1991) *First Destination of Award Recipients in Higher Education (1990)*, HEA, Dublin.

HOPPER, T. and ARMSTRONG, P. (1991) 'Cost Accounting, Controlling Labour and the Rise of the Conglomerates', *Accounting, Organizations and Society*, 16(5/6), pp. 405–38.

HUMPHREY, CHRISTOPHER, TURLEY, STUART and MOIZER, PETER (1991) 'Protecting Against Detection: The Case of Auditors and Fraud?', paper presented at the 'Third Interdisciplinary Perspectives on Accounting Conference', Manchester University (July).

ICAEW (1988) *Council Members Briefing Handbook*, ICAEW, London.

ICAI (1910–91) *Members Handbook* (published yearly) ICAI, Dublin.

IRISH INDEPENDENT (1989) 'Penal Taxes "Driving Out" Graduates Needed Here', *Irish Independent*, 27 July 1989.

IRIZARRY, RAFAEL, L. (1980) 'Over-Education and Unemployment in the Third World – The Paradoxes of Dependent Industrialisation', *Comparative Education Review*, 24(3), pp. 338–52.

JACK, ANDREW (1992) 'Changing Patterns of Recruitment Repay Study', *Financial Times*, 16 April.

JACKSON, JOHN A. (1963) *The Irish in Britain*, Routledge and Kegan Paul, London.

JACKSON, JOHN A. (1986) 'The Irish in Britain', in P.J. Drudy (ed.), *Ireland and Britain Since 1922, Irish Studies*, vol. 5, Cambridge University Press, Cambridge, pp. 125–38.

JAMOUS, H. and PELOILLE, B. (1970) 'Changes in the French University-Hospital System', in John A. Jackson (ed.), *Professions and Professionalisation*, Cambridge University Press, London, pp. 111–52.

JENKINS, RICHARD (1986) *Racism and Recruitment*, Cambridge University Press, Cambridge.

JOHNSON, TERENCE, J. (1972) *Professions and Powers*, Macmillan, London.

JOHNSON, TERENCE, J. (1977) 'The Professions in the Class Structure', in Richard Scase (ed.), *Industrial Society: Class, Cleavage and Control*, George Allen & Unwin, London, pp. 93–110.

JOHNSON, TERENCE, J. (1980) 'Work and Power', in Geoff Esland and Graeme Salaman (eds), *The Politics of Work and Occupations*, Open University Press, London, pp. 335–71.

JOHNSON, TERENCE (1982) 'The State and Professions: Peculiarities of the British', in Anthony Giddens and Gavin Mackenzie (eds), *Social Class and the Division of Labour*, Cambridge University Press, Cambridge, pp. 186–208.

JOHNSON, TERENCE, J. (1986) 'The Professions', in Geoffrey Hurd (ed.), *Human Society: an Introduction to Sociology*, Routledge and Kegan Paul, London, pp. 152–70.

JONES, EDGAR (1981) *Accountancy and the British Economy 1840–1980: The Evolution of Ernst and Whinney*, Batsford, London.

JONES, GISELLE (1989) 'Wide Variance in Growth Reshuffles League Table', *The Accountant* (June), pp. 8–13.

JÖNSSON, STEN (1988) *Accounting Regulation and Elite Structures*, Wiley, Chichester.

JÖNSSON, STEN (1991) 'Role Making in Accounting While the State is Watching', *Accounting, Organizations and Society*, 16(5/6).

KEAT, RUSSELL and ABERCROMBIE, NICHOLAS (1991), *Enterprise Culture*, Routledge, London.

KENNEDY, KIERAN, A. and DOWLING, BRENDAN, R. (1975) *Economic Growth in Ireland Since 1947*, Gill and Macmillan, Dublin.

KERR, CLARK, DUNLOP, J.T., HARBISON, F. and MYERS, C.A. (1973) *Industrialism and Industrial Man*, Penguin, Harmondsworth.

KING, RUSSELL and SHUTTLEWORTH, IAN (1988) 'Ireland's New Wave Emigration in the 1980s', *Irish Geography*, 21, pp. 104–9.

KNIGHTS, DAVID and MORGAN, GLENN (1990) 'Management Control in Sales Forces: A Case Study from the Labour Process of Life Insurance', *Work, Employment and Society*, 4(3), pp. 369–90.

KUMAR, KRISHAN (1978) *Prophecy and Progress*, Penguin, Harmondsworth.

LASH, SCOTT and URRY, JOHN (1987) *The End of Organised Capitalism*, Polity Press, Cambridge.

LAWRENCE, PETER (1980) *Managers and Management in Germany*, Croom Helm, Beckenham.

LEINSTER SOCIETY OF CHARTERED ACCOUNTANTS (LSCA) (1990) *Salary Survey 1990*, LSCA, Dublin.

LEYSHON, A., DANIELS, P.W. and THRIFT, N. (1987a) *Large Accountancy Firms in the UK: Operational Adaptation and Spatial Development, Working Papers on Producer Services* 2, University of Bristol and The Services Industries Research Centre, Portsmouth Polytechnic.

LEYSHON, A., DANIELS, P.W. and THRIFT, N. (1987b) *Internationalisation of Professional Producer Services: The Case of Large Accountancy Firms, Working Paper On Producer Services*, 3, University of Bristol and The Services Industries Research Centre, Portsmouth Polytechnic.

LEYSHON, A., THRIFT, N. and TOMMEY, C. (1989) *'South Goes North?' The Rise of the British Provincial Financial Centre, Working Papers on Producer Services*, 10, University of Bristol and The Services Industries Research Centre, Portsmouth Polytechnic.

LIPIETZ, ALAIN (1986) 'New Tendencies in the International Division of Labour', in Allen Scott and Michael Storper (eds), *Production, Work, Territory – The Geographical Anatomy of Industrial Capitalism*, Allen and Unwin, Boston, pp. 16–40.

LIPIETZ, ALAIN (1987) *Mirages and Miracles: The Crisis of Global Fordism*, Verso Publications, London.

LOVELL, ALAN (1992) 'Accounting Education: A Developing Debate', *Management Accounting* (March), pp. 20–23.

LOVERING, KEN (1990) 'A Perfunctionary Sort of Post-Fordism: Economic Restructuring and Labour Market Segmentation in Britain in the 1980s', *Work, Employment and Society*, Special Issue (May), pp. 9–28.

LYNN, RICHARD (1968) *The Irish Brain Drain, Economic and Social Research Institute (ESRI) Paper* 43.

MACASKILL, JON (1989) 'Beating the Big Eight', *The Accountant* (January), pp. 6–8.

MACKENZIE, GAVIN (1982) 'Class Boundaries and the Labour Process', in Anthony Giddens and Gavin Mackenzie (eds), *Social Class and the Division of Labour*, Cambridge University Press, Cambridge, pp. 63–86.

MAGEEAN, D.M. (1985) 'Nineteenth-Century Irish Emigration: A Case Study Using Passenger Lists', in P.J. Drudy (ed.), *The Irish in America: Emigration, Assimilation and Impact, Irish Studies*, 4, Cambridge University Press, Cambridge, pp. 39–62.

MARSHALL, GORDON, NEWBY, HOWARD, ROSE, DAVID and VOGLES, CAROLYN (1988) *Social Class in Modern Britain*, Hutchinson Education, London.

MARTIN, RON (1988) 'Industrial Capitalism in Transition', in Doreen Massey and John Allen (eds), *Uneven Re-development: Cities and Regions in Transition*, Hodder and Stoughton, London, pp. 202–31.

MARX, KARL (1976a) *Capital*, vol. 1, Penguin, Harmondsworth.

MARX, KARL (1976b) *Capital*, vol. 3, Penguin, Harmondsworth.

MARX, KARL and ENGELS, FREDERICK (1967) *The Communist Manifesto*, Penguin, Harmondsworth.

MASSEY, DOREEN (1988a) 'What is an Economy Anyhow?', in Doreen Massey and John Allen (eds), *The Economy in Question?*, Sage Publications, London, pp. 229–59.

MASSEY, DOREEN (1988b) 'Uneven Development – Social Change and Spatial Divisions of Labour', in Doreen Massey and John Allen (eds), *Uneven Redevelopment: Cities and Regions in Transition*, Hodder and Stoughton, London, pp. 250–76.

MAYCOCK, JOHN (1986) *Financial Conglomerates: The New Phenomenon*, Gower, Aldershot.

McCANN, BILLY (1988) 'Accountancy to Become More Polarised', *Finance* (January), pp. 21–2.

McCURDY, SHAUN (1988) 'A Study of the Role of Marketing in the Big Eight Accountancy Firms', unpublished MBA thesis, Trinity College Dublin.

McGOVERN, PATRICK (1992) 'On the Bench: The Integration of Technical Workers into Multinational Companies in the Republic of Ireland', unpublished PhD in progress, Nuffield College, University of Oxford.

McHUGH, GERARD and STAMP, BILLY (1992) 'Big Changes Proposed in Ireland', *Certified Accountant* (March), pp. 10–11.

McMANUS, JOHN (1982) 'Education or Exploitation?', *Irish Times Working and Living Supplement*, 20 June 1992.

McNEIL, IAN (1992) 'Auditors Lead Way to Accountability', *The Observer*, 29 March 1992.

MEENAN, JAMES (1970) *The Irish Economy Since 1922*, Liverpool University Press, Liverpool.

MITCHELL, AUSTIN (1992) 'Why Auditors must be Brought to Book', *The Observer*, 5 March 1992.

MOORE, MATTHEW and MOORE, MARTIN (1991) *Managing Lawyers: Recruiting and Retaining Staff in Private Practice*, Chancery Law Publishing, London.

MURRAY, F. and KNIGHTS, D. (1990) 'Inter-Managerial Competition and Capital Accumulation: IT Specialists, Accountants and Executive Control', *Critical Perspectives on Accounting*, 1(2), pp. 167–89.

MURRAY, FERGUS (1988) 'The Decentralisation of Production – The Decline of the Mass Collective Worker?', in R.E. Pahl (ed.), *On Work: Historical, Comparative and Theoretical Approaches*, Basil Blackwell, Oxford, pp. 258–78.

NATIONAL ECONOMIC AND SOCIAL COUNCIL (NESC) (1991) *The Economic and Social Implications of Emigration*, NESC, Dublin.

NEU, D., MURRAY, D. and WRIGHT, M. (1991) 'Price Is Not Enough: The Influence of the "Social" in the Auditor/Client Relationship', paper presented at the 'Third Interdisciplinary Perspectives on Accounting Conference', Manchester University (July).

NICHOLS, THEO (1969) *Ownership, Control and Ideology*, George Allen and Unwin, London.

NICHOLS, THEO (1986) 'Introduction', in Peter Armstrong *et al.* (eds.), *White Collar Workers, Trade Unions and Class*, Beckenham.

O'MALLEY, EOIN (1987) *The Irish Engineering Industry*, ESRI, Dublin.

O'ROURKE, MARY (1988) 'Estimates Address on Education Spending', paper presented to the Dail, 26 October 1988.

OFFE, CLAUS (1976) *Industry and Inequality*, Edward Arnold, London.

OFFE, CLAUS (1985) *Disorganised Capitalism*, Polity Press, Cambridge.

OPPENHEIMER, MARTIN (1973) 'The Proletarianisation of the Professional', in Paul Halmos (ed.), *Professionalisation and Social Change*, University of Keele, Sociological Review Monograph, No. 20, pp. 213–27.

PARKHOUSE, JAMES (1991) *Doctors' Careers – Aims and Experiences of Medical Graduates*, Routledge, London.

PATERSON, ALAN (1983) 'Becoming a Judge', in Robert Dingwall and Philip Lewis (eds), *The Sociology of The Professions*, Macmillan, London, pp. 263–85.

PERRONS, D.C. (1981) 'The Role of Ireland in the New International Division of Labour', *Regional Studies*, 15(2), pp. 81–100.

PESCHEL, R.E. and PESCHEL, E.R. (1986) *When A Doctor Hates a Patient*, University of California Press, London.

PIORE, M.J. and SABEL, C.F. (1984) *The Second Industrial Divide*, Basic Books, New York.

PORTER, MAUREEN (1990) 'Professional–Client Relationships and Women's Reproductive Health Care', in Sarah Cunningham-Burley and Neil McKeganey (eds), *Readings in Medical Sociology*, Tavistock/Routledge, London, pp. 182–210.

POULANTZAS, NICOS (1979) *Classes in Contemporary Capitalism*, New Left Books, London.

POWER, MICHAEL (1989) 'Educating Accountants – Towards A Critical Ethnography', paper presented at the Accounting and Social Workshop Conference, London School of Economics (November).

QUIN, TIMOTHY (1988) 'A Centenarian Renders – His Account', in David Rowe (ed.), *The Irish Chartered Accountant Centenary Essays*, Gill and Macmillan, Dublin.

RAJAN, AMIN (1987) *The Second Industrial Revolution?*, Butterworths, London.

RICHARDS, ARCHIBALD, B. (1981) *Touche Ross and Co 1899–1981: The Origins and Growth of the UK Firm*, Touche Ross and Co, London.

ROBINSON, H.W. (1983) *A History of Accountants in Ireland*, 2nd edn, ICAI, Dublin.

ROSLENDER, ROBIN (1990) 'The Accountant in the Class Structure', *Public Interest Accounting*, 3, pp. 195–212.

ROWE, DAVID (1988) 'The Changing World of the Smaller Firm', in David Rowe (ed.), *The Irish Chartered Accountant Centenary Essays*, Gill and Macmillan, Dublin.

RUNCIMAN, W.G. (1990) 'How Many Classes are There in Contemporary British Society?', *Sociology*, 24(3), pp. 377–96.

SALAMAN, GRAEME (1982) 'Managing the Frontier of Control', in Anthony Giddens and Gavin Mackenzie (eds), *Social Class and the Division of Labour*, Cambridge University Press, Cambridge, pp. 46–62.

SALT, J. (1986) 'International Migration: A Spatial Theoretical Approach', in Michael Pacione (ed.), *Population Geography: Progress and Prospects*, Croom Helm, Beckenham, pp. 166–93.

SARGENT, J.R. (1986) 'UK Performance in Services' in Frank Blackaby (ed.), *De-industrialisation*, 2nd edn, Gower, Aldershot, pp. 102–16.

SASSEN, SASKIA (1988) *The Mobility of Labour and Capital*, Cambridge University Press, New York.

SASSEN, SASKIA (1991) *The Global City – New York, London, Tokyo*, Princeton University Press, Princeton, NJ.

SASSEN-KOOB, SASKIA (1984) 'The New Labour Demand in Global Cities', in Michael P. Smith (ed.), *Cities in Transformation*, Sage Publications, California, pp. 139–71.

SASSEN-KOOB, SASKIA (1987) 'Issues of Core and Periphery: Labour and Global Restructuring', in J. Henderson and M. Castells (eds), *Global Restructuring and Territorial Development*, Sage Publications, California pp. 60–87.

SAVAGE, M., DICKENS, P. and FIELDING, T. (1988) 'Some Social and Political Implications of the Contemporary Fragmentation of the "Service Class" in Britain', *International Journal of Urban and Regional Research*, 12(3), pp. 455–76.

SCASE, RICHARD and GOFFEE, ROBERT (1982) *The Entrepreneurial Middle Class*, Croom Helm, Beckenham.

SEERS, DUDLEY (1979) 'The Periphery of Europe', in Dudley Seers, Bernard Schaffer and Marja-Lisa Kiljunen (eds), *Underdeveloped Europe: Studies in Core–Periphery Relations*, The Harvester Press, Hassocks, pp. 3–35.

SHUTTLEWORTH, IAN and KOCKEL, ULLRICH (1990) *Aspects of Irish Emigration*, APRU Discussion Paper, 90/3.

SIMMONS, JOHN (ed.) (1980) *The Education Dilemma*, Pergamon Press, Oxford.

SMITH, CHRIS (1987) *Technical Workers: Class, Labour and Trade Unions*, Macmillan Education, London.

STACEY, NICHOLAS, A.H. (1954) *English Accountancy 1800–1954*. Gee & Co., London.

STANLEY, CHRISTOPHER (1991) 'Justice Enters the Marketplace', in Russell Keat and Nicholas Abercrombie (eds), *Enterprise Culture*, Routledge, London, pp. 206–15.

STEINMETZ, GEORGE and WRIGHT, ERIK OLIN (1989) 'The Fall and Rise of the Petty Bourgeoisie: Changing Patterns of Self-Employment in the Postwar United States', *The American Journal of Sociology*, 94(5), pp. 973–1018.

STERNE, JOHN (1987) 'Where Do All the Computer Graduates Go?', *Irish Computer* (November), pp. 18–21.

STEVENS, MARK (1984) *The Big Eight*, Collier Press, New York.

STEWART, A., PRANDY, K. and BLACKBURN, R.M. (1980) *Social Stratification and Occupations*, Macmillan, London.

STRAUSS, ANSELM (1975) *Professions, Work and Careers*, Transaction Books, New Brunswick, NJ.

TANSEY, PAUl (1990) 'Graduating to Jobs Abroad', *Labour Market Review*, 1, pp. 37–52.

TELESIS CONSULTANCY GROUP (1982) *A Review of Industrial Policy, NESC Paper*, 64, National Economic and Social Council, Dublin.

THOMPSON, PAUL (1989) *The Nature of Work*, Macmillan Education, London.

THRIFT, NIGEL (1988) 'The Geography of International Economic Disorder', in Doreen Massey and John Allen (eds), *Uneven Re-development: Cities and Regions in Transition*, Hodder and Stoughton, London, pp. 6–46.

TINKER, TONY (1985) *Paper Prophets: A Social Critique of Accounting*, Holt, Rinehart & Winston, Eastbourne.

TODARO, MICHAEL (1980) 'The Influence of Education on Migration and Fertility', in John Simmons (ed.), *The Education Dilemma*, Pergamon Press, Oxford, pp. 179–88.

TRICKER, R., IAN (1967) *The Accountant in Management*, Batsford, London.

WALSH, ANTHONY (1988) 'The Making of the Chartered Accountant', in David Rowe (ed.), *The Irish Chartered Accountant Centenary Essays*, Gill and Macmillan, Dublin.

WATSON, KEITH (1982) *Educational Neo-Colonialism: The Continuing Legacy*, Croom Helm, Beckenham.

WATTS, ROSS, L. and ZIMMERMAN, JEROLD, L. (1990) 'Positive Accounting Theory: A Ten Year Perspective', *The Accounting Review*, 65(1) (January), pp. 131–56.

WHITELY, NIGEL (1991) 'Design in Enterprise Culture – Design for Whose Profit?', in Russell Keat and Nicholas Abercrombie (eds), *Enterprise Culture*, Routledge, London, pp. 186–205.

WICKHAM, JAMES (1987) *Technicians and Engineers in Irish Electronics Plants*, NBST Discussion Paper, Dublin.

WICKHAM, JAMES (1989) 'The Over Educated Engineer? The Work, Education and Careers of Irish Electronic Engineers', *IBAR – Journal of Irish Business and Administrative Research*, 10, pp. 19–33.

WICKHAM, JAMES and MURRAY, PETER (1987) *Women in the Irish Electronics Industry*, Employment Equality Agency, Dublin.

WILKINSON, BARRY (1983) *The Shopfloor Politics of the New Technology*, Heinemann Educational, London.

WILLIAMSON, OLIVER, E. (1975) *Markets and Hierarchies: Analysis and Antitrust Implications*, Free Press, New York.

WINSBURY, REX (1977) *Thomson McLintock – The First Hundred Years*, Thomson McLintock and Co, London.

WOOD, P.A. (1988) 'Employment Change and the Role of the Producer Service Sector', in Doreen Massey and John Allen (eds), *Uneven Re-development: Cities and Regions in Transition*, Hodder and Stoughton, London, pp. 91–106.

WOOD, STEPHEN and KELLY, JOHN (1988) 'Taylorism, Responsible Autonomy, and Management Strategy', in R.E. Pahl (ed.), *On Work: Historical, Comparative and Theoretical Approaches*, Basil Blackwell, Oxford, pp. 175–89.

WRIGHT, ERIK OLIN (1985) *Classes*, Verso Editions, London.

Index